Emergency Preparedness and Survival Guide Volume One

The articles that appear in this book were previously published in *Backwoods Home Magazine*.

ISBN: **0-9718445-2-6**

Cover art by Don Childers

Manufactured in the United States of America

Published by *Backwoods Home Magazine*, Inc.
P.O. Box 712, Gold Beach, OR 97444
www.backwoodshome.com

Table of Contents

Introduction

Welcome to Volume One of our best selling anthology, Backwoods Home Magazine's *Emergency Preparedness and Survival Guide Volume One*. It is intended to give readers a one-stop manual on how to prepare for a major disruption of society, whether it is caused by terrorists or natural disaster.

The newly published Volumes Two and Three are written in the same vein and, like Volume One, each contains articles taken directly from *Backwoods Home Magazine*, along with several which are entirely new and were commissioned specifically for these guides. The articles in each volume are stand-alone articles taken from the issues of *Backwoods Home Magazine*, along with some new material written specifically for these guides, making it easy for the reader to go directly to a topic of interest. If there is a practical difference between this and the two new volumes, it's that this is a general volume while Volume Two leans a little toward winter weather and Volume Three leans toward the warmer months.

This anthology is divided into three sections:

Section 1 — The Threat
This section describes the ongoing terrorist threats currently faced by Americans, including biological, chemical, and nuclear terrorist acts.

Section 2 — Immediate Preparation
This section contains articles outlining the immediate preparations you can make to safeguard yourself and your family not only against terrorist attack or natural disaster, but also against personal misfortune. It contains articles on storing food and water, alternative sources of electricity and warmth, medical preparation, emergency survival gear, and firearms.

Section 3 — Long-term Preparation
This section addresses long-term preparation, including growing a garden so you can feed your family without relying on the supermarket, and canning food.

Dave Duffy
Publisher
Backwoods Home Magazine

Section 1
The Threat

Terrorist attacks can shake the foundations of our biggest buildings, but they cannot touch the foundation of America. These acts shatter steel, but they cannot dent the steel of American resolve.

— George W. Bush, Address to the U.S. after hijack attacks on the U.S. World Trade Centers and Pentagon, September 11, 2001

Chapter 1
Preparing for disaster

By Gary F. Arnet, D.D.S.

Are you prepared for a disaster that could affect the daily function of your life or the lives of your family members? Or do you even believe a disaster will ever affect you?

Earthquakes, blizzards, hurricanes, electrical power outages, and who knows what else happen all the time. And now we have the added threat of terrorist attacks. Still, most Americans ignore the warnings. "It can't happen here," some say. "The government will take care of me if it does," others think.

But not only do sudden disasters happen, they can happen to you. And when they do, you will be on your own. The tragedy of September 11 illustrates this well. Look at the total disruption of transportation and emergency services in New York City immediately following the terrorist attack. This was followed by the immediate and complete paralysis of air transportation throughout the United States. Thousands were stranded for days on their own in strange cities.

Anthrax attacks followed, paralyzing the mail service and spreading terror across the nation. Hazardous materials teams and health departments throughout the nation were swamped with false calls from citizens fearing anthrax-laced letters.

As serious as these attacks were, they pale in comparison to the possibilities. Consider a major biological or nuclear attack or accident. Hundreds of thousands of casualties are predicted in some scenarios. Even the major earthquake predicted for the Midwest is expected to cause widespread destruction and casualties.

These disasters or attacks could overwhelm local, regional, and national emergency resources and cause widespread panic. Transportation could stop, markets could be stripped of food within hours, essential emergency services could be overwhelmed, and food, medical supplies, and emergency service workers would be sent to the disaster area, leaving critical shortages in local areas. After Hurricane Andrew devastated Florida, plywood was in short supply throughout the country as it was being sent to rebuild the state.

Many do not prepare for these emergencies. During one earthquake in southern California, people were lined up outside hospitals to get Band-aids. They were so unprepared that they did not even have basic first aid kits,

FEMA recommends you have a portable disaster supply kit that contains all of the food, water, and emergency supplies that your family would need for three days.

overwhelming medical personnel who were trying to deal with the severely injured.

Are you prepared?

Now, more than ever, you need to prepare for the possibility of disasters or attacks on a scale and type never before imagined. It is your duty to yourself, your family, and your country to be prepared.

Some of us need to be prepared for being at "ground zero." Certain areas are the most likely direct targets of terrorists or natural disasters. All of us need to be prepared to be indirect targets, those affected by the temporary collapse of our nation's infrastructure.

In short, we all need to be able to live self-sufficiently for a period of time.

What to prepare for will depend on your geographical area. Natural disasters and the risk of major terrorist attacks vary by where you live. The first thing you need to do is make a list of the possible disasters for which you need to prepare. Some of the things you will want to consider include natural disasters, such as blizzards, floods, earthquakes, hurricanes, and wild fires, as well as technological disasters, such as nuclear, biological, chemical (NBC) attacks, and hazardous material accidents.

Don't forget cyber-attacks, the possibility that an enemy could attack our computer systems, shutting down electrical, gas, communications, transportation, and emergency and medical services. What about attacks on our farms and agricultural processing plants? While they would likely affect only a small number of people directly, they would completely shut down food production and distribution systems.

While there are many things to plan for, your response to all of them is one of two things: *stay at home* or *evacuate*. For blizzards, earthquakes, cyber-attacks, nuclear fallout, quarantine after biological attacks, and collapse of the infrastructure, you will want to stay at home. For floods, hurricanes, or with some advance notice of NBC attacks, evacuation may be your course of action.

Whenever possible, staying at home in your own environment and with your own emergency supplies is the best choice. When you evacuate, you are essentially a refugee at the mercy of government evacuation centers or the compassion of the local population. In a major disaster, don't expect to be welcomed by the locals who are struggling with their own survival.

In all situations, you will need to be able to think for yourself. Confusion always accompanies a major disaster and initial information and instructions may be conflicting and incorrect. Some caught in the World Trade Center were initially advised that everything was fine and they should stay at their desks. Those who took matters into their own hands immediately evacuated the building. So, monitor the radio and television for official instructions on what to do, such as whether to evacuate or not, but don't assume they are correct. Make your own decisions based on your plans and preparation.

Full face respirators can be part of your preparation if you live in an area where hazardous materials spills or chemical attacks are possible.

Riding it out at home

Key to your survival is preparing a disaster supplies kit, essentially the stockpiling of all materials that you would need to live on if you are cut off from outside utilities, water, and supplies. Once a disaster occurs, there won't be time and materials may not be available.

How long you will need to be self-sufficient is hard to say. The Federal Emergency Management Agency (FEMA) advises everyone to store enough food, water, and supplies to take care of their family for three days. Preparing a "72-hour kit" is a good idea. It can be used for immediate evacuation and part of your overall disaster supply kit. Place items in a portable, easy-to-carry container, such as a large plastic box or duffel bag, ready to grab at a moment's notice.

But, is it enough? A blizzard, earthquake, quarantine, or nuclear fallout could confine you for much longer. You need to be able to take care of all the needs for your family for a period of at least two weeks and possibly longer. Having supplies for one to three months is not all that unreasonable or hard to accomplish.

There are six basics that should be part of your home disaster supplies kit: water, food, first aid supplies, tools and emergency supplies, clothing and bedding, and special needs items.

Water. An individual must drink at least two quarts of water per day to avoid dehydration, and as much as four to five in hot weather or if they are

Foods that have a shelf-life of 5 to 10 years are available from many disaster supply companies and are a good way to be sure that your food does not spoil.

exercising or working hard. Store at least a gallon of water per person per day (two quarts for drinking and two for food preparation and sanitation) in food-grade plastic containers, such as water containers or empty two-liter soda bottles. Thirty to fifty-gallon containers are also available and can be stored in a garage or shed. Rotate water supplies every six months so they stay fresh.

For extended disasters, additional water may need to be obtained. Rain is pure water and can be used without further purification. Water from lakes, streams, or reservoirs should be purified by boiling, using a portable water filter, or by adding a water purification chemical, such as *Polar Pure* or *Potable Aqua*.

Food. Non-perishable foods that require no refrigeration or cooking and which use little or no water to prepare are the best for your disaster kit. Ready-to-eat canned foods including meats, stews, beans, fruits, and vegetables are the mainstay of the food supply, along with canned juices, milk, and soups. Include high energy foods, such as peanut butter, crackers, granola bars, energy bars, or trail mix and some comfort foods, such as cookies, hard candy, coffee, or tea.

For foods that must be cooked, be sure to have a camping-type cook stove and fuel, Dutch oven and briquettes, or other cooking source. This will allow you to prepare more types of food, such as rice, dehydrated foods, flour biscuits, and cornbread.

Consider shelf life of stored foods. Rotate regular canned goods and food every six months. Eat the stored food as part of your regular meals, replacing it with newly purchased food.

Numerous companies sell emergency foods that are packaged to last for 5 to 10 years and are good to have around since you don't have to worry about rotating food as often. Military MREs (Meals Ready To Eat) are also available and have a long shelf-life, although they are bulky and expensive. They are convenient to have in your vehicle disaster kit, however.

First aid supplies. First aid kits should be available in your house and vehicles. Your local American Red Cross chapter can supply you with a basic first aid manual and list of first aid supplies. Your home kit should include items to treat injuries such as lacerations, sprains, and burns, as well as medicines, such as aspirin or non-aspirin pain relievers, anti-diarrhea medicine, laxatives, and antacids.

Tools and emergency supplies. Tools and emergency supplies should include such things as battery-operated radio and flashlights with extra batteries, cups/plates/utensils, non-electric can opener, matches, lantern, fire extinguisher, hand tools for repairs and to turn off household water and gas, a whistle, and plastic sheeting. For sanitation, include toilet paper, towelettes, soap, toothpaste, personal hygiene items, disinfectant, and household chlorine bleach. Many more items can be added. Think through the things you use on a daily basis.

Clothing and bedding. Clothing and bedding would include a change of clothing and footwear for everyone in the household, rain gear, cold weather clothes, hat and gloves, and blankets or sleeping bags. Remember, a house or car can get very cold without heat. Prepare for the worst weather that you might encounter.

Special needs items. Special needs items may include formula and diapers for infants, prescription medications, contact lenses and supplies, extra glasses, and other supplies or equipment for infant, elderly, or disabled individuals. Ample pet food should also be stored. Confinement in the house during a disaster can be boring, especially for children, so remember books, games, and other entertainment.

Store your disaster supply kit in a convenient place that is known to all family members and make sure they know your family's disaster plan. Evaluate your kit once a year and update it according to family needs.

Evacuation

You may not have much time to prepare when you need to evacuate. A hazardous materials spill could mean instant evacuation, so always have a smaller version of your home disaster supply kit in the trunk of your car.

When you have advance warning of an evacuation, bring your portable "72-hour" disaster supply kit, along with additional food, water, and clothing. Keep important family documents in a waterproof, portable container, ready to bring with you in an evacuation. These may include your will, insurance policies, contracts, deeds, stocks and bonds, passports, social security card, bank and credit account numbers, family documents (birth, marriage, and death certificates), inventory of valuable household items, and important telephone numbers. It would be a good idea to always keep some cash in this container, so you have it for an emergency. If there is time, valuable family heirlooms or photographs can be added.

Keeping a checklist of what to bring in an evacuation is a good idea. In the stress of the moment, it is easy to forget an important item.

Now that you have a basic plan for any emergency, let's consider plans for some specific risks.

Weapons of mass destruction

Weapons of mass destruction are chemical, biological, or nuclear weapons developed by countries for war, but now being sought by terrorists for use against civilian populations. Some in the government agree that their future use against the civilian population within the borders of the United States is almost guaranteed.

Despite the horror this will cause, it is possible to protect yourself and your family from the effects of many of these attacks by using common sense, avoiding panic, becoming informed, and preparing ahead of time. This article is intended to help you start doing just that.

Chemical terrorism

NATO defines a chemical weapon as a chemical substance intended for military use to kill, injure, or incapacitate people. Not only do they cause death and injury, they can have devastating psychological effects, crippling not only the affected population, but the nation in general. Depending on the chemical used, the weapon will affect the nervous system, lungs, skin, eyes, nose, throat, or a combination of these.

Relatively inexpensive to produce or obtain, it is fairly certain that terrorists have access to such chemical weapons which they would use against civilian populations without hesitation. This was proven on March 20, 1995, when the Aum Shinrikyo religious cult attacked the Tokyo subway with sarin nerve gas, killing 12 and injuring more than 5,000.

Unfortunately, chemical attacks against a civilian population is a reality today. Israeli civilians have been living with this possibility for some time. Civilians are issued gas masks and chemical "safe rooms" are being built in new homes. American civilians must be prepared also.

Just as we could not believe that terrorists would fly airplanes into buildings, we cannot begin to think of all the ways terrorists might use chemical weapons. Logic says that confined areas with large numbers of people would be likely targets. Subways, tunnels, office buildings, hotels, apartment building, and airports seem to be potential targets.

However, nothing is to stop terrorists from spraying football stadiums, parades, or any other large gathering of people with chemicals from aircraft or chemicals released upwind. For military applications, chemical weapons are also dispersed via missile, rocket, bombs, artillery shell, and land mines and it is possible these could be obtained for use against civilians.

To understand the actions to take during a chemical attack, it is important to first understand the chemicals and their effects. Thousands of poisonous chemicals are known, but only a few are suitable as weapons and have been stockpiled for war. While about 70 different chemicals have been produced as weapons, two main types of chemical agents are currently available, poison gases, and nerve agents.

Mustard gas is felt by experts to be the most likely gas used in a terrorist attack, although Iraq also has cyanide gas weapons. Germany introduced and effectively used mustard gas during World War I, causing thousands of casualties. Since then, it has been used many times, including by Iraq against the Iranians and Kurds in the 1980s. It is widely available in Third World countries and former Warsaw Pact countries. The United States still has a stockpile in its arsenal that is awaiting destruction.

Chemical protection masks (gas masks) have been issued to 23,000 workers at the Pentagon and to Israeli citizens. Most Americans will probably not need them, but those who may live or work in areas that could be targets of chemical attack may want to obtain their own.

In a class called vesicants, mustard gas does not immediately kill people, rather taking hours for symptoms to develop. Vapors of mustard gas penetrate most fabrics quickly and the chemical is absorbed into the skin. A sunburn appearance of the skin develops within 2 to 48 hours, with itching and stinging pain often present. After this, small blisters on the skin can form, eventually enlarging into very large blisters called bullae. Eyes can develop a mild inflammation (conjunctivitis) or severe ulcerations of the cornea, causing blindness. Death from mustard gas is most often from inhaling the gas. Irritation of the nose, throat, and sinuses is the first sign of inhaled gas, followed by laryngitis, nose bleeds, and a cough. The cough worsens as damage to the lower lungs leads to respiratory failure and death.

The Germans used cyanide gas during World War II in their gas chambers and it was used by Iraq against the Kurds in the 1980s. Deadly when used in enclosed spaces, cyanide gas is lighter than air and rapidly dissipates outdoors. It causes death by starving the body's cells of oxygen, being especially toxic to heart and brain cells.

Nerve agents are some of the most potent chemicals known to man and are a more likely terrorist threat than poison gases, often killing the victim within minutes of exposure. German scientists developing pesticides in the 1930s observed that chemicals called organo-phosphate compounds affect transmission of nerve impulses and kill humans rapidly. Although 12,000

Surgical or dust masks prevent inhalation of biological agents or fine dust and debris caused by explosions that can damage the lungs, but will not adequately protect against chemical agents.

tons of chemical weapons were made for the German military during World War II, they were not used on the battlefield. Although many countries have the ability to produce nerve agents, the only time they have been used in war so far was by the Iraqis in the Iraq/Iran war.

Early types of organo-phosphate weapons are classified in American nomenclature as "G agents" and include tabun (GA), sarin (GB), soman (GD), and cyclohexyl methylphosphonofluoridate (GF). In the 1950s, while researching insecticides, the most toxic nerve agents ever known to man were developed by American and European scientists. Called "V agents," they are 10 times more deadly than sarin. VX is the most common V agent.

Nerve agents are all colorless liquids. Sarin easily vaporizes and may be inhaled into the lungs as well as absorbed through the skin. An area contaminated by sarin decontaminates itself within a few days because of this easy vaporization. VX is more of a thick oil that does not vaporize as rapidly and is, therefore, mostly absorbed through the skin. VX may remain on the ground for several weeks. The effectiveness of tabun, soman, and GF contamination are somewhere between those of sarin and VX.

Nerve agents kill people by inhibiting acetylcholinesterase, an enzyme in the body that stops conduction of nerve impulses. When a nerve impulse gets to a junction, called a synapse, a chemical called acetylcholine allows the impulse to move to the next nerve cell. Acetylcholinesterase then degrades the acetylcholine so the nerve impulse will stop. When nerve agents block acetylcholinesterase, the muscles of the body continue to be stimulated by acetylcholine until they fatigue and breathing muscles no longer function.

The effects of exposure to a nerve agent depend on the dose and route of exposure. When exposed to a low dose, symptoms may include a runny nose, excess saliva, constriction of the pupils of the eyes, headache, or tightness of the chest. Slurred speech, tiredness, nausea, and hallucinations may occur.

Exposure to high doses of nerve agent, especially when inhaled, lead to muscle twitching, convulsions, and loss of consciousness. In large exposures, this may happen so quickly that symptoms previously mentioned may not have time to develop. Paralysis of the muscles of respiration and effects on the breathing centers of the brain cause death by suffocation. High doses of inhaled agent can cause death in two minutes, while exposure through the skin only takes longer for symptoms to develop.

Protection from chemical attack

We have all seen news photos of our soldiers in chemical protection gear, but what can we as civilians do? First, remember that an attack anywhere in the United States will bring nationwide panic, which is one of the goals of the terrorists. An attack in one city will be a local disaster, however, affecting only those in immediate contact with the chemical agent. If it is an airborne attack where wind could spread the agent, there could be an effect to the downwind population.

Signs of a possible chemical attack include many people suffering from watery eyes, coughing, choking, twitching, or having trouble breathing. Large numbers of dead or sick birds, fish, and small animals may be present.

There are three main ways to protect against chemical weapons: physical protection, medical protection, and decontamination. At the first sign of a chemical attack, quickly determine where the chemical is coming from and get away. When the chemical is in the building in which you are located, leave the building without passing through the contaminated area. If you can't get out, get as far away from the chemical release as possible.

Physical protection involves protection of the body and respiratory system. Military and front-line civil-defense rescue units who will need to be in the contaminated area will have full body suits and respirators that are not going to be available to the civilian population.

Civilian exposure to chemical agents will be mostly during the time that they are evacuating the attacked area. When doing so, individuals should make sure all areas of their skin are covered and they are wearing a protective mask.

Protective masks provide barriers preventing the chemical agent from being inhaled through the nose or mouth. While useful in chemical attacks, they are also useful in biological attacks and after major explosions that release fine dust and debris that can damage the lungs, such as the September 11 attacks on the Trade Center. They may also protect against smoke and chemicals released from attacks using conventional explosives on oil refinery or other industrial targets.

Surgical masks or masks made of dense-weave cotton that tightly cover the nose and mouth work to prevent inhalation of biological agents or dust, but will not adequately protect against chemical agents. Still, they are better than nothing in a chemical attack.

Protective chemical masks (gas masks), such as those issued to the Israeli civilian population, are available for adults and older children. In February, 23,000 workers at the Pentagon were issued chemical masks by the Department of Defense, so the government is taking the threat seriously.

Protective masks are not something that we can expect the government to be able to provide in an emergency. Those individuals who live or work in an area where a chemical attack is a possibility might want to have their own mask. For most people, they probably are not necessary. To be effective, they would need to be immediately accessible at all times.

Protective masks are available through stores that sell emergency preparedness or industrial safety supplies, as well as some military surplus stores. Since your life depends on it, purchase a new one designed for this purpose, not a used "army gas mask." Costs vary, but expect to pay as much as $190 for a good quality mask.

The population downwind of a chemical attack may be advised to "shelter in place" by authorities. If so, go indoors and create a "safe room" that is isolated from outside air. Turn off air conditioning, heaters, and fans that can draw outside air into the room. This would be the time to use plastic sheeting and duct tape to seal cracks around the door, air ducts, and any vents into the room.

Since some chemicals are heavier than air, they may seep into basements even if windows are closed, so a room above ground level is best. Listen to information provided by authorities over radio or television. Further actions depend on the type of chemical weapons used.

Medical protection

Since nerve agents work very rapidly, any medical treatment must be immediately available. The military provides kits with auto-injectors of antidote to those personnel at high risk of exposure to nerve agents. While these are not available to civilians and are reportedly not on the surplus market, these antidotes are standard pharmaceutical drugs. It may be possible to obtain them through a friendly physician or pharmacist if you believe you are at high-risk for exposure to chemical attack. For most of us, this is probably not the case.

Atropine is an anticholinergic compound that reduces the effect of excess acetylcholine and should be injected when exposure to nerve agent has occurred or is imminent. Pralidoxime chloride (Protopam chloride or 2-PAM), restores normal activity of acetylcholinerterase, blocking the effects of the nerve agent. Each combat soldier in the military is issued three MARK I kits, each containing an auto-injector with 2mg of atropine and 600 mg of pralidoxime chloride.

Diazepam (Valium) is an anti-seizure drug that is used as a pre-treatment drug or at the onset of severe symptoms from a nerve agent. As a pre-treatment, it is taken when an exposure is expected. A tablet is taken at least 30 minutes prior to exposure, with the best effect two hours later. Treatment can be repeated every eight hours for several days, if necessary. U.S. soldiers carry an auto-injector containing 10 mg of diazepam to be injected in case of severe nerve agent symptoms.

Decontamination

Once exposed to a chemical, rapid decontamination is important before it can be absorbed through the skin. Because decontamination works best within the first few minutes after exposure to chemical agents, self-decontamination is a priority. Strip off any contaminated clothing and wash with any source of water, using soap if available.

Flush contaminated skin with large amounts of water to remove or dilute the chemical agent. A wooden stick can be used to scrape off chemical agents, as can absorbent materials such as dry powders, soil, flour, and soap detergents. It is reported that applying flour and wiping with tissue paper is particularly effective in removing VX and soman, although all methods work for all agents. You don't need to know what you are dealing with to decontaminate.

Soap and water hydrolyze and inactivate VX and nerve agents, while chlorine can be used to oxidize mustard gas. The military recommends using a 0.5% solution of sodium or calcium hypochlorite solution (diluted bleach) for skin and a 5% solution for equipment. Household bleach is generally 4-6% chlorine and can be diluted for use.

Biological terrorism

Biological weapons are bacteria, viruses, and toxins that cause disease in humans, livestock, or crops. Attractive to terrorists because they are relatively inexpensive compared to nuclear, chemical, or conventional weapons, they can be manufactured with readily available scientific equipment and biological cultures.

Projections on the casualty rate from bioweapons are staggering. A government study estimated if 200 pounds of aerosolized anthrax was released over Washington D.C., there would be up to 3 million deaths. Smallpox killed over 500 million people in the world during the 20th century before it was eradicated in 1977.

Biological agents are odorless, colorless, and tasteless, and can be distributed by crop duster aircraft, boats, or trucks. With low wind speeds and inversion conditions, they can be sprayed upwind of the intended target, increasing the number of casualties.

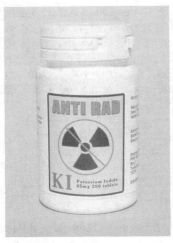

Potassium iodide is useful in preventing thyroid cancer from radioactive fallout. The National Pharmaceutical Stockpile program has large amounts stored, but many individuals prefer to have their own supply, which is inexpensive to purchase and does not need a prescription.

Bioweapons must be inhaled, eaten, or enter through a cut in the skin. Some, like smallpox, are contagious and are spread from person to person, while others, like anthrax, are not contagious. Terrorists would likely prefer inhaled agents, since they can be spread rapidly and a large number of individuals can be infected before anyone is aware of the attack.

Of twelve different agents mentioned repeatedly in biological warfare literature, six are considered most likely to be used: anthrax, smallpox, botulism toxin, plague, tularemia, and hemorrhagic fevers such as Ebola. Anthrax and botulism toxin have already been weaponized and are likely to be available to terrorists.

Smallpox is highly contagious and can be easily made in large quantities. The secret Soviet program of the Cold War reportedly made tons of weaponized smallpox. Since a good portion of the population has never been vaccinated, it is considered an ideal terrorist weapon.

Ricin is also something that has been in the news lately, having been found in an apartment in London.

Volumes of information have been written about all known biological warfare agents and detailed information can be found on the Internet and in medical books. Since the precautions we can take are the same no matter the biological agent, I will review only the few most likely agents.

Anthrax is a bacterial infection that causes diseases that affect the skin, gastrointestinal system, or respiratory system (inhalational anthrax). Inhalational anthrax is most severe and begins 3 to 5 days after inhaling anthrax spores. Respiratory symptoms begin slowly and then rapidly progress to shortness of breath and lack of oxygenation of the blood. Shock and death occur within 2 to 3 days after respiratory distress begins. Treatment with antibiotics is usually not effective once symptoms begin.

If exposure has occurred or is imminent, antibiotics are advised. Cipro 500 mg twice a day or doxycycline 100 mg twice a day are used. Vaccine is given to those not previously vaccinated.

Botulism toxin (Botox) is produced by Clostridium botulinum bacteria. It is the strongest toxin known, being 100,000 times stronger than sarin nerve gas. Working by blocking nerve transmissions, botulism toxin causes muscle paralysis and respiratory failure. Symptoms may appear 2 to 3 days after exposure and death occurs in as little as 24 hours after the first symptoms.

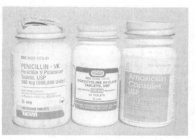

Antibiotics are used to treat bacterial infections caused by biological weapons and are being acquired by the National Pharmaceutical Stockpile program for use throughout the country. Authorities do not recommend that individual store antibiotics, although some are doing so with the help of their physicians.

No medicines are available to reverse this toxin and extensive hospital care is required which could take weeks or months. While this was fatal 60% of the time in the 1950s, medical care today has reduced the death rate to less than 5%. However, it should be expected the death rate would increase after a terrorist attack, as it would be difficult for hospitals to provide intensive care for hundreds of victims who might become simultaneously infected.

Smallpox is a virus that was eradicated from the world in 1977. Only two secure facilities in the world were supposed to have stored virus samples in case it was needed for a vaccine. One was in the United States and one in the Soviet Union. It is known the Soviet Union did research to weaponize smallpox pox, and to combine smallpox and Ebola viruses to make a weapon. A 1998 intelligence report concluded that smallpox for military use was possessed by Iraq, North Korea, and Russia.

Spread by coughing, sneezing, or dust on clothing and bedding, smallpox is highly contagious. After an incubation period of 12 days, fever, vomiting, and headache begin, followed by rashes and blisters of the skin. Smallpox kills about 30% of its victims and scars and sometimes blinds the survivors..

A smallpox pox vaccine recently has become available for first responders and health care workers, and will be offered to the public in the future. Vaccination after exposure will protect if it is taken within four days..

Ricin is a deadly poison in the form of a powder, mist, or pellet that can be made by amateurs from the waste of castor beans. It was found recently in Afghanistan while searching Al-Qaeda caves and is suspected of being used in the Iran/Iraq war. Within hours of exposure, the victim starts coughing and their lungs fill with fluid. There is no antidote and treatment is aimed at supporting respiration until the victim recovers or dies. Death occurs within 3 to 4 days of exposure.

Protection from biological attack

A biological attack may not be immediately obvious, as biological agents cannot be detected until people become sick. Usually, hospitals will notice an unusual pattern of disease or there will be a large number of people seeking help.

Once a biological attack is suspected, local public health officials will notify the public via radio, television, and, possibly, door-to-door advising the public what steps to take. Expect mandatory quarantines of infected victims, possibly the entire civilian population.

Travel may be stopped with any significant biological attack on the United States. Long-term disruptions to the infrastructure of the country could affect the economy and food supply. This is another reason to consider a long-term preparedness plan, with three months to a year supply of food, water, and essentials.

It doesn't hurt to protect yourself if you become aware of a suspicious release of an unknown substance. Move away rapidly while covering the nose and mouth with a cotton filter, such as a handkerchief, towel, or T-shirt. Once safe, wash with soap and water, and contact authorities.

If a biological emergency is declared for a contagious disease, such as smallpox, follow health department instructions, use common sense, and practice good hygiene to avoid spreading the disease. If you have Internet access, www.cdc.gov has extensive descriptions of possible terrorist agents and decontamination procedures. Depending on the severity, this might be a good time to consider a self-imposed quarantine, avoiding contact with others. Definitely, it would be a time to wear a mask when in public. If a family member becomes sick, be suspicious, but do not automatically assume it is a result of the attack since symptoms of many common illnesses overlap with symptoms of biological weapons.

The National Pharmaceutical Stockpile program has stockpiled antibiotics, vaccines, and medical supplies that can be rapidly sent anywhere in the country for use in biological attacks. If antibiotics or vaccines are recommended, public health officials will give information about who should get them and where they are being offered.

Nuclear terrorism

A nuclear disaster, called a "nuclear emergency" by government agencies, is any accidental or intentional large-scale release of radioactive material. This could occur from any number of terrorist attacks in the United States or from fallout from a nuclear war in Iraq, Korea, or between India and Pakistan.

A relatively small nuclear bomb detonated in New York City could kill over 100,000 people and spread radiation over much of the east coast. Authorities worry that nuclear weapons could be bought, stolen, or built by terrorists or obtained by the fall of a nuclear power, such as Pakistan. Nuclear bombs, missiles, and "suitcase" bombs are all in demand by terrorists and Third World countries.

Nuclear power plants are also potential terrorist targets. An attack on one of the 103 nuclear power plants in the United States using a commercial jet or large bomb would have some of the same effects as the detonation of a nuclear weapon. A meltdown of the core or dispersal of spent fuel waste would spread radiation in lethal doses over large areas.

Nuclear waste material is transported by ship, truck, and rail throughout the United States. Radioactive waste from Asia actually is transported by rail through heavily populated areas of California to be stored in the West. Terrorist attacks against such largely unguarded rail transportation could spread radiation locally.

"Dirty" bombs are the most accessible radiological weapons available to terrorists. Islamic terrorists placed, but did not detonate, such a weapon in a Moscow park in 1996.

Relatively easy to make, "dirty" bombs are conventional explosives wrapped with radioactive waste material. Upon detonation, radiation is scattered widely. Cars, trucks, or shipping containers can easily hide such a bomb. It is estimated that forty percent of the inbound shipping into the United States could be affected if such a bomb were detonated at a major shipping port.

A nuclear disaster brought about the detonation of an actual atomic bomb would affect us in three ways. First, the population in the immediate area affected by the thermal effects (fireball), shock wave, and intense radiation would have to deal with death, injuries, and radioactivity.

Second, those living downwind would have to deal with radioactive fallout. Fallout is radiation that is scattered into the atmosphere and carried by the wind until it settles to the ground or is washed to the ground by rain or snow. Plant crops and animals used for food are contaminated and unusable, as are exposed sources of drinking water.

Third, there would be general panic throughout the United States and possible disruption of transportation, food, and supplies. Everyone, whether or not affected by radiation, will be affected by a major nuclear disaster in the United States. Understanding the effects of a nuclear explosion allows us to develop a rational plan of what to do if faced with a nuclear disaster.

Many disaster preparedness experts suggest having enough food and water to last several weeks or more. Foods stored can be a combination of everyday foods that are rotated every six months and foods designed to be stored for years.

Detonation of a nuclear weapon would cause a fireball of blinding light and heat, causing blindness, burns, and death. Everything nearby would catch fire and burn. Superheated air would cause a shock wave with winds traveling at supersonic speeds and blowing over every building, train, vehicle, or person in their path. Such winds travel several hundred miles per hour and cause damage over a mile away.

Severe radiation will cause immediate death and injury to those in the area of detonation and radiation sickness to those somewhat further away. Radiation sickness can cause hair to fall out, nausea, vomiting, diarrhea, bleeding, or infection. An individual can be shielded from the initial radiation blast by being sheltered by a concrete or dirt structure. Nuclear weapons also produce an electromagnetic pulse, causing localized disruption of electrical equipment, communications, and computers, but not injuring humans.

Fallout is the least serious consequence of a nuclear explosion, however it affects many more people than the initial blast since, depending on the winds, it can travel hundreds or thousands of miles. It causes deaths in the future due to cancer or birth defects.

Radiation exposure from fallout is either external or internal. External exposure occurs when radioactive material contaminates the skin or clothing and internal exposure occurs when radioactive material is swallowed, inhaled, or absorbed through open wounds. Most of the victims from the Chernobyl accident received internal radiation from drinking milk produced by cows that ate contaminated grass.

The human body normally produces hormones in the thyroid gland from iodine in our diet. One of the byproducts of a nuclear explosion is a form of radioactive iodine that is also absorbed and can cause cancer of the thyroid gland, especially in children, years later. Thousands of cases were reported after Chernobyl.

Time, distance, and shielding are factors that minimize exposure to radiation. Most radioactive fallout loses its strength rapidly and the farther from the source of radiation, the less radiation exposure. Concrete, dirt, and other dense building materials will block out radiation. For radioactive fallout, staying indoors may be all the shielding needed.

Protection from nuclear attack

Depending on the amount of notice that you have and the distance from the nuclear disaster, you will either need to stay put in a sheltered place or evacuate.

In the case of nuclear power plant disasters, the Federal Emergency Management Agency (FEMA) has plans in place and residents within 10 miles of nuclear power plants are given information on what to do in such an emergency.

After a nuclear device explodes, move quickly away from the explosion site, going home or to a protected indoor site. If you are advised to "shelter in place" by authorities, go indoors and bring pets with you. Protect the inside of your home or business from fallout by turning off air conditioning, heating, vents, and fans, closing and locking windows and doors, and closing fire place dampers.

Cover air conditioners and vents with plastic, aluminum foil, or waxed paper taped in place to prevent radioactive dust from entering the room. Cracks around windows or doorways should be closed with duct tape or wet towels. Fill sinks, bathtubs, and containers with water and shut pipes off as a protection in case reservoirs become contaminated. If possible, go to a basement or other underground area, as these areas would give more protection from radiation.

When coming inside after exposure to fallout, remove clothes and shoes worn outside, place them in a sealed plastic bag, shower, and put on clean clothes and shoes. Stay indoors until authorities report that the level of radiation outside has subsided enough to be safe.

When going outdoors after it is safe, remember that fruits and vegetables in home gardens will be contaminated. Safety information on eating farm and home garden products should be provided by public health authorities, but, if you must use home grown products that have been exposed to radiation, wash and peel vegetables and fruits.

Use water that has been stored, or comes from underground sources, such as a well. Make sure water from exposed sources, such as rivers, open reservoirs, or lakes, is deemed safe by authorities before drinking. Normally, collecting rainwater is a pure source of drinkable water during a survival situation, but in this case rain may wash radioactive particles out of the atmosphere.

Potassium iodide is used to prevent thyroid cancer after exposure to radioactive fallout. It blocks the radioactive form of iodine from being absorbed by the gland by filling up the thyroid gland with normal iodine. It prevents only thyroid cancer, not the other effects of radiation.

After the Chernobyl accident, thousands of cases of thyroid cancer occurred years later in children in Russia, which did not give its population potassium iodide. Poland was also subjected to radioactive fallout but gave potassium iodide to over 17 million people and did not suffer increases in cancer rates.

During the Three Mile Island crisis, the U.S. government found itself without potassium iodide for the population and scrambled to find some from manufacturers. It turned out that it was not needed for that incident and the stockpile was discarded when it became old.

On September 11, although it wasn't needed, it turns out that the U.S. government again had no stockpile. Since then, the National Pharmaceutical Stockpile program has purchased large quantities of potassium iodide and people who live near some nuclear power plants have been issued pills to have available.

Should potassium iodide be needed on a large scale in the United States, it is likely that enough would not be available. Since it is cheap, safe, and does not require a prescription, it may be a wise idea to have some available as part of a disaster preparedness plan.

The FDA recommends adults and children over one year of age take one 130 mg tablet per day for 10 days. One-half tablet (65 mg) is the dose for children under one year of age. Individuals allergic to iodide should not take this product as it can cause severe allergic reactions. If you are considering having potassium iodide as part of your survival kit, you should talk to your physician to make sure it is safe for you and check the FDA web site for additional information. It is widely available over the Internet or through your pharmacy.

Radiation monitors are available to test for the presence of radiation. It is questionable if they are necessary or worth the cost. A nuclear disaster today is likely to be localized in one or several parts of the country and nuclear response teams will be equipped to monitor the environment. Waiting in a sheltered place until local authorities report it is safe is probably the best thing to do. Still, for those interested, information and radiation monitors are available through the Internet or surplus stores.

Preparation

The current government buzzword for "hunkering down" in your house or place of work after a chemical, biological, or nuclear attack is "Shelter in place." Basic preparations are the same for any terrorist act, as well as any natural disaster.

FEMA and the Department of Homeland Security advise people to have enough food, water, and supplies on hand to take care of their family for three days "until help from the government can arrive." Preparing the "72-

Red Cross and government agencies recommend everyone have food, water, and supplies to take care of themselves for at least 72 hours. A "72 hour kit" should be able to be easily loaded into a car in case evacuation is necessary during a terrorist attack or natural disaster.

hour kit" that they recommend is a good idea and can be used for immediate evacuation or as part of your overall home disaster supply kit.

However, in a major terrorist attack or disaster it is unlikely that government relief agencies will be able to help everyone within three days. They will be overwhelmed by disaster and the massive job of caring for the number of people who failed to prepare ahead of time.

It is not unreasonable to expect to have to take care of yourself for several weeks or longer. Some scenarios in which the economy or infrastructure is damaged by biological or nuclear terrorism suggest the need to care for your own needs for a year or longer. Be prepared by storing needed water, food, first aid materials, tools, emergency supplies, and special needs items.

One can live a while without food and comfort items, but cannot live long without water. The body needs at least two quarts of water per day to avoid dehydration, with exercise, hard work, and hot weather increasing the need to as much as four to five quarts per day.

It is recommended that at least a gallon of water per person per day (two quarts for drinking and two for food preparation and sanitation) be stored in food-grade plastic containers. Plastic water containers, empty two-liter soda bottles, or thirty to fifty gallon containers all work well. Two-gallon bottles of water available at markets are a convenient size to move and use. Water supplies should be rotated every six months to maintain freshness.

Non-perishable foods requiring minimal water to prepare, no refrigeration, and no cooking are ideal for part of your food supply. It is good to have a variety of ready-to-eat canned foods including canned meat, tuna, chicken, stews, beans, fruits, and vegetables, along with canned juices, milk, and soups. Canned foods don't require cooking and can be eaten unheated right out of the can, if necessary. Have a mechanical-type can-opener available in case there is no electricity to run electric ones.

Peanut butter, crackers, granola bars, trail mix, or energy bars are easy to store and are high-energy foods. Cookies, hard candy, coffee, or tea are nice comfort foods that will help brighten spirits in stressful times.

A good way to start out buying a supply of emergency food is to visit a large warehouse distributor, such as Costco or Sam's Warehouse, or some of the suppliers who advertise in this magazine. By buying in bulk, a large quantity of food can be purchased at a great discount. At Costco, a 25-lb. bag of rice sells for as little as $3 and a 25-lb. bag of pinto beans for $7. So, while it may get boring eating only beans and rice, you can feed a family for a long time during an emergency for only $10.

Stored food should be rotated every six months. To keep costs down and food fresh, store foods that you normally would buy and use these food supplies for your regular meals. Replace food used with newly purchased food.

Emergency foods packaged to last for 5 to 10 years are available from many sources. Their advantage is you don't need to remember to rotate food on a regular basis, they are convenient in evacuation situations, and they can be stored in a vehicle. Military MREs (Meals Ready To Eat) have a long shelf life, although they are expensive. Emergency Essentials (ad on page 15), Ready Reserve Foods, and Maple Leaf are among suppliers of #10 size cans of food intended for long-term storage. Their huge selection of foods would allow tasty, complete meals that could be stored for years.

Other emergency supplies should include a first aid kit, battery-operated radio, flashlight with extra batteries, non-electric can opener, matches, lantern, portable cooking stove and fuel, fire extinguisher, hand tools for repairs and to turn off household water and gas, a good knife, and, of course, the recommended plastic sheeting and duct tape to seal doors and vents.

Remember to include toilet paper, towelettes, soap, toothpaste, personal hygiene items, disinfectant, household chlorine bleach to purify water, and other sanitation items. These things will normally be in your home, but make sure you have a supply that will last at least two weeks. Don't forget formula and diapers for infants, prescription medications, contact lenses and supplies, extra glasses, and pet food.

Be prepared

The world is a new place. Terrorists today have the means, power, and desire to attack civilian populations with no hesitation. Who would have believed that we would be facing weapons of mass destruction on our own soil?

Terrorist attacks using weapons of mass destruction could be minor, causing fear and a few injuries, or could be devastating, killing hundreds of thousands and crippling our country. Whatever the case, there will be widespread panic and chaos. Now is the time to become informed about the possible threats, develop a plan for each threat, and prepare by storing the food, water, and emergency supplies that would be needed.

While future terrorist attacks are almost certain, it is possible to protect yourself against chemical, biological, and nuclear terrorism. Δ

Chapter 2
Biological & chemical terrorism

By Dave Duffy

A merica wages war against terrorists with cells in 60 nations. The enemy is willing to die in order to kill us, and they may have access to biological and chemical weapons.

How much danger are we in? Can they really unleash plagues of genetically altered bacteria and viruses among us, for which there are no vaccinations or treatments? Will they attack us with a nerve gas that can kill thousands of people in minutes?

No one has definite answers to these questions, but the military and the civilian medical establishment are both gearing up to treat biological and chemical casualties. The American Medical Association website (ama-assn. org) is packed with the latest information for physicians on how to treat biological and chemical patients.

But a lot of perspective is needed when trying to assess the actual danger we are in. It is not as great as the constant news coverage of anthrax, for example, would indicate. But it is *real*. In fact, one could argue that whoever first mailed anthrax through the U.S. mail did us a favor as a nation, because at long last we are taking seriously a threat that has existed for years.

Perspective

First the perspective:

If America was at war with a sophisticated military power such as the former Soviet Union, we *could* be attacked along the frightening scenarios mentioned above. The Soviets had hundreds of tons of genetically altered anthrax that even their own vaccine appeared defenseless against, they had hundreds of tons of nerve gas that could kill thousands of people in minutes, and they had the missile means to deliver both to our shore. In fact, Dr. Valdimir Paschenick, a defector from the secret Soviet biological warfare program of the 1980s, told Western intelligence that the Soviet's view of a possible World War III included biological and chemical-tipped missiles being lobbed into the United States.

But we have not been attacked by a sophisticated state; we have been attacked by terrorists who spend a lot of their time living in caves. Terrorists may be able to catch us by surprise and hijack planes and drive them into buildings, and they may be able to grow batches of anthrax bacteria and send them through the mail to kill a few unsuspecting people, but actually waging biological or chemical war on us is quite another matter.

Producing germs and being able to disseminate them widely among a civilian population requires hundreds of millions of dollars of research and a country with a large scientific infrastructure. Terrorists do not have that combination, nor do the third world countries who support terrorists and are reportedly attempting to develop biological weapons.

Iraq, for example, had the hundreds of millions of dollars and they made a concerted effort to develop anthrax, botulinum toxin, and other biological agents into weapons. They succeeded only in developing a liquid form of anthrax, which they put in the warheads of a few SCUD missiles but never used, because even Saddam Hussein realized they were totally ineffective as weapons.

The only countries to have succeeded in developing biological agents as weapons have been the former Soviet Union and the United States, and it is not at all clear just how effective those bioweapons would be if used.

Anthrax

Let's take anthrax as an example of just how difficult it is to turn a bacteria into a weapon. Anthrax is a good example because it is considered by military analysts as one of the most promising bacterial candidates to be weaponized. It is relatively easy to grow, stable, and has a good ability to infect people. Cutaneous (through the skin) anthrax is 20% fatal if untreated, and untreated inhalation anthrax is 90% fatal.

Both the making of the bacteria and the delivering of it successfully to the intended target must be considered together because there is no point in making a germ unless you can deliver it to targets. Nature is full of terrifying bacteria and viruses, but they don't always reach humans.

Anthrax lives in the ground in rural areas and typically infects only grazing animals because they spend so much of their time with their noses in the ground. A few anthrax spores cannot create an infection in humans; it takes about 10,000 or more. Wool sorters often inhale small quantities of anthrax spores, but do not get infected.

To be used as a weapon, anthrax spores must be converted to a dry powder one to five microns in size so it can be inhaled. It usually attacks the lungs, but it can also enter the body through cuts or undercooked meat. In a bad year about 10,000 people worldwide get anthrax, usually from tainted meat in third world countries.

The dry powder is necessary so the anthrax can stay in the air to be inhaled. If wet it will simply fall to the ground. Creating the powder is technically very difficult, requiring washing the spores in large, expensive centrifuges, then drying it by spraying a mist into a vacuum. It's expensive, technically demanding, and requires a lot of sophisticated equipment with several PhDs guiding the process.

Once the powder is made and disseminated, presumably through some sort of sophistical aerosol device (crop duster nozzles won't work) it still needs the help of wind to keep it from falling to the ground. If it falls to the ground it can't be inhaled. But the wind will also rapidly spread the powder too thin so most of the intended victims would not inhale enough to cause infection.

An aerosol attack with a large quantity of anthrax, which terrorists would probably not be able to do, may kill a few hundred people but not the hundreds of thousands some media people are suggesting. Opening an envelope full of the powder would be another matter. There may be millions of spores present so it would be easier to inhale the 10,000 or so necessary for infection to occur.

Once someone is infected, anthrax is also not contagious from human to human, and antibiotics are effective against it.

It is important to realize the difference between terrorists attacking us with biological weapons and being able to kill large numbers of people, and terrorists scaring the hell out of us by sending anthrax germs through the mail, or disseminating it in some other inept way, and killing a few unfortunate people. Mailed anthrax has a tremendous terrorizing effect, but that is probably the only effect the terrorists can achieve.

Even if the terrorists managed to somehow get hold of a quantity of the former Soviet Union's purported supply of genetically altered anthrax, against which there is no vaccine or antibiotic, they probably could not use it effectively except as a terror weapon. It does not spray well through nozzles, as bacteria likes to clump together and clog up the nozzles.

Some of the anthrax sent through the U.S. mail was contained in a powder, which may mean it came from the Soviet Union or the United States military anthrax stocks, since they are the only countries capable of making anthrax into a powder. The fact that the anthrax, when caught in time, apparently responded to antibiotics tends to indicate it may have come from the U.S. stocks. But that's only my speculation.

Living with terrorists and other nuts who set about to infect us with disease may be something we must learn to live with, at least until these people realize they can't do a lot of damage and we become immune to the terror aspect of it.

While doing research for this article, I encountered a lot of information in the mass media that talked about the terrible lethality of a lot of these disease agents. For example, botulism toxin, which some countries are developing as an agent and which folks can encounter while eating improperly canned food, is pound for pound the most toxic substance on earth. It sounds scary, and it is meant to be for the sake of readership, but it really has no relevance when you are talking about weaponizing diseases. As I said before, Nature is full of horrifying diseases, but if they can't get to you easily who cares. When we can food, we do so under strict rules so as to guard against botulism, just as when we eat in restaurants we avoid those that operate under third world conditions. We are so used to being conscious of cleanliness in America to safeguard our health—unlike many third world countries where diseases often run rampant—that we forget Nature has many diseases and toxins all around us.

Influenza kills about 20,000 Americans in a typical year, but most of us manage to carry on our lives in spite of that terrifying fact. My own daughter has asthma so is in a high risk group for influenza, and she doesn't get a flu shot because it gives her the flu. So she is vulnerable, but both she and I do not walk around terrified. Life has its risks.

This is not the first time bungling terrorists will try to attack us with disease, and it won't be the last. As recently as 1984, the Bhagwan Shree Rajneesh cult had a beef with local officials in The Dalles, Oregon. They grew salmonella typhimurium in a laboratory at their Oregon ranch and used it to contaminate salad bars in four local restaurants. No one died, but nearly 800 people became ill. The culprits were all jailed for a few years, then deported.

Smallpox

Now that we're feeling a little more secure against anthrax and bacteria, and a few other germs, there *is* something to worry about. It is viruses. Many are contagious through the air, or from human to human. In many cases, one infected person can infect 10 or 20 more very quickly, so infections can multiply rapidly.

One virus in particular is worrisome—smallpox. Smallpox is a very contagious virus that is fatal in 30% of cases. Most people my age (59) were vaccinated against smallpox when children, but vaccinations stopped in 1977 when the disease was eradicated. The World Health Organization decided that only two laboratories should possess the eradicated smallpox: one in the former Soviet Union and one in the United States.

The former Soviet Union is believed to have developed smallpox as a biological weapon in its secret biological weapons program of the 1980s. In 1992, amidst the economic ruins of what had been the Soviet Union, Boris Yeltsin admitted the existence of the secret program and promptly discontinued it. Some 60,000 scientists and technicians who had become expert at developing biological weapons during the 20-year existence of the secret program were thrown out of work. The fear is that some of them may have sold their expertise, or perhaps samples of the smallpox, to other nations who wanted to pursue biological warfare research.

The United States still has some smallpox vaccine (15 million doses), but it is at least 25 years old and we are not sure how viable it is. It could take two to three years to develop a new vaccine. As for my vaccination, it may still offer some protection against a smallpox strain that was not genetically altered, but it has most assuredly lost a lot of its effectiveness in the 50 odd years since I got it.

Compounding the concern is that the Soviets may have made a genetically altered smallpox. Dr. Ken Alibek, former deputy chief of Biopreparat, the civilian arm of the Soviet Union's secret biological weapons program, stated recently that the Soviets had been working to genetically alter the smallpox virus, and had explored combining it with Venezuelan equine encephalomytlitis and with the Ebola virus.

The entire thrust of the Soviets' biological warfare program, according to Dr. Alibek, was to develop agents "for which there was no prevention and no cure," which was in sharp contrast to the U.S. program which created vaccines and treatments for each agent studied.

The danger is that suicidal terrorists, if they were able to get hold of some of the smallpox, will infect themselves and walk among us in crowded cities. Once infected, people are contagious for 7 to 10 days. Even smallpox that has not been genetically altered is still a virus, and viruses do not respond to antibiotics.

The Soviet breakup

Since the ending of the Soviet Union's biological program, not all of their biological stocks have been accounted for. The Soviets amassed hundreds of tons of anthrax, smallpox, tularemia, botulinum toxin, and a host of other diseases and toxins. Have terrorists bought some from unemployed biowarfare scientists desperate for money?

Another concern is the way the Soviets disposed of their biological weapons. For example, in 1988 they secretly buried tons of supposedly deactivated anthrax spores on the remote island Vozrozhdeniye (Renaissance Island) in the Aral Sea in Uzbekistan, just north of Afghanistan. A subsequent ill-thought-out irrigation project has drained 75% of the water from the Aral Sea so that the island can now be reached by land.

The United States is working with Uzbekistan to secure the anthrax. Analysis has determined that 6 of the 11 burial sites on the island contain live anthrax spores. This island was also used by the Soviets to test other germ warfare agents, such as smallpox, tularemia, plague, Q-fever, typhus, brucellosis, glanders, Venezuelan Equine encephalitis, and botulism toxin. Uzbekistan is also home to former Soviet chemical weapons plants.

Chemical weapons

Chemical agents, including some nerve agents, are much easier to make than biological weapons, thus earning them the reputation as "the poor man's atom bomb." Iraq manufactured several nerve agents, which it used with deadly effect against Iranians in their 1980s war, and again against its own people, the Kurds, in 1988.

Chemical agents are particularly frightening because many of them can be made with chemicals that are readily available to terrorists. They can be made in a home laboratory, and many of them can be disseminated fairly easily.

The agents come in several varieties: **choking agents** like the chlorine and phosgene used in World War I; **vesicants (blister agents)**, like mustard and lewisite; **nerve agents**, which are closely related to the insecticides and pesticides we use around the house and garden; and **blood agents** like cyanide, which is used in many manufacturing processes and is always being transported on our nation's highways.

The most deadly chemical agents are the nerve agents, which include VX, GF, soman, sarin, and tabun. They may also be the most likely choices as terrorist weapons. They are chemically similar to pesticides, and like pesticides they can be disseminated through spraying devices such as those on crop dusters.

Many of us are familiar with the Japanese cult, Aum Shinrikyo, which in 1995 released sarin gas, a nerve agent, in the Tokyo subway system, killing 12 people and injuring 5,500. The cult was also implicated in a sarin gas attack that occurred in 1994 in Matsumoto, Japan, killing 7 and injuring 200. The cult had produced an impure form of sarin that was not nearly as lethal as military grade. The same cult was unsuccessful at developing a successful biological agent, even though it had six laboratories and a budget of $300 million.

Some nerve agents, such as VX, are at least 10 times more powerful than sarin, and it is known that some countries that are sympathetic to terrorists possess it. In the case of VX, a single drop on the skin can kill a person.

Nerve agents are acetylcholinesterase inhibitors and interfere with the nervous system's ability to control muscles, causing muscles to spasm. They are absorbed through the respiratory tract or skin, and symptoms include chest tightness, pinpoint pupils, shortness of breath, drooling, sweating, vomiting, stomach cramps, involuntary defecation and urination, and extreme muscle twitching and seizures. It is very nasty stuff.

In the Persian Gulf War, Hussein's possession of nerve agent, and his suspected possession of biological weapons, caused the U.S. to arm troops with chemical defense kits and immunize them against anthrax and botulinum toxin. The U.S. said he never used the agent, but some veterans groups claim that Gulf War Illness (GWI) exhibits symptoms that are consistent with nerve agent poisoning.

Possible methods of delivery by terrorists would be to modify aircraft with tanks designed to spray the agent. Iraq was working to develop such a method in 1990, according to CIA reports. An aerosol system mounted on a remotely controlled Unmaned Aerial Vehicle (UAV) is another method.

The Aum Shinrikyo cult that attacked the Tokyo subway possessed a Russian helicopter and two radio-controlled drone aircraft that could have been modified to spray chemical agent over a city. The cult used exploding canisters to distribute their nerve agent in the subway system.

Tanks mounted under a car and crop dusters are obvious ways to deliver nerve agents. A crop dusting manual was found among the belongings of Zacarias Moussaoui, a material witness detained by the FBI as having links with the terrorists who destroyed the World Trade Center towers. Moussaoui had also sought to take flying lessons.

Most nerve agents tend to dissipate fairly quickly, but VX agent was designed to be sticky and so stays on a surface for a long time, making an area unusable. It is mainly absorbed through the skin, while other nerve agents are mainly absorbed through inhalation.

When I was attending CBR Warfare School in the Army 35 years ago, atropine injected into the thigh was the life saving antidote against nerve agent. That is still the antidote today, but rapid decontamination is also critical for survival. In many countries, military personnel carry an auto-injector containing atropine and pralidoxime chloride. Pretreatment to withstand an attack is also available to the military in the form of pills that lessen the effect of the nerve agent.

Recovery from nerve agent takes about two weeks, but long-term effects that include mental disorders are possible. As I said, this is very nasty stuff.

The "terror" aspect

During the Persian Gulf War in 1991, 39 Iraqi SCUD missiles reached Israel. Even though none carried the nerve agent anticipated, 230 Israelis were treated for atropine overdoses, and an additional 544 people were hospitalized for anxiety. Just the threat of attack by a biological or chemical agent is intimidating to civilian populations, and an actual attack with its ensuing panic has the potential to cause major disruptions in society.

During the Cold War we lived under the specter of sudden nuclear annihilation; now we live under the specter of imagined annihilation by germs we cannot see or smell, and chemicals that our enemy can make in the neighbor's bathtub.

At least 17 countries, some of whom sponsor terrorists, currently have biological and/or chemical weapons programs. They include Egypt, Iran, Iraq, Libya, Syria, Cuba, Vietnam, Laos, Bulgaria, India, North Korea, South Korea, Vietnam, Russia, China, Taiwan, and Israel.

There are hundreds of bacteria, viruses, and toxins that could be used to attack people, but the military has chosen to develop only a handful because of they meet criteria involving ease of production, stability, and ability to infect. They include anthrax, smallpox, plague, cholera, Venezuelan equine encephalitis, Q fever, brucellosis, tularemia, staphylococcal enterotoxins, ricin toxin, and botulinum toxin. There are also many harmful and deadly chemicals being developed.

Some American officials have long realized that the nerve agent attacks in Japan's subway could just as easily have occurred in any subway system in America, and some analysts have been trying to warn us that a terrorist biological attack on America was just as possible. Few people listened to them until now.

America is in a new type of war with terrorists, with part of the battlefront on our own shore. They can certainly inflict casualties upon us by surreptitiously inserting diseases in American society, and by surreptitiously releasing chemical agents that can harm, even kill us. But they cannot do it with effectiveness, especially in light of a now alert America.

For the initial stages of this new type of warfare, there will be a learning curve. But this is not the Middle Ages when plagues of various sorts visited generation after generation and went unchecked. We now have the science to quickly ascertain any threat and to develop preventive measures.

The learning curve will involve some casualties but mostly anxiety because we won't know when or where or how the terrorists will strike. Our loyal ally Britain has lived with that anxiety for decades at the hands of IRA terrorists. Now we have even more in common with them. Δ

THE HISTORY OF CHEMICAL & BIOLOGICAL WARFARE

The Germans are given credit for introducing both chemical and biological weapons into modern warfare during World War I.

Modern chemical warfare began April 22, 1915 near Ypres, Belgium, when the Germans released 160 tons of chlorine gas from 6,000 pressurized cylinders into the wind blowing toward the Allies. The gas choked to death 5,000 Allied troops. They repeated the attack two days later.

The Germans introduced Phosgene, which was 10 times more deadly than the chlorine gas, in 1915, and mustard and cyanide later in the war. Before the war was over, both sides had released 113,000 tons of chemicals, killing 92,000 and wounding 1.2 million.

Modern biological warfare was introduced as an antianimal weapon in 1915 by an American-educated surgeon and German agent who grew anthrax and glanders in his Maryland home laboratory, then passed them on to another German agent who inoculated horses bound for the Allies.

After the war the combatant nations signed the Geneva protocol, which barred both gas and bacteriological warfare. During World War II, no combatant used chemical or biological agent on the battlefield, even though the Germans by then had developed nerve agents that were 15 to 100 times more potent than the World War I agents. (There is some evidence that the Japanese may have released plague-infected rats in China that killed several thousand civilians.)

Even though the agents were not used on World War II battlefields, the Germans did murder millions of civilians using Zyklon-B and other chemicals. Allied nations seized the German chemical weapons after the war and started their own programs. Most of the chemical weapons manufacturing plants were taken by the Russians to Volgograd.

In 1952, in England, during research on chemical agents being developed from insecticides, a new nerve agent many times more lethal than others was discovered. Codenamed VX, the United States took over the large-scale production of it from 1961 to 1968 in Dugway, Utah. In one accident at the plant, a cloud of the agent escaped and killed more than 6,000 nearby sheep.

In the 1960s and early 70s in Vietnam, chemical agents called "Agent Orange," "Agent Purple," "Agent Blue," and "Agent White" were used by the United States to defoliate the jungle surrounding the enemy, and unconfirmed human casualties were reported.

In 1969 President Nixon unilaterally discontinued America's biological weapons program and destroyed its stockpiles.

In 1972 the Biological Weapons Convention outlawed biological weapons, and in 1973 the Chemical Weapons Convention outlawed chemical weapons.

The Soviets, however, continued to operate a secret biological weapons program employing 60,000 people.

In 1979 an accident at a secret Soviet biological plant in Sverdlovsk (now called Ekaterinburg), Russia, caused at least 66 people living downwind from the plant to die of inhalation anthrax. In 1992 Boris Yeltsin admitted the existence of the secret program and discontinued it.

During the 1970s there were allegations that chemical agents were used in Laos against the Hmong tribesman who had supported the United States during the Vietnam War.

During the Arab-Israeli War of 1973, no chemical agents were used but captured Egyptian soldiers carried an antidote to the nerve agent soman.

There were allegations in the 1ate 1970s and 1980s that a biological agent, tentatively identified as a mycotoxin produced from a fungi, was used in Kampuchea, Cambodia.

During the 1980s in Afghanistan, there were frequent allegations that the Soviets were using chemical agents against Afghan rebels.

Also during the 1980s, during the eight-year Iran-Iraq War, it was confirmed that two types of chemical agents, the blister agent mustard and the nerve agent tabun, had been used by Iraq against Iran. Many Iranians were evacuated to Europe for treatment.

In 1988 it was also confirmed that Iraq had used nerve agents, mustard, and cyanide against Kurdish civilians when they bombed the village of Halabja in northern Iraq.

Although the U.S. says Iraq did not use chemical agents in the Persian Gulf War against Coalition Forces, some attribute "Gulf War Illness" to the possible use of them.

The use of chemical and biological warfare goes way back in history: Hannibal hurled poisonous snakes onto ships at Eurymedon in 190 BC. In 1346 DeMussis, a Mongol, catapulted bodies infected with bubonic plague into Kaffa, a seaport on the Black Sea in Russia. The British gave New England Indians smallpox-infected blankets in 1763. Even in America's Civil War, there were incidents of selling smallpox-infected clothing to unsuspecting Union soldiers.

Historical occurrences are numerous: Water wells have been poisoned by leaving dead bodies in them, arrows were dipped in blood and manure and decomposing bodies, wine was tainted with leprosy patients' blood, and artillery shells were filled with the saliva of rabid dogs.

Hurling plague-infected bodies at the enemy was a tactic used more than once in history's wars, and plague is still considered by the military as a good candidate for a modern biological warfare agent.

Chapter 3
Dark winter
A simulated terrorist attack on three American cities using weaponized smallpox

By Dave Duffy

Historically smallpox has been the most deadly of all diseases for humans, killing between 300 and 500 million in the last century alone, far more than the 111 million people killed in all that century's wars combined. It is easily spread, kills 30% of those infected, and terribly scars and sometimes blinds those who survive. It was declared eradicated from Earth in 1980, but the Soviet Union has acknowledged maintaining a secret biological weapons program since then that employed 60,000 technicians and scientists. One fear is that some of the smallpox the Soviets worked with has gotten into terrorist hands, or that unemployed Soviet scientists desperate for money have been hired by Iraq, Al Qaida, or other terrorists.

June 22-23, 2001, nearly three months before the attack that toppled New York's World Trade towers, the United States conducted a major simulation of a terrorist smallpox attack against three American cities. It was named *Dark Winter*, and it lived up to its name. Within seven weeks, one million Americans were dead and the disease had spread to 25 states and 13 foreign countries. In the face of the out of control epidemic, panic had spread across America, interrupting vital services such as food deliveries to supermarkets, and our Government considered the possibility of a nuclear response, although against whom it was not clear.

Following is a reenactment of that exercise, edited for brevity but containing all the essential elements. The exercise took place at Andrews Air Force Base in Maryland, and was attended by many senior level government officials. Participating institutions included the *Johns Hopkins Center for Civilian Biodefense Strategies, the Center for Strategic and International Studies, the Oklahoma National Memorial Institute for the Prevention of Terrorism,* and the *Analytic Services Institute for Homeland Security.*

Former U.S. Senator Sam Nunn of Georgia played the President of the United States, Governor Frank Keating of Oklahoma played himself, five senior journalists who worked for major news organizations participated in mock news briefings, and a number of other participants played various key government positions ranging from the Director of Central Intelligence to key Government health advisors. Fifty people connected with U.S. bioterrorism policy preparedness observed the exercise.

The goal of the exercise was to increase awareness among Government officials of the danger of such an attack, and to examine the decision challenges the highest levels of Government would face if confronted with a biological attack. The ultimate aim was to improve strategies of response.

Smallpox was chosen as the disease because historically it has been the most feared and deadly of diseases, and one of the more likely choices for terrorists. It is not only easily spread from one person to another, but there is no effective medical treatment. It may also be unstoppable in an unvaccinated population, and since the United States' mandatory vaccination program was stopped in 1972, the U.S. population is very susceptible to smallpox. Even that part of the population that was vaccinated as late as 1972 may have little or no protection against the disease.

Although smallpox was declared eradicated in 1980, two official repositories of the variola virus were kept: one at the *Centers for Disease Control and Prevention* in Atlanta, and the other at the *Russian State Research Center for Virology and Biotechnology* in Koltsovo, Novosibirsk in central Siberia. Those supplies were to be used for scientific research and vaccine development, but it is now known that both countries maintained secret biological weapons programs since 1980. By 1990 the Soviet Union had a facility capable of producing 80 to 100 tons of smallpox a year, and it typically warehoused 20 tons. Although Russia and the United States have since abandoned their biological weapons programs, other countries still have them. It is thought that several rogue states like North Korea and Iraq and possibly terrorists have obtained samples of the smallpox virus.

Although the exercise took only two days, it simulated a time span of two weeks occurring between December 9-22, 2002. The exercise involved three *National Security Council (NSC)* meetings taking place on Dec. 9, 15, and 22, with the participants being made aware of evolving details of the attack and being required to establish strategies and make policy decisions to deal with it.

Exercise controllers acted as special assistants and deputies, providing facts and suggesting policy options to deal with the smallpox outbreak. Simulated newspaper coverage and TV video clips of the ensuing epidemic were also shown to participants, and various simulated memoranda, intelligence updates, and top level assessments of the spread of the epidemic were provided to key players whose jobs would normally require such information.

Each of the three NSC meetings began with controllers giving the NSC players briefings on the progress of the attack, an assessment of who the perpetrators might be, the response of the public, the comments of foreign governments, and any other information they would normally receive in such an emergency.

Assumptions

Several assumptions were made for this exercise, based on historical evidence and a variety of data related to susceptibility to smallpox:

- *Assumption 1: It was assumed that the initial attack was from "weaponized smallpox," similar to what the former Soviet Union would have developed in its secret bioweapons program.*

This would be a far more efficient way of attacking the U.S. than with, say, infected jihad volunteers walking among the U.S. population. Weaponized smallpox can be aerosolized and dispersed in a variety of ways, such as attaching an aerosol device filled with weaponized smallpox, complete with a timer, to the wall of a shopping mall, airport, or ventilation system of an enclosed stadium, or attaching a spraying device to an unmanned drone (UAV) that has been programmed with global positioning (GPS) maps and flying it over a populated area.

- *Assumption 2: The U.S. population's "herd immunity" to smallpox was 20%, so that 228 million of its citizens were highly susceptible to infection.*

This is a matter of debate. It is known that 42% of the population has never received a smallpox vaccination, and the remainder have declining immunity from vaccinations about 30 years ago. No one knows for sure, but epidemiologic data suggest that initial vaccination gives protection for 5 to 10 years, while revaccination gives even greater protection, possibly more than 10 years. Those who have been vaccinated twice, then, say as a child and while in the military, should have the greatest immunity.

- *Assumption 3: The transmission rate of the disease was 10 to 1, that is, each infected person infected 10 others.*

Although transmission rates have varied widely historically depending on susceptibility of a population, the strain of disease, and various social, demographic, political, and economic factors, the simulation designers considered a 10 to 1 transmission rate a conservative estimate. The U.S. population, they pointed out, is highly susceptible because vaccinations stopped in this country 30 years ago. Also, we are a highly mobile society. By the time the first victims are diagnosed with smallpox (9-17 day incubation period), the disease will have already begun spreading to a second generation of victims. Some of the initial victims and the second generation of victims will have travelled to other cities by that time. Since few American doctors have ever seen a case of smallpox, and since the initial symptoms resemble flu, diagnosis is liable to be slow.

For this simulation, the 10 to 1 estimate was based on 34 smallpox outbreaks in the past involving cases of smallpox being accidentally imported into a country that no longer had endemic smallpox. Twenty four of the outbreaks occurred in winter, which is the time when smallpox spreads most readily and which is the time within which the simulated attack occurs. Of these 24, 6 outbreaks most closed paralleled the conditions of the *Dark Winter* exercise, and they were used to make the 10 to 1 estimate. The number of second generation cases in those 6 outbreaks ranged from 10 to 19.

One reason the 10 to 1 estimate is thought to be on the conservative side is because of the 1972 outbreak in Yugoslavia, which encompassed many of the aspects one finds today in American society, namely, a great number of susceptible people and a wide geographic dispersion of cases. In that outbreak a man on a religious pilgrimage to Mecca and Medina was infected with smallpox while in Iraq, then brought it back to Yugoslavia. His infection was not diagnosed, nor were the 11 people he infected suspected of having smallpox. Not until 140 new cases developed was the epidemic recognized as smallpox. Some 35 people died from this single initial infection.

- *Assumption 4: The U.S. Centers for Disease Control and Prevention (CDC) had 12 million doses of vaccine available at the time of the exercise.*

The CDC actually had 15.4 million doses, but practical experience from the 1960s and 70s smallpox eradication programs showed that it was common to lose 20% of a vial's vaccine due to inefficiencies and waste.

- *Assumption 5: In the initial attack at three shopping malls in Oklahoma City, Philadelphia, and Atlanta, 3,000 people were infected.*

This is considered a plausible scenario scientifically since it would take only 30 grams of weaponized smallpox to infect 3,000 people via an aerosol attack.

The 1st NSC meeting, Dec. 9, 2002
The initial attack:

On December 9, 2002, during the first of three NSC meetings that will take place in this simulation, the 12 NSC members are told that a smallpox outbreak has occurred in the U.S. In Oklahoma, 12 cases of smallpox have been confirmed, with 14 more suspected. There are also suspected cases of smallpox in Georgia and Pennsylvania.

The governor of Oklahoma, Frank Keating, who is in town to make a speech, attends the meeting. NSC members are briefed on the disease, its lethality, its contagion, and the availability of smallpox vaccine.

All this takes place against a backdrop of the following geopolitical situation:

- Iraq is again threatening to invade Kuwait, and leaders of Kuwait, the United Arab Emirates, and Bahrain have requested the U.S., Britain, and France deploy troops to the region. The NSC meeting has been called to consider deploying forces.
- Since sanctions against Iraq had been lifted six months prior, it has been discovered that Saddam Hussein is aggressively pursuing a bioweapons program.
- Several top scientists from the former Soviet secret bioweapons program are believed to have been working in Iraq and Iran for the past year.
- An Al Qaida terrorist was recently caught trying to buy plutonium and biological pathogens from Russia.

President Nunn informs the NSC members that the agenda of the meeting has changed, that the U.S. has been subjected to a suspected smallpox attack, and that it could be related to their anticipated decision to deploy troops to the Mideast. No one has yet taken credit for the attack.

He introduces Governor Keating, who says hospital emergency rooms in Oklahoma City hospitals are very crowded and that many in the hospital staff have failed to show up for work, fearing a smallpox infection they might bring home to their families. The media is broadcasting nonstop news about the smallpox outbreak, and the Governor is already considering calling out the National Guard if fear continues to grow among the populace. He has already declared a state of emergency and requests the President do the same. He goes before the news cameras in a few hours, he says, and he'd like to be able to tell the people of Oklahoma that all 3.5 million of them will get the smallpox vaccine within 72 hours.

The NSC is then briefed on smallpox, using various slides of actual smallpox cases and statistics relating to the progression, spread, and lethality of the disease: U.S. doctors have no experience with smallpox and there is no rapid diagnosis or treatment. Isolation or vaccination are the only defenses. Only 12 million doses of vaccine are available, and a CDC contract for an additional 40 million doses will not be filled until 2004. The worldwide supply of vaccine is 60 million doses, but some of it is believed worthless due to inadequate storage by some countries.

The NSC members are told that the CDC has sent 100,000 doses of smallpox vaccine to Oklahoma, with vaccinations restricted to infected people, their close contacts, and investigators.

Council members are also told that the attack most likely occurred about Dec. 1, due to at least a 7-day incubation period for the disease. The second generation of cases, then, would be about Dec. 20, 11 days away. Urgent action is needed to halt the spread of the disease, but a modern, urban, mobile population, coupled with a limited supply of vaccine, does not offer encouraging prospects for controlling the outbreak.

The FBI tells the Council they will have 200 agents vaccinated and sent to Oklahoma within 24 hours, but they have no leads as yet. Several possible culprits are named: Iraq, Iran, North Korea, China, Russia all

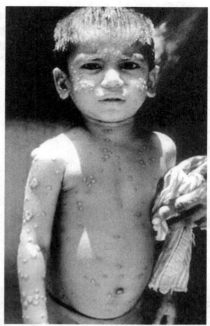

Child with full-body distribution of smallpox eruptions, Pakistan, 1955

have the capability. But anyone who has obtained samples of smallpox, possibly from an unemployed Soviet scientist, could grow smallpox and launch an attack.

Council members consider their options. The CDC and local authorities would already be isolating victims and their closest contacts. Should public gatherings be curtailed and schools closed? How should the available vaccine be distributed? Should the National Guard be activated, and should it be under state or federal control? Should there be mandatory or voluntary vaccinations? What should the public be told? What should be done about the deployment of troops to the Mideast?

They agree to inform the public quickly and completely to ensure cooperation with disease control measures. They decide to use the "ring method" of vaccination, which worked so successfully in eradicating the disease in the 1960s and 70s. With the ring method, all first contacts with the victim are vaccinated, then a second ring of secondary contacts are vaccinated. The NSC decides the ring method should also be used in other states, should the virus break out there. For strategic purposes they reserve 1 million doses of vaccine for Department of Defense (DOD) needs, and instruct the DOD to determine its priorities. They also decide to deploy an additional aircraft carrier battle group to the Persian Gulf to join the one already there.

The final action of the NSC is to prepare a presidential statement for the news media, which the President delivers to a nationwide audience from the press room.

The 2nd NSC meeting, Dec. 15, 2002
The outbreak spreads:

The second NSC meeting opens with a review of the following *news video clips*:

- 300 people are dead and 2000 are infected in 15 states. Hospitals are overwhelmed as tens of thousand of sick or fearful people seek medical help. Many hospital employees are not showing up for work.
- The epidemic has spread to Canada, Mexico, and the United Kingdom, with Canada and Mexico asking the U.S. for vaccine.
- Violence has broken out in some areas, with riots around a vaccination site in Philadelphia leaving two dead. Police and the National Guard are trying to control the crowds.
- Many countries have closed their borders to people travelling from the U.S. unless they can show proof of recent smallpox vaccination.
- Governor Keating is considering closing all stores to try and halt the spread of the disease. Malls across the country are already virtually deserted. The Governor has closed all schools and universities and cancelled all sporting events.
- The federal government is being widely criticized from all quarters for failure to have an adequate smallpox vaccine on hand. The lone pharmaceutical company capable of making smallpox vaccine says that at most it can produce 4 million doses per month, even if all FDA regulations are waived. Russia has offered to provide 4 million doses of vaccine.
- Panic buying is beginning to occur in some cities as food deliveries are slowed by the reluctance of truckers to go into areas with smallpox. There are sporadic reports of people of Arab appearance being assaulted on the street.

A *memo* is given to the Attorney General. It clarifies the *Stafford Act, the Posse Comitatus Act, the Federal Quarantine Law,* the *Insurrection Act,* and *Martial Law,* all laws designed to invoke federal authority in a national emergency. Among other things, the laws would allow the President to declare a national emergency and use military troops to quell civil disturbances, authorize the forced inoculation and isolation of people who could spread a communicable disease, restrict travel, dispose of bodies in ways contrary to personal beliefs, suspend habeas corpus (that is, arrest without due process), and curtail other liberties as needed.

Another ***memo*** to the FBI Director and Attorney General states there is a high probability that the attack came from another state or a state-sponsored terrorist group, and that an initial analysis of the smallpox used indicates it came from Soviet Union stocks or North Korea. The memo notes that as little as two years ago North Korean Special Forces were still receiving smallpox vaccine.

The President is handed a ***memo*** suggesting it may be problematic going forward with a war in the Persian Gulf, given the severity of the domestic crisis. He addresses the council members, announcing that the Secretary of State is ill and hospitalized. He says the lack of vaccine and the tactics of some states to stop the epidemic has led to serious economic disruption and civil unrest in some areas.

The Chair of the Deputies Committee, Dr. Tara O'Toole, outlines the progress of the epidemic and says all cases appear related to three initial attacks in Oklahoma, Georgia, and Pennsylvania. Vaccine, unfortunately, is running out amid growing political pressure to vaccinate more broadly. One million doses of vaccine are still being held for military personnel facing the potential war in the Persian Gulf. With all the vaccine that has been distributed, 1.25 million doses remain.

Dr. O'Toole further states that there is growing public demand for the forcible relocation of infected people to isolated facilities. She says contacts of infected people are not complying sufficiently with voluntary home isolation. There is also dangerous misinformation in some media about good vaccine and bad vaccine, advice to flee cities, claims that poor neighborhoods are being denied vaccine, and hate speech directed at certain ethnic groups.

The FEMA Director delivers his remarks: Health care facilities have become nonfunctional in some communities due to overcrowding and workers staying away from their jobs. At least 20 hospitals have closed their doors in Oklahoma. In many states National Guard troops are providing security at hospitals, even delivering food and critical supplies. Many states have prohibited public gatherings, stopped transportation, and closed airports.

Once again the NSC considers its options. Members decide to leave the National Guard, as well as quarantine and isolation issues, in the hands of the states. They will accept the vaccine from Russia, and proceed with a crash program to manufacture vaccine even though liability issues have not been resolved. They opt for mandatory isolation of all smallpox victims in dedicated facilities. They will encourage voluntary isolation of contacts using National Guard and Defense Department resources to supply food. Federal travel restrictions will be established, and penalties will be imposed for the promulgation of dangerous information.

An intelligence memo is given to NSC members: It indicates that a new exclusionary zone has been established by Iraq around a suspected bioresearch facility near Samarra. Activity at the facility appears normal but villages for a 10-mile radius around it appear to have been abandoned.

In a memo delivered to the Attorney General, there are reports of increasing incidents of violence, mainly against people with dark skin or who appear Arab-American. Two mosques have been defaced and one burned in the last 24 hours. In downtown Chicago, three dark skinned youths were shot dead, apparently because they looked Middle Eastern. The ACLU has sued Pennsylvania over the issues of mandatory vaccination and curtailment of transportation.

The NSC watches a newsclip in which the Governor of Texas announces the suspension of all travel between Texas and Oklahoma. He urges other governors to do the same, and he strongly criticizes the federal government for being "unable or unwilling to prevent the spread of the smallpox virus."

President Nunn addresses the nation on national TV. He relates the gravity of the crisis and appeals for Americans to remain calm and work together to defeat the virus, and to heed the advice of their elected leaders and health officials.

The 3rd NSC meeting, Dec. 22, 2002
A crisis out of control:

The third and final NSC meeting opens with a review of *news video clips*:

- The number of smallpox cases has reached 16,000, with 1,000 people now dead. The epidemic has spread to 25 states and 10 other countries. Although investigation suggests all cases are related to the initial attack in three states, the evidence does not rule out additional or ongoing attacks.
- The U.S. is suffering severe economic damage. In Atlanta and Philadelphia, most businesses are closed and massive traffic jams are occurring across the state as people try to flee the disease.
- A New York Times poll indicates that most Americans think that the state and federal governments have lost control of the epidemic. A CNN/Gallup poll says nearly half of Americans think the President should use nuclear weapons against any nation proven responsible for the smallpox attack.
- Violence is spreading across the nation as individuals try to keep others suspected of having smallpox at a distance. In New York,

two police officers and three family members were killed when the police tried to escort two family members with smallpox to an isolation area.

Then Dr. O'Toole once again outlines the progress of the epidemic for the NSC:

- In the past 48 hours there have been 14,000 new cases. Of the 1,000 dead, 200 have been from reactions to vaccination. It is estimated that 5,000 more will die within the next two weeks.
- The vaccine has now been depleted, and the U.S. can produce only 12 million unlicensed doses a month, beginning in four weeks.
- A major impact on the U.S. economy continues and there are shortages of many types of food across the nation. People are fleeing cities after the announcement of new smallpox cases.

The NSC asks for a worst case scenario. It is stark:

- By the end of the second generation of smallpox cases (about Jan. 3), 30,000 will be infected and 10,000 dead.
- By the end of Generation 3 (Jan. 20), 300,000 will be infected and 100,000 dead.
- By the end of Generation 4 (Feb. 6, which is 7 weeks after the start of the epidemic), 3 million will be infected and 1 million dead.

A *memo* is given to the Secretary of State:
- Russia, France, and Nigeria are demanding the U.S. share any vaccine it has to help fight the overseas spread of the epidemic.
- Cuba has offered to sell smallpox vaccine to the U.S. Cuba claims it has the know-how to produce the vaccine quickly.

Another *memo* is handed to the Director of the FBI and the Director of Central Intelligence (DCI):
- A credible Iraqi defector claims Iraq is behind the smallpox attack. Iraq has previously denied involvement, but has also warned the U.S. that it will retaliate against any U.S. attack in "highly damaging ways."

Finally, a *printed message* is handed to all members of the NSC. It states that the *New York Times, Washington Post,* and *USA Today* have received anonymous letters demanding the U.S. withdraw its forces from the Persian Gulf and Saudi Arabia. The letter claims responsibility for the smallpox attack and contains a generic fingerprint of the smallpox strain matching the fingerprint of the strain causing the current epidemic. Unless the U.S. forces withdraw in one week, it warns of renewed attacks using smallpox, anthrax, and plague.

The *Dark Winter* exercise ends with the NSC discussing how to respond. If the American people demand they use nuclear weapons, against who? Should they withdraw U.S. troops from the Persian Gulf? And finally, with no vaccine remaining and the epidemic out of control, how do they control the current spread of smallpox and any new attacks with disease?

End of *Dark Winter* exercise

Astonishing! The United States had been brought to its knees by a virus delivered covertly by terrorists who lurk in the dark recesses of the world. Few thought it remotely possible before the exercise, but afterwards many inside and outside of Government became alarmed at the possibility.

The *Dark Winter* exercise was no trivial undertaking. It was carefully planned and orchestrated, primarily by the prestigious John Hopkins University in Baltimore, Maryland, to answer one question: Could America withstand an attack of human-inflicted disease. The answer was a resounding No! — at least in the case of smallpox. We flunked the exercise on a catastrophic scale.

Three months after the exercise the U.S. was subjected to the September 11 attacks against the World Trade Centers in New York City and the subsequent anthrax mail attacks in Washington, D.C. Suddenly the attacks of terrorists were not just the stuff of "what if" simulations like *Dark Winter*. Our Government began working on defense strategies against such attacks, and it started evaluating its stocks of smallpox vaccine.

The vaccine situation is different today than it was in June of 2001 when the *Dark Winter* exercise took place. The U.S. has found more vaccine than we thought we had, and we have diluted other vaccine to make it stretch far enough to cover the American population. There are still questions about the effectiveness of this diluted vaccine after so many years in storage, but new vaccine to cover the entire population is being manufactured and will be ready in early 2004. Δ

Chapter 4
Nuclear terrorism

How the bomb works...
...what happened in Hiroshima and Nagasaki...
...what will happen if terrorists detonate one here...
...how terrorists may get their hands on the bomb

By John Silveira

From the events of September 11 we have learned the extent to which terrorists are willing to go to commit an act of terrorism. They are willing to hijack planes and use them as suicide bombs, killing themselves along with thousands of innocents.

It is conceivable that, in the case of Moslem terrorists, the most ardent among them imagine starting a worldwide jihad, or holy war, involving Islam and the West. This, at least, seems to be what Osama bin Laden and his band of thugs, al Qaida, had in mind.

There is no doubt that the devastating American response to the events of September 11th was not what the terrorists expected. However, our response does not mean that terrorism will go away. On the contrary, because of what many call "the law of unintended consequences," as a result of our decisive response we may find ourselves confronted by even greater acts of sabotage and destruction as terrorists attempt to up the ante in the hope of gaining whatever political, philosophical, or religious objectives they may have.

And that's about all they can hope to achieve. Here in the early part of the 21st century no terrorist organization nor any countries that harbor or sympathize with them could conceivably mount an attack that could "defeat" the United States. We're not going to be invaded. And it's also unlikely that any of the terrorists are acting as they do because they imagine invading us is possible. More likely, they assume that an attack of sufficient magnitude will change American foreign policy into something they find more desirable.

There are possibilities of more terrorist attacks employing more terrifying methods. But it's not likely we will find ourselves enduring random local explosions, the likes of which are used by terrorists in Israel. Ted Kaczynski and Timothy McVeigh notwithstanding, those kinds of sustained bombings require a large domestic terrorist base which isn't yet present in the United States. (This isn't to say there won't be one in the future.)

Definitions:

The words used when talking about "the bomb" are sometimes used interchangeably, though there is some consensus. For example, *atomic bomb* is sometimes used to describe just fission bombs—those that use only uranium or plutonium; other times it's used to refer to both fission bombs and fusion bombs—those that derive most of their power from fusing hydrogen. For this article the words are used as follows:

Atomic bomb — a *fission* bomb, one that derives its power exclusively from the splitting of uranium or plutonium atoms.

Hydrogen bomb — a *fusion* bomb that derives most of its power from the fusing of hydrogen, though all hydrogen bombs are triggered with fission bombs.

Nuclear bomb — the class of bombs that includes both fission bombs and fusion bombs.

Thermonuclear bomb — a hydrogen bomb, so-called because they are triggered by the thermal radiation created by the fission bomb that gets them going.

There are other terms used such as dirty bomb and neutron bomb, but they are explained in the text.

Up the scale from random bombings is the possibility of biological or chemical terrorism. These attacks are more worrisome than car and truck bombs because an epidemic of small pox or some other disease may become self-sustaining as it sweeps across the country. Dave Duffy addresses the prospects of this kind of terrorism in Chapter 2, *Biological & chemical terrorism.*

As he points out, the infrastructure required to conduct a biological terrorist campaign may well be beyond the scope of any contemporary terrorist organization or their covert sponsors, and the start of an epidemic may be stemmed by medical aid and sanitary practices which could quickly be put in place.

But at the top of the scale, and the most fearsome of the possible terrorist attacks, is nuclear terrorism. And of all of the acts terrorists may engage in, this is the one that, though it's not likely to bring about the fall of the West, will most likely bring on the utter death of freedom—whether or not it brings on the change in American policy they desire.

And, almost as bad as actual nuclear terrorism, may be just the *threat* of nuclear terrorism. In fact, just trying to prevent such an attack may spell the end of freedom as we know it.

We could lose it all because of some crazy terrorist and a mushroom cloud. And we could lose it forever. We could trade away our rights for the feeling of security. It would be like George Orwell's *1984* where the government has become a dictatorship and justifies it with the excuse that a constant state of war exists.

Types of bombs

With the exception of what are now called "dirty bombs," nuclear terrorism is all about "the bomb." There are several types of nuclear bombs terrorists could employ and several ways they could use them. The bomb types depend on the materials they have available, the technology they have for producing one (if they don't just out-and-out steal one or buy one on the black market), and the size of the explosion they want to make—though there's no doubt that their philosophy will be "the bigger the better."

Militarily speaking, nuclear bombs are classified according to the size of the explosion they create, which determines the military use to which they will be put. The smaller ones are referred to as tactical and the larger ones as strategic.

Tactical bombs, sometimes called battlefield nuclear weapons, are small-yield nuclear devices meant to cause local destruction. Their beauty, from a terrorist's point of view, is that they are small enough (some of them were meant to fit into artillery shells) that some could fit into a suitcase and some may fit into something as small as an attaché case. The smallest bomb made by the United States is called a "Davy Crockett." It's a 0.1K (kiloton) bomb weighing 51 pounds and meant to be fired from a recoilless rifle that could be mounted on a jeep.

The radius of destruction of such a suitcase-size weapon depends on the amount of energy the explosion produces. This is called its "yield." If a single tactical nuclear weapon like this had been brought up to one of the top floors of either of the WTC towers, it would have acted like an airburst (this is the kind of explosion that causes the widest possible area of destruction) that not only would have destroyed both buildings, killing almost everyone in each, but it would have killed most people for a radius of several blocks. Depending on the time of day it was detonated, such a weapon could have killed hundreds of thousands of people.

Similarly, a larger bomb of this type, on the scale of the bombs dropped on Hiroshima and Nagasaki, could be fit into a car as small as a VW Bug, parked several blocks from the White House and Capitol Hill and detonated during the President's State of the Union Address, or some other event, killing most of the heads of our government. Or similarly, it could be flown at a height of two thousand feet over the capital, to effect an airburst, wreaking devastation on the scale of that we wrought at Hiroshima and Nagasaki to conclude World War II.

Strategic bombs, sometimes called "thermonuclear" or "hydrogen" bombs, are more powerful than the atomic bombs dropped on Japan. Thermonuclear bombs are much larger both in the size of the bomb itself and the size of the explosion they create. Some of these devices could destroy entire cities.

It is the actual securing of one and then delivering it that could pose problems. But their use by terrorists can't be completely ruled out.

The differences between atomic and hydrogen bombs is that an atomic bomb depends on fissionable matter, specifically uranium-235 (U^{235}) or plutonium-239 (Pu^{239}) to create an explosion, while a hydrogen bomb has, at its heart, an atomic bomb to get things going, but depends on the fusion of hydrogen into helium to generate most of its power.

The additional materials added to an atomic bomb to make it a hydrogen bomb are cheaper than the uranium and plutonium that go into making the atomic bomb, making hydrogen bombs, pound for pound, cheaper.

Furthermore, there's really no limit to how big of a hydrogen bomb you can build.

Getting a bomb into the U.S.

The most likely way to get one of these bombs into this country would be the same way drugs are brought in: a small plane (especially one landing at a remote airstrip) or a boat.

It is possible that either of these devices, a tactical or strategic nuclear bomb, could be brought into this country by boat, then detonated without off-loading it from the vessel. This was the delivery system suggested in the letter delivered to President Franklin Roosevelt just prior to World War II, and signed by Albert Einstein, in which Roosevelt was urged to embark upon a program to develop nuclear weapons before the Germans did.

Another delivery system could be to detonate a tactical nuclear weapon aboard a low-flying plane. A plane flying low over the heart of a city, or a crowded football stadium, would be guaranteed to kill in the tens if not hundreds of thousands. And if the crew delivering it is willing to die in the process—not an unthinkable scenario after September 11th—a bomb bay door isn't even necessary.

Dirty bombs. At one time this was the designation used solely for describing nuclear bombs that also disperse a large amount of radioactive residue upon exploding. Today it is also used to designate conventional bombs encased in radioactive material.

The blast and fire effects of a conventional "dirty bomb" are the least of such a bomb. There is no nuclear explosion with these devices. The intended effects are the dispersal of radioactive material. But it's unlikely a bomb set off by terrorists could send the material very far, and the number of people

kilotons *vs.* megatons

The explosive effects of nuclear bombs are so much greater than any of the explosions mankind's weapons had created before that there was little to compare them to. But right from the beginning it was decided to equate them to how much TNT it would take to create as much damage, and it was estimated that the bombs dropped on Hiroshima and Nagasaki were the equivalent of dropping 10,000 to 20,000 *tons* of high explosives—TNT— on each of the cities. It would have taken at least 3,000 of World War II's largest bombers, the B-29s, to drop what the lone B-29, the *Enola Gay*, dropped on Hiroshima. The Greek prefix for thousand is kilo, abbreviated "K," therefore the bomb dropped on Hiroshima was estimated to have the explosive equivalence of 10K to 20K of TNT.

Thermonuclear bombs are thousands of times more powerful than atomic bombs so there equivalence is measured in *millions* of tons. The Greek prefix for million is mega, abbreviated "M."

Several of the countries that currently belong to the "nuclear club" now have bombs (deliverable by missile or bomber) that are more than 1,000 times as powerful as the bombs dropped on Japan.

affected would be nowhere near the number affected by a real nuclear bomb or even a well dispersed biological agent.

Once such a bomb is detonated our strategy would be to avoid the area of contamination until we effect a cleanup. The real effect of such a bomb would just be terror.

Neutron bombs. These are the bombs that are supposed to kill people but leave property intact. It's worth knowing that *every* nuclear bomb is a neutron bomb, i.e., they all produce neutrons. Ordinarily, however, the radius of the blast is greater than the radius of damage done by the neutrons, so that almost everyone within range of the effects of the neutrons are killed by the blast, anyway.

But in what we today specifically designate a neutron bomb, the bomb is made so as to minimize the blast effects while maximizing the emission of neutrons so that while there is still a nuclear explosion it's much smaller, but the number of neutrons is maximized.

The neutrons can be deadly, depending on how they interact with atoms that make up the cells in your body. Generally speaking someone exposed to a blast of the neutrons doesn't die immediately. Depending on the amount of exposure, death will likely come after a few days as the cells in the body die.

Neutron bombs were designed for the battlefields of Europe where, if Warsaw Pact armies were speeding across West Germany or other countries, whole armies could be destroyed without destroying the countryside in the

Nuclear fission

There are two ways U^{235} or Pu^{239} can decay. One is by the emission of alpha particles from the nucleus (alpha particles are the same as the nucleus of a helium atom that has been stripped of its two orbiting electrons). What's left behind are other radioactive atoms—protactinium in the case of U^{235}; U^{235} in the case of Pu^{239}—and, once the alpha particle acquires two electrons, there's also a helium atom that didn't exist before.

The other way U^{235} and Pu^{239} can decay is that, on rare occasions, spontaneous *fission* that naturally takes place (the same kind of fission that takes place in an atomic explosion) results in two much smaller atomic nuclei, a *substantial amount* of energy, and two or three free neutrons.

It is this second kind of decay that starts a chain reaction in a fission bomb. In U^{235} if any of those extra neutrons that are produced are absorbed by a neighboring atom of U^{235}, that atom becomes unstable and it undergoes fission and also releases a substantial amount of energy while leaving behind two smaller atoms and two or three extra neutrons. And, if those neutrons are further captured by more U^{235} nuclei...well, you get the picture. More and more neutrons are produced and captured by more and more U^{235} nuclei and this is a chain reaction. First hundreds, then thousands, then millions, then billions, then trillions of nuclei are involved in the reaction, all releasing ever more neutrons and a *huge* amount of energy. And it all happens in a few millionths of a second. A similar but slightly more difficult process must occur to get Pu^{239} to undergo fission.

But, in either case, four conditions must be met:

1) There must be enough of the U^{235} or Pu^{239} atoms to sustain the reaction.

2) The atoms must be close enough together.

3) There can't be too many impurities that can absorb the free neutrons and stop the reaction.

4) The neutrons can't be too fast. (When the nucleus undergoes fission it isn't "exploding" like a pumpkin does when a rifle bullet goes through it. The neutron just goes right through it leaving it more or less undisturbed. The neutron must move slow enough to be "captured" by the nucleus. Then it is more like the "straw that breaks the camel's back" because the extra neutron makes the nucleus unstable and it splits.)

If there aren't enough neighboring U^{235} atoms or they're too far away, the neutrons are lost and the "chain reaction" can't be sustained.

process. From the war protesters' point of view, they were weapons of greedy capitalists who wanted to kill people while leaving property undamaged. From the the military perspective they were weapons that would kill invading armies while not desolating the entire countryside. People who fled their towns could go home and find much of the infrastructure intact.

How an atomic bomb works

The amount of fissile material (U^{235} or Pu^{239}) typically used to make fission weapons with the yield that destroyed Hiroshima and Nagasaki (about 13 kilotons of TNT) runs from about 6 to 15 pounds of Pu^{239} in a plutonium bomb to about 40 pounds of U^{235} for the uranium bomb. (The U^{235} bomb dropped on Hiroshima required 130 pounds, but that may be because it was the first uranium bomb and therefore more primitive.)

The difference in the amount of fissile material between the Pu^{239} and the U^{235} bombs is because, though the uranium bomb is much easier to set off, uranium is not as efficient at undergoing a chain reaction when it explodes and a great deal of it goes to waste. Approximately as much material undergoes fission in the uranium bomb as in the plutonium bomb, i.e., about 10 pounds, but the rest is just vaporized by the explosion.

This is one of the reasons that "Little Boy," the uranium bomb we dropped on Hiroshima, is, as far as I know, the only uranium bomb this country ever made. All of our other nuclear bombs, whether tactical atomic bombs or the detonators for hydrogen bombs, have been made from plutonium.

But despite the 6 to 15-pound limit I just gave, smaller bombs are possible. A recent report from the Natural Resources Defense Council states that nuclear weapons with a destructive power of 1 kiloton can be built with not much more that 2 pounds of weapon-grade Pu^{239}, while the smallest amount of Pu^{239} that could be used to achieve critical mass (actually critical density) is about a half a pound.

A bomb using half a pound of Pu^{239} would, naturally, have a yield of less than a kiloton. But the problems of achieving critical density is even more acute with such a small mass and not likely one to be solved by terrorists. It has, however, been solved by scientists in the U.S. and Russia. And that is a problem for us because, as we shall see, there are rumors that very small attaché case-size bombs are missing from the Russian inventory.

The effects of a nuclear detonation

The destructive effects of nuclear explosions are thermal (as in fire), blast, electromagnetic pulse (EMP), and radioactive fallout.

Thermal effects. When a nuclear bomb goes off there is an immediate pulse of x-rays. These x-rays superheat the surrounding air to white hot temperatures. This superheating of the air is the start of the *fireball*. It is also the source of a burst of light and heat that will blind, burn, and cause spontaneous fires. Both the x-rays and the heat will kill. This will all happen in less than one second. Most of the deaths from a nuclear explosion will happen in this first second.

The shock wave. The violent expansion of the superheated air also produces a shock wave—or pressure wave—that radiates out from the fireball at supersonic speeds. The overpressure of this wave knocks buildings down, and throws bodies, automobiles, trucks, and even trains through the air. Many of the deaths and injuries will result from flying debris caused by the shock wave.

And besides the spontaneous fires caused by the searing heat of the initial explosion, more fires yet will be caused by buildings that collapse as the pressure wave passes over them. The source of these secondary fires will be electrical and gas fires caused by buildings that collapse, from utilities that fail, gas stations that are destroyed, and automobiles, trucks, and even gasoline hauling tanker-trucks that are tossed through the air.

The shock wave or overpressure wave will also generate winds whose velocity will depend on the size of the blast and your distance from it. At the very least there will be hurricane-force winds. With a large thermonuclear bomb the winds near the blast will be several hundred miles per hour.

In both Hiroshima and Nagasaki winds as far away as a mile from the center of the blast threw masonry walls as much as 80 feet. If stone walls were tossed about by the winds, it's likely that people were too and the probability of surviving being thrown about in this way is slight.

As to effects of blast pressure on the human body: the human body is remarkably resilient and resistant to just the increase in pressure alone. It's thought that at both Hiroshima and Nagasaki that the people who may have been killed by the pressure increase alone would had to have been within a few hundred feet of the explosion, and they would have been killed by gamma radiation, heat, flying objects, and being thrown by the winds, anyway.

Radiation. In both Hiroshima and Nagasaki there were immediate injuries and deaths from radiation. They were from the ionizing radiation immediately created by the bombs in the first few seconds of the blasts.

For those exposed to the most intense blast of radiation, death was probably 100 percent certain. To lesser degrees this radiation resulted in injuries and illnesses that resulted in varying degrees of temporary hair loss, bleeding— both internal and external—and various other symptoms such as diarrhea. Those who survived more than two months generally recovered to live somewhat normal lives.

For those who serendipitously found themselves behind shielding, such as masonry walls, radiation injuries were minimized in even those victims who were relatively close to ground zero. If you weren't killed by the heat, the blast, flying objects, or fires that erupted after the damned things went off, well, the radiation wasn't a problem.

Other than that, it's thought that if you were ¾ of a mile from ground zero, in either of the Japanese cities, and fully exposed to the effects of the radiation blast, you had a 50 percent chance of living.

Residual radioactivity. Far behind these in importance is going to be residual radioactivity in the form of *fallout*. Elevated death rates due to cancers and birth defects in future years, along with other maladies, may become problems, but they will pale in comparison to the death and destruction that will take place in the first few minutes of a nuclear blast.

And as a historical aside, it's worth noting that both Hiroshima and Nagasaki are bigger and more vibrant cities today than they were before the bombings despite the fact that they were both ground zero for nuclear blasts.

EMP. The very least of the problems from nuclear terrorism will be electromagnetic pulse. All nuclear bombs generate EMP, which is only a danger to electrical equipment, and not a direct danger to humans. And though all nuclear bombs generate EMP, for bombs detonated in the lower atmosphere the range of the EMP is very short and the damage is only local. Really destructive EMP is the result of high-yield bombs detonated at very high altitudes, and this is not likely to be how a terrorist is going to set off a nuclear weapon.

What happened at Hiroshima and Nagasaki

From the two bombs dropped on the Japanese cities of Hiroshima and Nagasaki we have a fair idea of what the effects of the detonation of nuclear bombs in a populated area would be. Both explosions were blasts in the 10 to 20 kiloton range, probably the upper limit of what to expect from a terrorist weapon.

• In those cities everything within about a one-mile radius was totally destroyed, with the exception of reinforced buildings, and even they had doors and windows blown off and were gutted by fires. Flash fires, started by the heat from the blast, started as far as two miles from ground zero in Nagasaki. Heavy damage extended beyond that to a radius of about three miles in both cities.

• Though the two bombs were comparable in size, about four square miles of Hiroshima, directly under the burst, were completely destroyed (this is a circle roughly 2¼ miles across), whereas in Nagasaki the area completely destroyed was about 1½ square miles (a circle about 1¼ miles across). The difference in destruction had more to do with where the bombs exploded and the geography of the cities than with the bombs themselves. Hiroshima is a city that lies in a flat plain, so the effect of the blast traveled unimpeded across the countryside. Nagasaki, on the other hand, is a city of hills so various parts of the city were shielded or shadowed by the hills.

• In both cities all humans and animals within 1 kilometer (about ⁶/10 mile) of the blast died almost instantaneously.

• From 1 kilometer to about 2 kilometers (1.2 miles), there were still many deaths. Those that died also died almost instantaneously, but many others survived. However, the vast majority of those survivors were injured either seriously or superficially by the blast and heat.

• From 1.2 miles out to a distance of about 2.5 miles many were injured by the intense heat and flying objects.

• At five miles most of the injuries were from flying objects.

In Hiroshima, the layout of the city's buildings, their construction (mostly wood), as well as the flatness of the local terrain conspired to create a firestorm that razed much of the city and contributed to many of the deaths. But Nagasaki, due to its hilly geography and the layout of the city, did not suffer from a firestorm.

In both cities buildings were destroyed by either overpressure waves that resulted from the blast, fires caused by the heat of the blast, and fires caused by buildings that, though they were beyond the heat effects of the bomb itself, caught fire when they collapsed.

More fires were caused as initial fires spread.

People became casualties as a result of flash burns from the almost instantaneous heat generated by the explosion, the fires caused by the bomb, and blast effects that not only sent bodies flying but turned objects of all sizes into millions of missiles.

What would happen in an American city

Such a bomb, detonated at the proper altitude, in the core of a dense American city could conceivably cause 100,000 deaths and perhaps up to half a million injuries. The totals would depend on:

• the time of day (If set off in a city, people may be at work or at home in the suburbs.)

• the population density (The New York City borough of Manhattan is very dense with 1.4 million people living in 23 square miles. On a weekday, hundreds of thousands more come to the borough from other parts of New York, from New Jersey, and from Connecticut to work. Los Angeles, though it has a population of over 3½ million, is spread out over almost 470 square miles—20 times the area of Manhattan.)

• where the bomb was detonated in the city

How dangerous are U^{235} and Pu^{239} to terrorists?

The beauty of Pu^{239}, from the terrorist's point of view, is that, though of the 15 or so isotopes of plutonium only two are fissile (capable of being used in a nuclear bomb), the only one that is practical to use in a bomb also happens to be quite safe to handle.

There are four common ways in which radioactive elements decay. One is through fission, which is quite rare. The other three ways are that it can emit alpha particles (which are really just the nuclei of helium atoms that have been stripped of their electrons), positive or negative beta particles (which are positive or negative electrons), or gamma radiation (which is like x-rays). Some elements emit one of these when they decay, others emit a combination of them. There are also other decay particles we're not interested in here, such as neutrinos.

On a scale of how dangerous they are, alpha particles can be stopped by something as thin as paper. In fact, your skin serves as a good barrier to them. Beta particles can be stopped by a window pane. Gamma radiation is the stuff that causes cancer and, in sufficient quantities, can kill you.

Pu^{239} is an alpha particle emitter. You could sleep with it under your pillow. From the terrorist's point of view, the plutonium that he can create the most destruction with is also the safest for him to handle and it can easily be transported by individuals without harm to their persons.

However, the downside of a plutonium bomb is the difficulty of constructing the bomb, of detonating it, and the fact that they are generally encased in U^{238}, which is a gamma emitter which is not safe to handle, and emits radiation which is detectable.

• at what altitude (Airbursts are much more destructive than ground bursts, hence a terrorist may set one off near the top of a skyscraper or from a low-flying plane.)

• the nature of the local geography (flat, hilly, etc.)

• the weather (Overcast or foggy weather will cut down the intensity and the range of the thermal radiation from the blast.)

Had terrorists placed a nuclear device in either of the World Trade Center towers, death would have been from the heat, blast effects, and the near instantaneous collapse of both towers. On September 11th, most of the occupants of both towers escaped in the first 10 or 15 minutes, saving tens of thousands. Few, if any, would have escaped from the buildings in a nuclear blast. Many would have died in other buildings, also, but survival would have

U^{235} *vs.* Pu^{239}

There are reasons the United States and other developed countries use Pu^{239} as opposed to U^{235} in their bombs. But the main reasons are, first, that U^{235} is a naturally occurring element that is very rare while Pu^{239} is man-made element made by subjecting more plentiful U^{238}, the most common occurring isotope of uranium, to neutrons in nuclear reactors. Until the end of the Cold War, the United States made tons of Pu^{239} this way every year. The second reason is that, while Pu^{239} is harder to detonate in a bomb, once you start the fission, it undergoes the fission process much more efficiently, consuming more of the Pu^{239} in the process. A U^{235} bomb, on the other hand, is easier to get going, but the fission process is very inefficient and about 90 percent of the uranium is wasted.

The third reason is that, since bombs can be built with much less Pu^{239} than with U^{235}, the bombs themselves are lighter and missiles that carry them have longer ranges.

But there are also reasons why developing countries initially build U^{235} as opposed to Pu^{239} bombs. It is because, although U^{235} is rare, to manufacture Pu^{239} you must have a type of nuclear reactor called a "breeder reactor." In this kind of reactor you can literally actually produce more fuel than you are consuming by irradiating U^{238} with neutrons to create Pu^{239}. If you don't have a breeder reactor, and few countries do, you can't make Pu^{239}.

A second reason is that the triggering device in a U^{235} bomb can be quite crude. All you need to do is get enough of it in one place and BOOM. It's as if U^{235} is just dying to go off. But the triggering device in a Pu^{239} bomb is a technological marvel in and of itself. Neutron emitting isotopes of beryllium and polonium are introduced to enhance the production of neutrons required for fission, and the Pu^{239} core must be surrounded by a layer of explosives (usually 32 separate little bombs) to be imploded precisely.

been more likely due to chance. Most of the deaths would have been from thermal effects and blast. And other buildings in the area, though not immediately destroyed by the blast, would have been destroyed by ensuing fires. Scores would have been gutted and most would have collapsed.

In Hiroshima and Nagasaki, underground bomb shelters with earth-covered roofs, which were directly below the burst, collapsed. But those a half mile away or further survived. From this we can gather that those in subways would probably survive, though collapsing buildings, smoke, and fires could cause problems including the possibility of asphyxiation if raging fires above ground pulled enough air out of the subway system to feed the flames.

Depending on the size of a terrorist's bomb, surrounding skyscrapers may be pushed over. Most likely, however, those not near the blast would not fall immediately, though deaths and injuries within them would be extensive. Most of the damage would come from fires caused by the intense heat from the blast and secondary fires that come from short circuits and other things. Some of those buildings would eventually collapse due to fires, and most of those left standing would be damaged beyond repair.

Unlike being near ground zero, where (unless you're in a subway) death will be instantaneous and almost certain, a few blocks away your fate may be the result of dumb luck—good or bad. The further away you are from a blast, the more likely your fate will be tied to shielding or "shadowing" from neighboring buildings. It's quite likely that within a few blocks of such a blast there will be people who survive unscathed while people near them will be injured or killed by debris. And, most certainly, those shielded by buildings will not suffer the effects of ionizing radiation.

Those exposed to the light from the blast may be burned on only one side. In Hiroshima and Nagasaki, whether someone was burned through their clothes sometimes depended solely on the colors of the clothing they wore. Some people were badly burned through dark colored clothes while others standing next to them but wearing white clothing were relatively unscathed. Others wearing various colors of clothes found themselves burned in patterns that corresponded with the various lightness and darkness in the patterns of their clothes. In the meantime, even the way clothes fit determined how burns were dispersed. Tight fits tended to burn more than loose fits.

Given today's synthetic fabrics, it's conceivable that some people would find dark clothes melted into their skin from acrylics and such while the rest of their bodies will be relatively unscathed.

Different American cities, if targeted by nuclear terrorists, would suffer different effects. An airburst over Los Angeles, for example, may see destruction over vast amounts of the city with numerous pockets that are relatively unscathed because of the numerous hills and valleys in that city.

In both Hiroshima and Nagasaki most underground utilities were undisturbed by the blast because it was an airburst. Where there were breaks, it was due to collapsing buildings. However, aboveground utilities, such as power and phone lines, were damaged or destroyed depending on how close they were to the burst.

In American cites, where many of the utilities are underground, a surprising number would probably remain in service. In areas where large buildings collapsed, such as on Manhattan, losses in service would probably be local.

Within minutes after a nuclear detonation, the biggest threats to human life will be fire and collapsing buildings. On September 11th most of the victims died in the collapse of the towers. But we know from World War II that it is

The power in a 1-kiloton bomb

To give you an idea of how much explosive force a one kiloton bomb has, each of the Boeing 767s that flew into the World Trade Center carried no more than 70 tons of fuel. A one-kiloton bomb explodes with the energy of about 14 fully-loaded 767s crashing. And because the one-kiloton bomb releases its energy faster, its explosive characteristics are enhanced. (Think of this as comparing the energy released from a tankful of gasoline over a week's driving as opposed to how the same energy would be released if the same tankful were consumed in a hundredth of a second. In the former case we have a week of pleasant driving; in the latter we have a gigantic explosion that would level your home, all from the same tankful of gasoline. Yet, it's the same amount of energy being released.)

A one-kiloton bomb exploding at the top of a skyscraper or in a small plane 500 to 1,000 feet above a crowded city could, depending on the geography and population density of the city, result in tens of thousands, if not hundreds of thousands, of deaths.

To get a larger radius of destruction you must increase the yield of the bomb. The radius of destruction increases roughly as the cube of the bomb's yield, so to get a radius of destruction twice as great as the Hiroshima blast, which was equivalent to 13 kilotons (13K) of TNT, the bomb would have to be about eight times more powerful, or about 100 kilotons. (Incidentally, estimates of both the Hiroshima and Nagasaki blast have run from 10K to 20K, depending on who's doing the estimating. I've settled on 13K for this column.)

possible for whole cities to burn in a firestorm. While Hiroshima burned in a firestorm, Nagasaki did not. It was one of the reasons Hiroshima suffered more casualties than Nagasaki. Other cities, like Dresden, Germany, though they didn't suffer a nuclear detonation, also burned in firestorms.

A firestorm is usually the result of many smaller fires coalescing into one huge fire which causes an updraft so severe that it sucks air in from all sides. The air rushing in often has gale-force winds that prevent the fire from spreading. But the inrushing winds continue to feed oxygen to the flames, and if strong enough make it difficult or impossible for those who have been injured to leave the area. Such a fire continues to burn until it consumes everything within the flames.

Whether or not an American city that was subjected to a terrorist nuclear attack would be ravaged by a firestorm will depend on the weather, the layout of the city and the composition of its buildings, other sources of combustible materials such as gasoline storage, and the size of the bomb itself. In most American cites a firestorm would be possible.

How do you keep yourself safe?

You don't.

Kevlar vests aren't going to save you if you're too close to an exploding nuclear bomb, and if you are downwind from the fallout, neither will lead underwear. As in lightning storms, the real defense is just not being close to a target. Figuratively speaking, you don't want to stand under the trees.

Other than just not being too close to ground zero, there is a pill you can take—a potassium iodide (KI) or a potassium iodate (KIO_3) pill. One of the effects of a nuclear detonation is the creation of a short-lived radioactive isotope of iodine, that is quickly absorbed by the thyroid gland.

As this particular isotope (I^{131}), with its half-life of roughly eight days, degrades, it causes potentially fatal damage (including cancer) to your thyroid gland. If you are downwind from the fallout you may be affected.

What the pill does is flood your body with iodine so it doesn't absorb any more. This blocks the absorption of the radioactive isotope. Within a few months the radioactive iodine will have disappeared from the environment because of its short half-life.

Where terrorists may get a bomb

To get a bomb terrorists will either have to:
• get one already assembled
• get the parts for one and assemble it
• build one from scratch

All are possible, but it's just that some are more likely than others, and, of course, it's possible that they would get some parts prefabricated and have to make other parts from scratch. But no matter how they come up with a bomb, it would seem that they're going to have to have help from someone who's already done it.

There are unsubstantiated (and likely untrue) rumors that Osama bin Laden bought several of these suitcase-sized bombs for $30 million and two tons of Afghan heroin. But Jamal Ahmad al-Fadl, a Sudan native and one-time bin Laden associate, testified in the 1993 WTC bombing trial that bin Laden had unsuccessfully tried to obtain uranium suitable for building a bomb for $1.5 million.

The point is there are terrorists who are trying to obtain the material (U^{235}) to make a basic uranium bomb, which they probably could assemble, or to buy a stolen or smuggled plutonium bomb already assembled.

The so-called "nuclear club" is made up of just nine members. Following each name is the date they detonated their first nuclear device:

How a thermonuclear bomb works

A thermonuclear (or hydrogen) bomb is triggered by first setting off a "conventional" atomic bomb. Though there are several variations on how a specific bomb is made, in principle here's how one works:

The atomic bomb is made with a hollow sphere of Pu^{239}. At the center of this sphere is a heavy isotope of hydrogen called tritium (H^3). The Pu^{239} is encased in a layer of lithium deuteride. The neutrons from the exploding Pu^{239} compress the H^3 and begin fusing it. The combination of fissioning Pu^{239} and fusing H^3 turn the lithium deuteride into a mixture of another isotope of hydrogen, deuterium (H^2), and H^3. The extreme heat from the fissioning Pu^{239}, which now exceeds 100 million degrees, forces the H^2 and H^3 to fuse together and create helium. It is this fusing of hydrogen at the center of the sun that makes the sun shine, and in a thermonuclear bomb it is this same fusing that creates an even more fearsome explosion than an ordinary atomic bomb.

Very often, the outer casing that contains the thermonuclear bomb is made from the more commonly found isotope of uranium, U^{238}. Neutrons released by the fusing deuterium and tritium also create extra neutrons. These are high energy neutrons and not the type used to split Pu^{239} or U^{235} nuclei. They will, however, split U^{238} nuclei and this fission produces even more energy.

Thermonuclear bombs can typically be made hundreds and even thousands of times more powerful than atomic bombs.

But just as Pu^{239} bombs are more difficult to make than U^{235} bombs, thermonuclear bombs are more difficult to make than Pu^{239} bombs. However, once you perfect the method of making a thermonuclear bomb, it is easier to make bigger and bigger ones than it is to make bigger and bigger uranium or plutonium bombs. It's also cheaper.

The consolation is that thermonuclear bombs are currently beyond the technology of what terrorists are capable of and may remain that way for some time. However, stealing them is not. And it is also conceivable that if some third world country does make one, they could supply one to a terrorist group.

Delivery of such a weapon to its intended target then becomes a problem, but because it is larger, the bomb doesn't have to be nearly as close. Such a bomb, if large enough, could be detonated while still on a boat in a harbor or while resting in the back of large truck, or even flown in a chartered plane. It would, for all practical purposes destroy a city.

- **U.S.** (1945)
- **U.S.S.R.**—now **Russia** (1949)
- **United Kingdom** (1952)
- **France** (1960)
- **China** (1964)
- **India** (1974)
- **Pakistan** (1998)

Israel and the **Union of South Africa** have no doubt built bombs, and may even have detonated one, but South Africa claims to have left the club.

Israel had its first nuclear reactor in the 1960s and began building its own bombs in 1968. No one is really sure just how many they have, but it's likely they are building three to five each year.

When the Yom Kippur War started, catching the Israelis by surprise on October 6, 1973, Israeli positions were overrun all along its borders. The United States had already stopped supplying them with arms because of their stand on nukes. However, on October 9th, Israel notified then Secretary of State Henry Kissinger of its readiness to use its nuclear weapons if Israel's fortunes got worse. The United States reopened the supply lines that day and Israel turned back the invasion.

It is thought today the Israelis have between 80 and 150 weapons. But at this point in time none of them are considered to pose a terrorist threat to the United States.

For a terrorist to get the bomb in the foreseeable future it would seem as though at least one of the countries in the nuclear club would have to be involved.

Russia. When the former Soviet Union began to disassemble, one of the first concerns was what was going to happen with all of its nuclear weapons? They had between 13,000 and 15,000 strategic nuclear warheads and another 30,000 to 40,000 tactical nuclear warheads in their arsenal.

All the Soviet's strategic weapons were concentrated in Russia, Ukraine, Kazakhstan, and Byelorussia, and the tactical weapons were just in Russia, Ukraine, and Byelorussia. With the breakup the Russians intended to pull *all* of the nuclear weapons back behind their own borders and we can only hope they kept track of them all.

But there were several complications. One is that Russia has fallen on difficult economic times and the military arsenal they once held represents one of the few hard cash exports that can be readily sold for Western currency. An individual or group could make one or two of the 50,000 bombs "get lost" during the accounting and try to use them to strike it rich.

In September 1997 *60 Minutes* ran a story in which former Russian National Security Adviser Aleksandr Lebed claimed the Russian military had lost track of more than 100 suitcase-sized nuclear bombs. The bombs are supposed to be roughly 24 by 16 by 8 inches. The Russians reject this claim, as do many American intelligence experts.

But that brings about another aspect of the problem. Even if all the bombs can be accounted for, there are thousands of scientists and technicians who worked on the Soviet nuclear programs. They've become unemployed in their own homelands. They need jobs, they can build a bomb from scratch, and there are people who'll pay them to do it.

There was an estimated 100,000 scientists and technicians involved in the Soviet nuclear weapons programs, including 3,000 who had the highest levels of expertise. Now quite a few of them are out of work and the ones who have jobs are getting paid in worthless rubles.

Since the end of the Cold War, there have been at least 175 detected attempts to get plutonium out of Russia, either by smuggle or direct theft. There's no way to know whether any, which may have gone unreported, have succeeded.

But in 1994 three batches, amounting to a bit more than 12-ounces, of weapons grade plutonium (Pu-239) were seized in Germany. Theoretically, a bomb could be made from this amount. The good news is that its yield would be considerably less than a kiloton and not something that would impress an Air Force general in the Strategic Air Command. The bad news is that the havoc it would have caused would have been greater than that of the two planes that hit the World Trade Center. In fact, it's very unlikely that many of the people who were in either of those buildings could have survived the detonation of such a device.

The plutonium's source was immediately traced back to Russian nuclear weapons facilities.

Pakistan, which is roughly 97 percent Muslim, has the bomb. Apparently it has made its bombs from U^{235} using what is called the "centrifuge enrichment" method.

The difficulty is in acquiring a suitable centrifuge, and because of problems in balancing such a centrifuge properly this has proved to be difficult or impossible for all but the most technologically advanced countries. To get around this, the Pakistanis simply stole the plans for such a centrifuge.

In 1997, Pakistan detonated six atomic bombs. It's thought that the sixth and last may not have been a uranium bomb, as all the earlier ones were, but may instead have been a plutonium bomb. If it was, it means either Pakistan is now making its own plutonium at a nuclear reactor in Khushab, in the Punjab province, or it found a source of Pu^{239} from abroad.

Neither scenario is good. In the first, if Pakistan can manufacture its own Pu^{239}, though the country is stable today there's no way to know which way that nation will go tomorrow and one day they could surreptitiously become a supplier of the metal to terrorist groups. There are already extreme Islamic groups in Pakistan, and many of the Taliban volunteers came from Pakistan.

In the second scenario, if they purchased plutonium from abroad, it would seem apparent that so can others, including terrorist groups.

It's also thought that the same reactor at Khushab may be capable of creating tritium, one of the ingredients for a hydrogen bomb. If that's the case, then the stability of Pakistan may be one of the prime goals for the early 21st century.

The problem is not just that Pakistan's political picture could change, but it's more apt to have individuals sympathetic to the idea of jihad who may be willing to steal or smuggle a bomb out of the country. Of course, with probably no more than a hundred bombs, so far, they are probably much easier to keep track of than the tens of thousands the Russians have.

> # The first three bombs
>
> The very first atomic bomb exploded was a plutonium bomb nicknamed Gadget. It was detonated at the Trinity Test Site on what is now the White Sands Missile Test Range in New Mexico.
>
> Little Boy is a uranium bomb that weighed about 9,700 pounds and dropped on Hiroshima. It exploded 1,800 feet above the ground.
>
> Fat Man was a plutonium bomb weighing about 10,000 pounds and dropped on Nagasaki. It exploded 1,650 feet above the ground.
>
> The yield of all three bombs are estimated to have been in the 10 to 20 kiloton range.

India. India detonated its first atomic bomb back in 1974. With tensions building between it and Pakistan growing, it detonated another six in 1998. India claims that one of the bombs it detonated in 1998 was a low-yield thermonuclear bomb.

India is, at this time, one of the countries less likely to supply a terrorist group with a nuclear weapon. But theft cannot be discounted.

Iraq. In 1976 Iraq bought the Osiraq research reactor from the French. It was constructed outside of Iraq's capital, Baghdad. Its supposed purpose was as a reactor for making radioactive isotopes. In 1980 Iraq tried to buy 25,000 pounds of depleted uranium. This is the stuff you use to make plutonium (the bomb), not medical grade isotopes.

This was enough for the Israelis. In 1981 the Israelis flew American-made aircraft, F-16s, and in less than two minutes of bombing they leveled the reactor.

Other countries, such as the United States, the United Kingdom, France, China, Israel, and South Africa are low on the list of countries who may supply a terrorist group with an assembled bomb or the expertise to make one. But there is always the possibility of one being stolen, or of people with the expertise to build a crude one selling that expertise to the highest bidder on the black market. People have done stranger things for money.

Can terrorists develop one themselves?

The problems with terrorists actually building a nuclear bomb themselves are manyfold. The first is just getting the overall expertise to do it. This isn't something that some backyard tinkerer is going to do in his garage.

Procuring the fissionable material itself may be the least of the problem. As I said, the Germans intercepted Russian plutonium already.

Other than purifying uranium or plutonium to get weapon-grade material, making a detonator for a plutonium bomb may be the most difficult part of employing a nuclear bomb. This isn't just a matter of lighting a fuse and standing back. One of the challenges for scientists working on the Manhattan Project, America's atomic bomb project during World War II, was making a trigger for a plutonium bomb. Detonators for them are really high-tech stuff. Unfortunately, making a trigger for a uranium bomb is easier. If they had enough U^{235} to fashion a bomb, they could probably make the trigger in a cave in Afghanistan.

A few years ago a shipment of detonators being sent to Iraq was intercepted. Making a detonator for a plutonium bomb was one part that even their best scientists didn't want to tackle.

Testing to ensure they are manufacturing a working bomb is a problem. Testing one is difficult to hide, even if the test is an underground test, as even they have a characteristic seismic signature that differs from that of earthquakes, volcanoes, and other natural phenomena.

What can we do?

Detection of nuclear weapons on American soil requires both intelligence and technology.

The upside is that there are better and better detection methods for finding nuclear weapons terrorists may have, and using these gadgets are not intrusive in the way that many of the federal government's solutions to combating terrorism are. They are not likely to infringe on the one thing that makes Americans unique: our freedoms. The way some of them work is that fissionable materials that make nuclear bombs work emit a certain spectrum of gamma radiation that proper equipment can detect, often at quite a distance.

U^{235} and Pu^{239} are themselves very difficult to detect, because they emit only alpha particles which are very short range and easy to shield from detection. However, batches of U^{235} and Pu^{239} are never pure but often have other radioactive elements in them that are gamma emitters. Gamma radiation is very difficult to hide. Along with the impurities, the products U^{235} and Pu^{239} decay into are also radioactive and can be detected. For example, one of the decay by-products of U^{235} is protactinium-231 (Pa^{231}) which, when it decays, emits alpha, beta, and gamma radiation. The gamma radiation is detectable. With equipment that is sensitive enough, this kind of radiation is detectable even with equipment carried on aircraft over a city.

One of the ways "prospectors" looked for uranium in the '50s and '60s was by flying over wide stretches of the American West carrying Geiger counters "tuned" to the narrow spectrum of gamma radiation emitted by certain radioactive elements.

Also, the detonation of nuclear devices are started using conventional explosives. More and more, conventional explosives are also detectable using modern equipment. And, once again, this kind of equipment doesn't seem to pose problems by tampering with our freedoms.

The downside is that these detectors, for either radioactive materials or conventional explosives, are not yet widespread.

The President wants to install a $25 billion Anti-Ballistic Missile (ABM) System as a defense against missiles being launched by rogue countries or terrorists who somehow secure ballistic missile capability. The problem is that no banana republic is likely to strike at the United States in this manner and, within a few years, such a system is likely to be obsolete anyway.

Far more effective would be money spent on good intelligence and the latest detection technology for the Nuclear Emergency Search Teams (NEST), a little known and somewhat secret agency established in 1975 under the Department of Energy. NEST's task is to search, locate, and identify devices or material that may be nuclear bombs. Though its personnel have been called out on numerous occasions, as far as the public knows, they have never found a nuclear bomb. And given the complexities of making a bomb, it's probably an accurate assessment.

Currently working on a budget of about $100 million a year, which is less than ½ percent of that projected to build an ABM system, NEST is the only realistic safeguard we currently have against terrorist nukes. In the opinion of this writer, NEST is grossly underfunded and, in light of September 11th, it is where this country should seriously consider placing more emphasis. Δ

Section 2
Immediate
Preparation

Better three hours too soon than a minute too late.

— William Shakespeare, The Merry Wives of
Windsor, 1600-1601

Chapter 5
Overview

By Jackie Clay

Here's a brief overview of what you can do to prepare for emergencies, whether caused by terrorist acts or natural disasters.

Fuel storage

Store up fuel for heating, cooking, lighting, and your vehicle before you need it. Wood and other fuel can be stored a long time, will be cheaper before there is a great demand, and it will be easier to get. We have at least 12 cords of dry firewood in the lot, and only burn about one a year. It's nice to have... just in case. Likewise, a barrel of kerosene is good insurance against spending dark evenings. You may not be able to buy it during an emergency, but it's pretty cheap now.

Have alternative lighting, whether it is kerosene lamps, Coleman lamps, or propane wall lamps. Being scared and in the dark is not a good emotional combination. And be sure to have replacement wicks, globes, and other parts....just in case. We had one drop of condensation fall on a burning Coleman lamp, popping the globe instantly....and had to do without the lamp for a month, until we could get out of our snowed-in cabin for a replacement. Now we have replacements for each lamp type.

Store up some gasoline, where local regulations allow. With life-extenders, a barrel of gas can last a long time without getting too "old" to burn well. This gasoline can be used to travel or to cut wood to keep warm. (See Chapter 14 on storing LP gas, gasoline, diesel, and kerosene.)

Food storage

Have enough food stored up for at least a year, preferably two. This seems basic, but I know very few people, especially those with good jobs and "normal" incomes, who have a full pantry. With today's disposable society, many people shop daily for what they will eat for the next day's meals. The pantry (if they even have one) shelves are empty or filled with junk.

We keep two years' food stored up, from wheat to home-canned foods, just in case. (See Chapters 6-11 on canning and food storage.)

A medical kit

A good first aid book
Thermometer
Daily prescription meds for all family members
Antibiotics
Ointments for the eye, fungus & cuts
Antidiarrheal medication
Pain and anti-inflammatory medication such as aspirin
Burn treatment, such as *Burn Free*
Iodine/Betadine
Alcohol
Oral electrolytes (for dehydration from fever, diarrhea, stress)
Cold remedies
Cough medicines
Cough drops/throat discs
Bandages
Gauze
Cotton
Surgical tape
Scissors
Hemostats
Tweezers
Needles to remove slivers
A dental kit to patch dentures, replace fillings, etc.)
You may choose to include more, depending on your medical experience and background.

Medical needs

Build up an extensive medical kit. We use a large field box, which has two levels and many compartments. Get as much medical training as you can, such as EMT classes. You might not want to become an EMT, but you can learn much that will help your family in an emergency. Buy a good book or two, such as the *Red Cross First Aid* manual and the *Merck Manual*. Then stock up that medical kit.

Remember that "normal" things, such as cold medicine, may not be readily available.

Both my husband, a CNA, and I, a veterinary field technician, have extensive medical experience, so we include in our medical kit sutures and suture needles, injectable local anesthetic, an IV and IV electrolytes, epinephrine for shock due to allergies or drug reaction, a blood pressure cuff and stethoscope, plaster casting material, and more. One never knows if, and when, a doctor will be available during an emergency. Of course, if a doctor *is* available, one should never attempt to treat their own or others' injuries or illnesses. (See Chapter 18 on medical kits for emergencies.)

Other high priorities

A radio and batteries are other must-haves. This keeps you in contact with what's going on in the world. There are several brands of solar powered radios on the market today for not a lot of money. Batteries must be replaced or recharged. We also have a weather radio to keep up on weather conditions which can affect one's life much more when times are tough. Listening to this 9-volt radio each morning keeps us in tune to Mother Nature. This book's publisher, Dave Duffy, has a satellite internet connection to keep in touch with the news, weather, and friends. He needs no phone. A small generator will give him the little bit of electricity he needs to run the computer.

Does your family have adequate warm, sturdy clothing? If not, this is a high priority. Buy good hiking boots, jeans, and clothing that is practical, long-lasting, and warm. If you never need 'em, they won't take up much space in a closet. If you do, they will become essential.

How about alternate transportation...not your car or pickup? Walking is fine, but doesn't cover many miles in a day.

Some alternatives are bicycles, ATVs, motorcycles, snowmobiles (in snow country), and horses. All take much less gas to run than a car or truck, and bicycles and horses take none at all. Remember you don't have to use a car or truck, even though you are used to it. The Amish and other plain people have always used horses and other non-motorized vehicles for travel, and in Europe and many other countries bicycles are the norm for a lot of folks.

Stay-at-home emergencies

Some emergencies, such as severe ice storms, power outages, and blizzards occur every year or so in many cold-climate areas, more frequently in other areas. These create emergencies that largely demand people stay where they are out of common sense.

Remember, without power, you will not have access to stores for food and supplies, banks and ATMs for cash, a flush toilet, drinking water out of the tap, your furnace fan (or heat at all, if you have a "modern" all electric home), the electric kitchen stove, gas for your car, and many other "normal" conveniences you are used to.

Stay-at-home emergencies

- Food and water for family, pets & livestock for at least 14 days; 55 gallons of fresh water will last a family of four for over seven days.
- Daily medications for family for 14 days
- Alternative heat source & fuel
- Alternative cooking source & fuel
- Alternative lighting source & fuel
- Flashlights & batteries
- Transistor, crank or solar radio
- Medical kit
- Matches
- Butane lighters
- Magnesium, flint & steel fire starter

The food in your refrigerator will slowly spoil and the food in your freezer will slowly thaw, then rot, if your electricity goes off for a long period. (See Chapter 15 on "What if the electricity goes off?")

Getting along comfortably without electricity

There's a lot you can do without electricity. Number one, begin a game plan of *not* depending on electricity.

Trade in your electric stove for a gas range that does not have electric ignition. It will work when there is no electricity. Better yet, buy a wood range for the kitchen or basement. Trade in your electric refrigerator for a gas unit. Not only will it run without power, but it keeps food much better and lasts for many more years. Have at least a back-up heating unit that does not depend on electricity to run or to power the fan. A wood stove, a propane or natural gas wall furnace, or a space heater are all more dependable than a central furnace requiring electricity to provide heat for the home. (A good book to buy is *Living Without Electricity and Liking It* by Anita Evangelista. It's available from *Backwoods Home Magazine*, 1-800-835-2418.)

Alternative lighting

Decide on what emergency lighting you will use. A lot of folks prefer to buy a generator to power their entire home during a short to moderate power outage. In our remote setting, we prefer not to have to depend on generators running 24 hours a day; we use one for an hour or so and then only as truly needed. Remember, gasoline or diesel fuel may be exceedingly hard to get. Don't waste it for luxury.

We have used propane wall lamps, which give good light and are cheap to run; Coleman lamps, which also give good light, but must be pumped up to pressure from time to time; and kerosene lamps. Candles can do once in a while, in a pinch, but are easily upset, and are dangerous to use.

Be sure you have a good supply of matches, as you'll need more than you think. A few butane lighters also come in handy. I also keep a flint, steel, and magnesium fire starter, just in case. The magnesium burns very hot so it will light a fire, whether your fuel is wet or dry.

Drinking water

Have enough food and emergency water stored up if you don't have an alternative water supply, such as a well with hand pump, spring, or cistern. **Never** drink *any* surface water, such as from a lake or stream, that is not either filtered with a good filter to remove contaminants such as giardia, which causes terrific diarrhea, or boiled for five minutes after straining off the major silt. You can treat questionable water with iodine, in drop or tablet form, but personally, I think the taste is awful. I prefer boiling, cooling, then shaking the water container vigorously to re-oxygenate it, which dramatically improves the taste. **Never** drink any water from a lake or stream in or downstream from agricultural land (leaching nitrates from fertilizer) or factories/mines (heavy metals, toxic wastes), as these may escape all but the most expensive filters. Boiling will not make the water drinkable.

You can obtain water for washing and flushing the toilet from several sources: melting snow, ditches, ponds, livestock tanks, rivers, and other surface water. These will all do the job. When your water goes into an urban sewer, be sure you can "dump flush" the toilet, however, as some systems depend on pumps (electricity) to move the sewage. Check it out *before* you need to. (See chapter 11 on storing water for an emergency.)

Vehicle emergencies

A lot of our day-to-day emergencies involve being stranded with our vehicle. A mechanical failure, a flat tire, being stuck in the snow, stuck in the mud and so on can make life miserable. We need to make it less miserable— and not life-threatening as it can sometimes be.

Vehicular emergencies are compounded by other emergencies. If you are stranded in a blizzard, possibly because of an evacuation or civil disturbance, it can quickly lead to a life-threatening situation. You should prepare for these situations also.

It may seem basic, but always know where you are, and know the best route to take to get to where you are going. Carry and use a map.

In cities, avoid "bad" neighborhoods, even if it requires going out of your way.

Pay attention to weather conditions when you drive, and prepare accordingly. It's shocking to us to see folks in cars during cold, unpredictable winter weather, dressed in shorts and sandals. That's playing Russian roulette. Wear warm clothes during cold weather, or at least have them with you, including warm socks and boots.

Even in summer take some warm clothes along with you. Some evenings get downright cold in many areas, especially when there is a drizzly rain pouring all night.

If the weather is really bad, don't drive. Seems logical, but a lot of unprepared folks set out into the teeth of a blizzard or hurricane because *nothing* is going to disturb their plans. Waiting a day or two is a lot safer. Listen to a weather radio or current weather forecast before setting out. Even a four wheel drive can run into icy roads or drifted snow and have trouble.

A year's food supply for your family

This is a sample list for my family, which is a family of three. Your family needs may differ quite a bit, due to your meal preference. However, if you use this list as a base, you won't go hungry. It also allows for "company" meals. This is a realistic pantry supply to last a year comfortably. Remember to rotate your supplies, using the oldest first, replenishing as you use, in order to keep relatively fresh foodstocks. If you have a family of 4, increase the amount by 25%, a family of 6, by 50%, etc.

GRAINS

· 300 pounds of hard wheat or in combination with 150 pounds
  of wheat and 150 pounds of flour.
· 50 pounds of dry corn to grind for cornmeal
· 50 pounds of soft wheat
· 50 pounds white rice
· 50 pounds brown rice
· 50 pounds oatmeal
· 25 pounds of masa harina de maize (corn flour for tortillas and tamales)

PASTA

·15 pounds spaghetti
·6 pounds assorted noodles
·6 pounds lasagna

LEGUMES

· 50 pounds of pinto beans
· 50 pounds of combined other beans, such as navy, kidney, etc.
· 20 pounds of split peas
· 20 pounds lentils

DAIRY

· 18 #10 cans dry milk or in combination with boxes of store-bought dry milk
· 2 #10 cans cheese powder
· 5 #10 cans dehydrated eggs
· 3 #10 cans butter or margarine

SUGAR

· 50 pounds white granulated sugar
· 10 pounds brown sugar
· 10 pounds powdered sugar

SHORTENING/OIL

· 10 3# cans shortening
· 5 48 fl. oz. bottles vegetable oil
· 2 16 fl. oz. bottles olive oil

SALT

· 10 pounds iodized table salt (for pickling & meat preservation as well as table use)

VEGETABLES

· 104 pints of green beans
· 104 pints of sweet corn
· 104 pints of carrots
· 104 quarts of tomatoes

- 104 pints of tomato sauce
- 104 half pints tomato paste
- 104 quarts of potatoes and/or 22 pounds instant potatoes
- 26 quarts of squash or pumpkin
- 26 pints beets
- 2 #10 cans dehydrated sweet corn
- 4 #10 cans dehydrated peas
- 1 #10 can dehydrated onions
- 2 #10 cans dehydrated broccoli

FRUITS

- 52 pints peaches
- 52 pints apple sauce
- 52 pints fruit cocktail
- 52 quarts apples (includes pies, etc.)
- 52 pints pears
- 104 pints misc. fruits
- 1 #10 can raisins
- 1 #10 can dehydrated strawberries
- 2 #10 cans dehydrated apple slices
- 2 #10 cans dehydrated banana slices

MEAT

- 52 pints lean beef/venison roast
- 52 pints chicken/turkey
- 52 pints ham/fish/misc.
- 52 cans tuna
- 52 cans Spam
- 52 pints home canned hamburger for tacos, casseroles, etc.

- 1 #10 can ea. TVP (textured vegetable protein), bacon, chicken)

SEEDS

A heavy selection of garden seeds to replenish your food supply, should the period of hard times last longer than a few months. Always opt for the worst and prepare ahead.

Most garden seeds last for years, if kept dry. One notable exception is onion seed, which should be replaced yearly.

MISCELLANEOUS

- 1 pound baking soda
- 3 pounds baking powder
- 1 pound dry yeast
- spices usually used
- 25 dozen canning jar lids, wide mouth & regular
- coffee, tea, powdered drink mixes in sufficient quantity
- A grain mill to grind grains
- An Amish or other "cooking with basics" cookbook or two
- 1 gallon inexpensive pancake syrup
- An assortment of "treats", such as pickles, jams, preserves

If you do get stuck or stranded by a mechanical failure in bad weather, stay with the vehicle. A lot of folks lose their lives by trying to hike for help. In a vehicle, there is absence of wind, making comfortable survival much more certain. Your candle can heat the inside, warn other motorists of your presence, and attract the attention of rescuers. **But be careful!** Everything inside a vehicle ignites easily and burns with toxic smoke. Keep a down-wind window cracked to prevent carbon monoxide poisoning, especially if you run the vehicle (with the tailpipe in the clear) from time to time, to keep warm. (See Chapter 23 on emergency gear for your vehicle.)

A plan, a truck, and a survival pack for short-term evacuation

There are many situations where you may be suddenly called upon to evacuate your home: forest fire, hurricane, earthquake, chemical spills by truck or train, flood, or even radical emergencies such as terrorist activity or riots. To prevent panic, be prepared before anything of this sort happens.

We also have our favorite photo albums, important papers, and keepsakes localized for instant grabbing.

Have a "plan of action" worked out, discussed with all family members. Where you will meet? Who will carry what, and where you will go—a relative's house, a campsite on state or federal land?

If you always keep on top of the weather, the news, and local conditions, you will have a jump-start on evacuation, allowing you to prepare beforehand and avoid panic.

Have the car/truck fully gassed up and carry some reserve gas in cans....just in case. Carry not only your "grab and get" supplies, but be sure you have maps and your vehicle emergency equipment, as well. Try to stay out of main traffic areas/jams and stay out of dangerous areas, i.e., near the path of a fire, the chemical attack, the riot, etc.

It's a good idea if every member of the family has his/her own survival pack. Even a cheap backpack containing warm clothing, food, water, a lighter, candle, first aid supplies, etc. will provide extra security if family members become separated or if someone forgets something.

A survival retreat for long-term evacuation

All families today should have a safe place they can evacuate to should things get dangerous in their home area. This is especially true for city-dwelling people. Such possible realistic scenarios as riots and severe economic depression or collapse, which, considering the current global economic mess, may be the most likely scenario of all.

This retreat can be called a summer home, a vacation home, hunting cabin, or whatever. Calling it a survival retreat immediately brands you as a nut-case radical. Just quietly go about your business, not making waves or attracting attention, and secure your hideaway.

This safe spot should be located at least an hour's drive from a city—two hours from a large urban area such as an L.A. or Chicago-type metropolis. A rural location is great, but a more remote place is even better. Some folks freak out at this, preferring a small rural town setting. That'll work, too, as a close small community can work together. But we've found that that is not always the case, and we prefer to keep to the boonies.

You want something with a little acreage in case you must raise all of

Supplies to store

- 25 pounds laundry soap
- 12 28 oz. bottles dish soap
- 73 rolls toilet paper
- sanitary napkins in sufficient quantity
- 8 gallons bleach (used for sanitation as well as laundry)
- 12 bars hand soap
- 6 24 oz. bottles shampoo
- personal products, such as toothpaste, deodorant
- chainsaw oil and other items to keep things running
- pet foods
- livestock feed
- 55 gallons kerosene for lighting
- 25 gallons Coleman fuel or other lantern fuel

your food. Some people claim you can raise all your family's food on a small 50 x 50-foot garden. Nope, you cannot! When you must can all winter's food, raise all of your small grain and corn, and grow feed for any livestock you have (chickens, rabbits, etc)—and take into consideration weeds, drought, and predation—you will need more land, at least two acres to feed your family well.

Your retreat needs to have non-electric capabilities (or alternative power such as solar, wind, hydro, or generator—see Chapter 15 on electricity), well or spring water, wood heat, and alternative lighting, with appropriate fuel stored up in advance.

The sooner you get started the better, for you can plant an orchard, berries, and perennial vegetables, such as Jerusalem artichokes, asparagus, etc., allowing time for them to mature to bearing age. You can also have adequate time to slowly stock up on food and other supplies, work the garden plot up very well, fence any land you need to, develop irrigation, etc.

Where should the survival retreat be located? That's largely a personal preference. We love the very remote country: central Alaska, northern British Columbia, the Montana and Wyoming and Idaho high country. But it's certainly not for everyone. Many more folks would be happier with the plains states: Maine, Arkansas, Missouri, or Minnesota. You can still find very rural areas, far from a freeway or big city, and find it easier to raise food for the family.

And the survival retreat does *not* need to be expensive. I have personally priced many retreats, in diverse locations, nationwide, priced below $35,000.

Choose the retreat with care, taking into consideration such things as nearness to a freeway (dangerous refugee traffic in some scenarios), nearness to a military or other strategic government location (possible missile or terrorist strike), nuclear plant (possible malfunction or terrorist strike), below a dam (possible rupture and flooding), or near any factory, chemical plant, etc.

The decision to evacuate

The decision to evacuate for long term, perhaps forever, of one's home is stressful and highly personal.

It's best to leave before a situation becomes very serious. There are several reasons for this. First, there will still probably be gasoline available. The roads will be relatively uncongested, as most people have a tendency to wait until the last moment to leave, hoping desperately that things will get better. Travelling will be less stressful and much safer. A hoard of panic stricken, angry, hopeless people, even the "nicest" people in the city, could become dangerous.

Take a good map and trace out a route, avoiding freeway-congested areas and large cities, even if it means going miles out of the way. We would prefer to stick to backroads and minor highways. Drive this route often during normal times to familiarize yourself with it and work out any possible problems.

Δ

Vehicle kit

- Jack & lug wrench
- Spare tire
- Shovel
- Battery jumper cables
- Basic tool kit
- Fix-A-Flat
- Oil
- Lighter air pump
- Gallon of drinking water
- Blankets
- Basic first aid kit
- Flashlight
- Emergency food
- Candles with matches
- Map
- Cell phone or C.B. can be a life saver.

EVACUATION NEEDS

Storage food in large cooler #1

Instant potatoes
Dry milk
Canned tuna
Dehydrated eggs
Dry noodles
Flour
Shortening
TVPs
Dry soup mixes
MREs (military instant Rice
meals; meals ready to eat)
Dry beans
Margarine powder
Dehydrated fruit
Dehydrated vegetables
Tomato powder
Baking powder
Salt
Spices & condiments
Pudding mixes
Cornmeal
Instant coffee, tea,
drink mixes
Sugar

Kitchen box in large cooler #2

Frying pan
Large pot
Smaller pot
Mixing bowl, steel (can double as
cooking utensil)
Matches & lighters
Toilet paper
Paper towels
Dish towel
Dish soap
Candles
Dish scrubber pad
Bowls for family
Silverware for family

Metal spatula
Roll of duct tape
Small roll of wire
Metal cups for family
Small water filter
Propane stove & tanks
Flashlight & batteries
Hatchet

Medical Kit (as previously detailed)

Sleeping Gear (in large plastic box)

Sleeping bags
Candles & lighters
Coleman lantern
Unopened gallon of lantern fuel
Bow saw
Warm socks & jackets
10' x 12' plastic tarp
lightweight tent
Radio

Rifle/shotgun and ammunition (food procurement, signaling, and family protection)

Personal backpacks

Warm clothes
Emergency food
Socks
Stocking hat
Basic fishing gear without rod
Small first aid kit
Space blanket
Flashlight
Roll of wire & rope
Pocket knife
Canteen with cup
Lighter
A few dollars in quarters & bills

Chapter 6
Canned and dried storage foods

By Jackie Clay

To avoid panic and discomfort, it is provident and wise to stock up on food for not only survival, but reasonable comfort and happiness, should we need to live off what we have stored in our pantry, root cellar, basement, or attic.

We should also rotate the foods we store in order to have wholesome foods to choose from. But just how long are foods actually good?

Some items at the store have a "freshness date" and it is commonly believed that after that date the products will not be good. And even preparedness companies cite a shelf life of five years in their storable foods. Then along comes some strange person, such as myself, who tells a different tale. As a long-time survivalist and home canner, with nothing to lose or gain from telling you anything but the truth, you might listen to my experiences.

I have always kept at least a two year supply of food stored against bad times, whether it be an illness, injury, loss of a job, storm, or worse. This is a practice I learned from my parents and grandparents who lived through and learned from the Depression. Every year I home-can hundreds of jars of food, most filled with home-raised produce and meat, some with meat from hunting, some with items purchased at great sales at the market throughout the year.

In one year we canned two deer, a tremendous tomato crop in another, a bumper apple crop in yet another, and so on. I always can all I am able, as in other years the crop may not be so good and the hunting may be sparse. In this way, my pantry leapfrogs, as we do not consume all of last year's canned food. So, through the years, the canned goods build and build, and despite rotating the shelves to try to use up the oldest, our supply expands.

Likewise, other pantry supplies, bought from the stores, grows and grows as one great sale follows another.

Okay, the bottom line: Just how long will this stuff keep? Do I really have to throw it to the chickens after a year? Two years? Five years? The answer is one word.

No.

Tins and sealed jars hold dry foods such as beans, peas, corn, pasta, and seeds for future gardens.

Canned goods

No matter what you read in canning books (the newer ones, of course), on labels, in magazines, and no matter what your neighbor or friend tells you, canned foods will last nearly indefinitely.

Now, you *must* store all canned foods, including home canned foods, in a cool, dark, dry place for optimum shelf life. Storing them in hot, light conditions will sometimes result in changes in texture, color, and taste as well as hasten the breakdown of vitamins. (It is this breakdown in vitamins that most often gives the warning, which sounds so dire: *use before such and such a date.*)

It is true that most canned foods will lose some vitamin content. But if you've ever been hungry—I mean real hungry—you don't worry if the vitamin C in the canned tomatoes is below national standards. Besides, we figure we make up any vitamin shortfall with the fresh produce we eat nearly every day from the garden.

Storing canned foods in damp conditions, as often found in basements or root cellars, can shorten the shelf life, and sooner or later the cans and jar tops will rust, weaken, and the contents will spoil. If this is your only storage facility, be certain to use up any cans or tins that are beginning to rust before they go bad and always check such containers for mold, cloudiness, odor, or an unsealed or bulging condition. All indicate spoiled foods. Likewise, boil all vegetables or meats for 15 minutes to kill pathogens, even if not apparent. Just to be sure.

A full pantry is great insurance.

I have home-canned jars of food that are at least 20 years old, which we use from time to time. For instance the cherries we picked from Dad's orchard, which we parcel out frugally until we get our own trees bearing. These foods taste, smell, and look great, despite their age. Plenty good for an emergency situation, for sure.

Dry goods

Okay, let's move on to the more nebulous items, such as dry goods, like flours, dry milk, sugar, etc. Will all of these store indefinitely as well? Yes and no, depending on the product. Let's start with those that have an extremely long shelf life, given good storage practices. By this I mean kept dry, sealed, and stored in a fairly cool, dry, dark location.

Beans, dry peas, wheat, and other dry grains, unprocessed, will keep in storage a long, long time. I have some beans that are more than 700 years old, and they still germinate and grow.

You know I could eat them, if I wanted to. But, of course, I don't as they are treasures from the past.

Because these grains store so long, it is best to store whole grains, including corn, and grind them as needed. For once they are ground, the shelf life decreases, often dramatically. Take whole wheat flour and corn meal for instance. Both of these products can become rancid after a period of from two weeks to a few years, because of the oils in them.

White flour from the store has been "processed," which removes the oily germ and, of course, much of the nutrition. Therefore, it will store for a much longer time than will whole wheat flour. My grandmother did not like to use fresh white flour, preferring to use older flour as it baked better. Right now, I'm using a bin of six-year-old white flour, and it is fine. I do sift it twice to fluff it up because when it sits in the bag for a long time, it settles and packs together. Without the extra sifting, it bakes pretty solid biscuits and bread. Corn meal will usually last, unrancid, for about a year or two in a sealed glass jar.

Other than dampness, a bag of flour or grain's worst enemy is the meal moth. This little bugger is a small, nondescript greyish moth who gets into our grain and lays eggs which hatch out into flour weevils, ruining the flour in a short time. The first sign of weevils are tiny dark specks in the flour, followed by webbing in the can or jar. The moths initially come into our pantry in a bag of flour with a small tear, hole, or unglued section of bag.

Always thoroughly check all new bags of flour or meal at the store, rejecting any that have a tiny leak. Taping the hole at the store is not a cure. Buy solid bags, and immediately get them into good, airtight storage. For long term storage, I put two 25-pound sacks in a good food grade garbage bag, stick a few bay leaves in for good measure, and seal the bag with duct tape. The bay leaves discourage any moths that could possibly get into the sealed plastic bag. These sacks are then either stored in a clean garbage can or sturdy cardboard box, which is also taped shut when full.

I usually freeze five-gallon pails of whole grains in case some minute friends are hitching a ride in our food. The freezing kills them before they become a problem.

It is a very good idea to buy a package of meal moth lures/traps, which attract the moths before they attack your stored flours. The cost is minimal and they do afford good protection. These traps sit discreetly on your pantry shelf, trapping any moths that happen by.

Sugars will last indefinitely. They must be kept dry and sealed to prevent hardening. When I store brown sugar, I dampen a piece of folded washcloth and place it on top of the sugar, then seal the jar. This keeps the sugar from hardening, which is a problem with brown sugar. If a bag or jar of sugar does get hard or crumbly, it is still good, although a bit inconvenient. Just warm up the sugar and add it to the liquid in the recipe to soften it.

Dry milk, dry eggs, dry margarine and butter powder, cheese powder, and powdered cheese sauce are foods that keep very well, if unopened and well sealed. I buy dry eggs, powdered cheese, margarine, orange drink mix, and many other long-storage items from a preparedness company as they are sealed in #10 cans.

I've used some of these foods that were seven-years-old and older and all were perfectly fine. And I've used dry milk from the store which was well sealed and stored for 10 years on our pantry shelf. The milk smelled and tasted normal and resulted in great pancakes, rolls, and sauces.

Home dehydrated vegetables and dehydrated vegetables purchased from preparedness companies in #10 cans make an excellent lightweight, nutritious, long-term storage item. I dehydrate everything from sliced potatoes and corn to tomatoes and peppers. Perfectly dried and securely sealed, they will last for years.

I buy two one-pound foil bags of granulated dry yeast at a time. One I open and pour into a jar, which is stored in the fridge. The other is stored, unopened, in the freezer compartment of the fridge. As yeast only keeps a shelf life of about a year, unrefrigerated, I rotate this yearly, using the frozen yeast to replace the one in the refrigerator at the end of the year and buying a new one for the freezer. But, in an emergency, one can always use a bit of this old yeast or even develop wild yeast to make a sourdough starter.

Salt will keep forever if stored with care.

Baking powder will keep well a long time if stored properly. In fact, the can of Rumford I'm using now was purchased five years ago and it just sits on my shelf. And if it starts to weaken, you can just add a bit more or boost it by adding warm liquid to the mix. Baking soda lasts even longer. I'm using some off the pantry shelf that is nine, count 'em, nine years old. And no one has ever whined about my cooking.

More perishable foods

How about more perishable foods? When we lived on our remote homestead in Montana's high country, we were snowed in for at least six months out of the year, so preparation was a must. We learned that we could stick frozen stick margarine in a cooler we placed in a snowbank and have it last all winter. Unfrozen but refrigerated margarine would keep for about two months, then begin to pick up odors and tastes. We learned that tubs of margarine would keep for nearly all winter in a cold spot on the floor of our pantry, but we did need to protect it from not only our cats and an occasional mouse, but from the dogs as well. Butter lasts a much shorter time, unless kept strictly frozen.

Shortening, bought and kept sealed, will last many years before going rancid. I have used some that was 7 years-old, and it was fine.

Eggs are a big joke with us. Many folks insist on "fresh" eggs, throwing out those a few weeks old. I worked part time for an egg ranch. The fresh eggs were picked up weekly, hauled to a warehouse where they were distributed to wholesale companies, who kept them around awhile before trucking them to super markets where they were finally bought. How much time elapsed? Who knows?

We raise our own chickens but before we snowmobiled our day-old chicks up the mountain one April we had to buy eggs for the winter. We found that if we bought really fresh eggs from a rancher in November, we'd have good eggs in May. I did crack them into a cup, as an occasional one would be bad.

You can waterglass your eggs, but a crock full of those eggs is nasty to reach into. Kind of like dipping into snot for breakfast eggs. It takes your appetite away and it is a bit costly.

We found that keeping the eggs boxed in the fridge or cold corner of the pantry was sufficient to keep them all winter. All eggs to be stored should be carefully inspected for even the most minute cracks as it can allow bacteria to penetrate the egg.

Without a flock of chickens to depend on, it is a good idea to have several #10 cans of powdered eggs on hand to be available in an emergency.

Just a note: home-raised eggs, fresh from the hen, are fine unrefrigerated for many days. I've found hidden nests in the weeds with eggs that have not been sat on by the hen yet, and though they sat out in 90° weather for as much as a week, I used them, finding every one was like it was fresh from the hen.

Meats and meat substitutes

Unless your family is vegetarian, meats in storage is necessary. No, I do not mean in the freezer, as no matter what "bad times" entail, the first thing to go is the power. Lose a job, get injured, not enough to pay the power bill, storms, earthquakes, fires, floods—all can quickly zap the power. While there are steps you can take to keep a freezer from thawing out quickly, they are not enough for a long-lasting emergency.

I have home-canned meat for years, and found it extremely easy, quick, and convenient. Any canning book can help you get started today. This meat, including stews, soups, sauces, fish, poultry, and wild game will keep indefinitely if properly stored in that dark, dry, cool pantry.

Want to store meat before you get that two years' supply of home-canned meat on your shelf? Just look on your supermarket shelves. There's a lot to choose from: tuna, salmon, hash, chicken, ham, sauces, beef, and even bacon. For long-term storage I try to stay away from those convenient "pop tops" with a handy pull ring. They are nice, but can easily get unsealed in the hustle and rush of an emergency. You have to handle and pack them very carefully, or the weakened area that pops can be poked, unsealing them, often without a sign it has happened. Yes, our family does have Spam on the shelves of our pantry, but I handle it very carefully. Soups, stews, canned spaghetti, and so forth, purchased from the store shelves, will also last indefinitely, if kept dry to prevent rusting.

Jerky? Well, to tell the truth, few people ever dry it long enough for safe, dependable long-term storage without canning it as well. In many climates, the meat goes bad or begins to mold in as little as two weeks without refrigeration. If it is dried to a brittle stick, it will keep longer, but it is like chewing on a piece of rawhide. Indians did it, but they were much less fussy than today's urban population.

A popular meat substitute that is lightweight, nutritious, tasty, and long keeping is a product called TVP (textured vegetable protein). You probably best recognize it as the bacon-bits that aren't really bacon. We keep about 15 pounds in factory sealed #10 cans or aluminum bags in our pantry. As most recipes only need about a quarter cup, you can see these lightweight crumbles last a long time.

They come in several flavors: chicken, beef, bacon, ham, and even taco. I've found that keeping several jars of dried soup base next to the TVPs makes a nice couple. Simply adding the flavored soup base to soup, noodles, or whatever, then tossing in the matched TVP, makes a very quick, lightweight, satisfying, and *cheap* dinner, even on the go.

Snacks for storage

Okay, I know goodies may get raised eyebrows, but they sure make an emergency less depressing. Unfortunately, potato chips and other "normal" snacks are primarily grease which turns rancid pretty quickly. But there are still a lot of snacks out there perfect for the pantry. On the top of our list is home-dried fruit. I dry about as much as I can and have gallon jars of dried apples, apple bits, peaches, peach bits, strawberries, pineapple, apricots, pears, and more. I have 10-year-old dried apples in a test jar and I've pulled out a few to nibble on each year for five years now. They are a bit brown, but still very tasty. These dried fruits can either be eaten as a great snack, added to mixes such as pancake or muffin, or rehydrated and eaten soft and juicy.

Don't have a dehydrator yet? While you shop or build, you may want to consider dried fruit from the store. While quite expensive, it is readily available and there are good choices: apples, prunes, raisins, cranberries, strawberries, apricots, pineapple, and more. The down side is that most are heavily laden with sugar, but they are light and tasty.

Jello and instant pudding mixes are another long-term storage goody. Lasting indefinitely, they make a great snack, treat, or reward.

Dried beverages, whether they be coffee, tea, or powdered drink mixes, all store well, even in very long-term plans. It is best, as in all the other above items, to rotate your stock, because powdered drinks, especially, have a tendency to cake. Of course they are still usable, but it doesn't take much to use the old stuff as you go and replace it with new.

Nuts and sealed packages of sunflower seeds make another great storage snack. They will usually last several years, factory sealed or home canned. Otherwise, they will become as rancid as those opened holiday salted nuts. I can a variety of nuts at home, especially walnuts and pecans from friends' orchards.

Search stores and preparedness catalogs for other snacks that sound good to you. A person can always experiment (before spending money stocking up on an item) with just about any food.

MREs? For those of you who are uninitiated, MRE stands for "meals ready to eat," a meal in a pouch developed for the military, with no cooking necessary. Here I'll put myself on the firing line and say they just plain cost too much for this frugal person. They taste fairly good—about like a TV dinner—are reasonably nutritious, are certainly fast and easy to grab and run with, but they are expensive and heavy if you have to carry them.

However, their shelf life is quite good. It is claimed that they will store for five years, but I'd suspect quite a bit longer if kept away from heat. But, for the cost of an MRE to feed one person, I can fix a meal—a real meal where you get filled up—for four people, even in the boonies.

So there you have it—the truth according to Jackie on long-term food storage. Try it yourself and find out how creative your family can be. Mine certainly is.

Just remember these tips:
- 1. Keep food cool, dark, and dry.
- 2. Make sure the food is factory or home-sealed as well as it can be.
- 3. Rotate all storage food regularly, marking the date on which you entered each item into the pantry. Use the oldest first.
- 4. Don't be afraid to experiment.
- 5. Have fun.

After all, it's a real joy and very reassuring to know that your family can get by nearly any period of bad times, eating good, nutritious food that they enjoy. Δ

Chapter 7
Long term food storage

By Jackie Clay

You've decided that you're going to put at least a year's worth of food away for your family just in case. Great! Everyone should do that. We store enough to feed friends, extended family, and neighbors from time to time, as well. We could not turn down anyone who came to us saying, "I'm hungry." So I stock up more than most people do.

Flours and grains

Man may not live by bread alone, but grains form the base for many meals, especially during a period of hard times. With flours and whole grains stored, you have the main ingredient for homemade pastas, breads, rolls, biscuits, pancakes, waffles, tortillas and other flat breads, pie crusts, cookies, cakes, and more.

I store unbleached (who needs bleaching compounds in their diet?) flour, at least 200 pounds, in 25-pound store bags, wrapped in plastic bags and duct tape, in Rubbermaid garbage cans with locking lids in my pantry. This will feed three of us, plus extra for friends and family, for over a year, coupled with other flour products and whole grains.

You can add any specialty flours your family likes, such as rye, amaranth, or Durham (for specialty pastas).

In addition to this flour, I like at least 100 pounds of hard wheat (sometimes called "wheat berries"). As ground whole wheat goes rancid fairly quickly, I like this wheat on hand to grind for all of my whole wheat recipes. In addition, whole wheat grain will grow when planted, making wheat growing on a fairly small plot possible to restock my supply. As little as a 50x50-foot plot will grow enough wheat for a small family's needs.

I also stock about 20 pounds of corn meal, 20 pounds of masa harina de maize (corn flour) which I use to make tamales and corn tortillas, along with 25 pounds of popcorn (grinds nicely for cornmeal, as well as popping for treats), and 25 pounds of hominy corn (makes hominy and also masa harina de maize).

Rice, both brown and white, fit nicely in our storage pantry. We also store about 25 pounds of a combination of white and brown rice with a few pounds of wild rice mixed in.

Home canning helps fill the pantry. Note decorative
popcorn tins in the background, filled with dry foods.

And don't forget rolled oats. They are much more versatile than just using them for oatmeal. I include them in several multi-grain breads, breakfast cake, bars, meat loaf, granola, and cookies. And as for oatmeal, we like it cooked up with peaches, strawberries, and apples, with cinnamon for a treat.

Any grains that are ground, especially corn meal, masa harina de maize, and whole wheat will get rancid quicker than do whole grains, which usually stay good for many years. Even so, flours (except whole wheat flour) will stay perfectly good for five years or more if kept dry and stored in air tight and bug and rodent-proof containers.

I buy my white flour, cornmeal, etc. on sale at local supermarkets, usually just before Thanksgiving, as it is cheaper then. Otherwise, I pick it up at Sam's Club or other restaurant supply houses.

I pick up whole grains from local grain farmers. Sometimes the wheat needs a bit more cleaning if dusty, but a few pours from one basket to another on a windy day ensures very clean wheat. (And my wheat is *not* treated with toxic fumigants in storage bins before being ground into flour, as is most wheat sold to flour mills.)

When buying flour to store, be absolutely sure the bags are completely sealed, with no flour leaking out, to prevent flour weevil problems. In areas where there is a weevil problem (webs and "bugs" in unsealed cornmeal and flour), some folks freeze each bag of flour for several days before wrapping and storing it in completely bug-proof containers. I have not done this, but I am exceptionally careful not to store any flour products that were not very well sealed from the processing plant, and I keep them in insect proof containers. Remember that these moths are very small and squeeze through very tiny openings.

It is not necessary to buy flours and grains from long-term storage companies unless you fear flooding. In this case, sealed tins or buckets of flours would be a good idea. I've had plain white flour stored for over five years, which is just as good today as it was when I bought it.

Beans and other legumes

When one thinks of long-term storage, usually dried beans come first to mind. I guess this is because they remain good for so long, are nutritious, and taste pretty darned good to boot. But, for heaven's sake, don't just buy a hundred pounds of navy beans and say you're all set for whatever may come your way. All beans do not taste the same. There's a big, big difference between a large white lima and a Jacob's cattle bean, for instance. Some taste nutty, some bland. Some

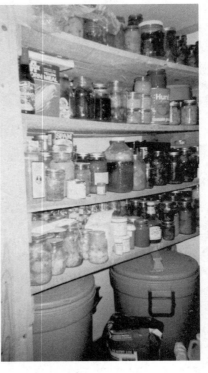

A full pantry staves off hunger.

cook up quickly, some require hours of cooking. Some remain firm after cooking, others get mushy and soft. Experiment with a wide variety of beans before committing to a choice.

We store about 50 pounds of combined legumes, which include pintos, Cherokee mixed cornfield beans, Jacob's cattle, Hopi black bush, navies, red kidney, and a dozen old Native American varieties, along with lentils, soup peas, blackeyed peas, and garbanzos.

Beans are a great protein source and combine well in many different dishes. Refried beans, fried dry pea patties, stews, soups, chiles, baked beans, and casseroles are just a few uses for these versatile legumes.

You can buy your beans in local markets, health food stores, and co-ops, or you can do like we do, and grow your own.

All beans store a long, long time in an airtight and bug and rodent-proof container. I keep mine in gallon glass jars and in decorative popcorn tins, right on handy shelves in the kitchen. While old beans do take longer to cook up tender, they last indefinitely; I've grown beans from 500-year-old seeds. And if you can grow plants from seed, you can certainly eat them.

Dried pasta

While I make a lot of homemade pasta, I still keep quite a bit in our storage pantry. When you're busy with a survival situation, you may not have time to make pasta. So I've put away 10 pounds of long spaghetti, 10 pounds of lasagna noodles, 10 pounds of wide egg noodles, 5 pounds of alphabet macaroni, 15 pounds of elbow macaroni, and a few pounds of assorted pasta noodles.

This dry pasta keeps indefinitely when stored in a dry, bug and rodent-proof container. As with my beans and other legumes, I use decorative pop-corn tins and gallon glass jars. After several years, the elbow macaroni smells a bit rancid, but it is still good when cooked with cheese or other sauces.

Sugar and honey

You will probably agree with me that we all eat too much sugar. And although honey is natural and better for us than refined sugar, it's still sugar. But in bad times, we usually feel better with "treats" from time to time. And these treats often include sugar. Also, much fruit is home canned with a sugar syrup, and if you're going to can to keep your pantry from running out in bad times, you'll need quite a bit for fruits, pickles, jams, jellies, preserves, etc.

Although my husband Bob is a diabetic, we do include sugar in our storage pantry. I keep a 25-pound sack in a plastic garbage can, along with assorted other dry foods. Much of this sugar is used in canning and desserts for my son, David, and myself. Bob needs a sugar substitute.

Sugar stores indefinitely if kept dry. If it should get damp and harden, you can still save it. Beat the bag with a hammer, being careful not to split the sack. (I would put the paper bag in a heavy plastic bag, just in case.) Soon the hard lump will be many smaller ones, easy to crumble with your hand.

Honey is a good long-term storage bet. Honey may crystallize if it gets too cool, but it is still good and will re-liquify if warmed up by sitting the jar in a saucepan of boiling water. Raw honey only needs to be put into quart or larger jars and sealed. I have 15-year-old honey that's still great. (In case you're wondering, I try to keep a little of each food for a long, long time, to see just *how* long it will remain good. I *do* rotate my long-term storage food, using the oldest and replacing it with newer food in an ongoing process.)

I keep two gallons of honey, stored in quart jars.

Besides these two sweeteners, I keep 10 pounds of brown sugar and 5 pounds of powdered sugar, stored in the bag they come in until I'm ready to use them. These bags are stored in the plastic garbage can, along with the white sugar and much more. The only problem I've had regularly with brown sugar is hardening in the bag. I've cured this by breaking the sugar into chunks, dropping them into a gallon glass jar and adding a piece of paper towel, dampened with water. Close the jar and in a few days the sugar will be soft again.

Miscellaneous dry goods

Powdered egg is a handy dry food to keep on the pantry shelves. The modern powered egg is much better than the old "green eggs" of military service days. Not only is it great in cooking, but it tastes pretty good too. I keep three #10 cans, which hold almost a gallon, on my pantry shelves.

Powdered margarine and butter are another "must have" for most families. These are reconstituted with either water or vegetable oil, with the oil tasting much better. I keep three of each, even though we have a cow and goats. One never knows when they may be dry and you need butter.

Powdered cheese is a great product that stores easily. I use it in macaroni and cheese, on popcorn, in potatoes au gratin, casseroles, and more. I keep about 10 pounds of a powdered cheese sauce that I buy from a local restaurant supply house quite inexpensively.

Dry yeast is a definite must in a long-term storage pantry, as well as in everyday use. I buy mine in 1-pound vacuum packed aluminum foil bags. Unopened and frozen, they last indefinitely. Unopened and on the shelf, they'll last for a couple of years. Opened and on the shelf, dry yeast is active for about a year or a little more. I keep an unopened bag in my propane fridge's freezer, figuring that if an emergency situation occurs, causing us to have to do without the fridge, my yeast will still be good for better than a year. I have another one on the shelf that I use every day.

Baking soda is also a necessary baking leavening agent, also useful for an antacid, deodorant, cleaner, and more. It keeps on the shelf forever. I keep 5 pounds.

Baking powder is hard to do without. You'll need it for quick breads, such as cornbread and biscuits, which are very important in emergencies because you can eat well and spend only minutes in baking. It keeps well for years without losing its leavening ability. I keep two large tins, one to use and one to store.

Salt is needed, not only to improve the flavor of foods but in meat preservation and canning. I keep 10 pounds of iodized salt in 1-pound boxes, and 10 pounds of canning salt. Canning salt is used in pickles because table salt contains chemicals that sometimes cause pickles to soften or discolor. Dry salt will keep forever. If it should harden, beat it with a hammer and it will be made useable.

Dry milk is a necessity, even for those of us who have dairy animals. One never knows when your animals may be dry and you need milk—today.

Dehydrated milk does *not* taste as good as fresh, no matter whose claims say theirs does. But it is great for cooking and it will work on cereal or for chocolate milk. The boxes at your local store will last for years with no change in taste. I keep about 10 pounds of dry milk, even though we have dairy animals.

Spices are indispensable. Be sure to store a wide variety of your favorites. True, spices do lose some of their flavor in a year or so. But better to have an old spice than no spice. They will "keep" forever, but will slowly lose their potency. I buy most of mine in oriental markets and restaurant supply houses.

Miscellaneous canned necessities

Peanut butter isn't just for kids, folks. It's a tasty, great protein source that's versatile, as well. No one guesses that the secret ingredient in my best stir-fry is a tablespoonful of chunky peanut butter. Remember that besides peanut butter sandwiches and spread on toast, you can bake cookies and other deserts with this protein-filled treat. Unopened, it'll last for years.

Shortening and **vegetable oils** will make cooking more of a pleasure, not to mention all the baking you may want to do. Most shortenings will store indefinitely in the pantry and unopened bottles of vegetable oils will be fine for over a year, usually longer. Rotate the oils more frequently than the solid shortening. You will probably like using corn oil to reconstitute your powdered margarine and butter, instead of water. You'll use more shortening and vegetable oil in a year than you'd guess. I store a dozen cans of shortening and 6 large bottles of vegetable oil.

Dehydrate foods at home

Unless you need sealed cans of dehydrated foods, you can dehydrate food for long-term storage yourself. It's amazing how easy it is to dry foods at home. While I home-can a huge variety of foods, I also rely on dehydrated foods, which compliment the canned foods. For instance, canned peas taste like nasty mush. Sorry Jolly Green, it's the truth. So instead of canning my peas, I dehydrate them. When rehydrated, they taste almost as good as fresh.

You can dehydrate foods on cookie sheets in a gas oven, with only the pilot on, in the oven of a wood cook stove with a slow fire and the door open, over a register, or in the back of your station wagon or Suburban on a hot day. I've dried foods on sheets, laid out on tin porch roofs, and in hay mows, protected from insects and dust by cheesecloth or old curtains. But, finally, I caught a killer sale at Wal-Mart and bought a round plastic electric dehydrator. (Vita-Mix also sells these.) I've dehydrated bushels of produce and it's showing no sign of weakening. I also bought two extra trays 10 years back, which help.

We live far off grid, but use the dehydrator when we have the generator on for a few hours for my writing or tool use. It's a little peculiar, but it works.

Peas are very easy to dehydrate at home. Simply shell your peas, then dip them into boiling water for one minute to blanch them. If you don't, the flavor will not keep as well. Let them drip dry, then spread them out on your trays, one layer deep. Dehydrate until they are hard and puckered. If using a cookie sheet, stir them a time or two.

Cool and pour into airtight, vermin-proof containers. I use odd shaped glass jars. I keep at least two gallons in storage, and they'll last for years. Rehydrate in boiling water and let them steep for an hour or two. For use in soups and stews, simply sprinkle a handful or two of dried peas into your stock. Simmer until done. Simple and tasty.

Not enough peas in the garden to dehydrate? Buy some on-sale frozen peas, thaw 'em, and go at it. They work fine.

Onions and **garlic** are about as easy as it gets. I peel them and slice whole round slices off, about an eighth of an inch thick. Place in a single layer on your tray and begin dehydrating. Dry until quite dry. I then chop them, either using a blender (when the generator is on) or in a food grinder. Dump the chopped onions out on a cookie sheet and dry further, until crunchy-dry. These may be stored as is or reduced to a textured powder to use in cooking as onion powder. I do some of each, and keep a quart of onion powder, a half pint of garlic powder, a quart of minced onion, and a half pint of minced garlic on my pantry shelf. I use these every day.

Sweet corn is another of my favorites. I briefly boil a couple dozen ears of corn, then cut the kernels off the cob and lay them on a drying tray in a single layer. Corn needs to be stirred often if on a cookie sheet, but is fine on a screen or regular dehydrator tray. Dry until tough and hard, then store in an airtight jar or other container. To rehydrate and use as fresh corn, I boil it for one minute, then place in the fridge overnight. The next day it's hard to tell from fresh corn. This sweet corn will keep for years in decent storage. If you run out of fresh corn, frozen or canned corn will dehydrate fine.

Carrots dehydrate great at home. Slice or dice the carrots into ¼-inch pieces. Blanch for one minute in steam or boiling water. Drip dry and put on a tray in a single layer. Dehydrate until leathery and quite hard.

Green beans dry fine, too. Simply cut into one inch pieces, blanch for a minute, dry, and lay in a single layer on the tray. They should be leathery-brittle. Green beans take a little more time to rehydrate. You can't just put a handful into a casserole and bake it. They'll still be tough. They should be rehydrated the night before and kept in the water they were boiled in over-night in the fridge.

Peppers of all kinds dehydrate wonderfully. The old way was to string them by the stems and hang in the sun on a porch wall. But if you live in a humid climate, you'll probably have molded peppers if you use this method. So use the dehydrator method. Seed the peppers, then halve thin-walled hot peppers or slice thick-walled peppers, such as bell peppers, in ¼-inch wide slices. Dehydrate in a single layer until crunchy.

Broccoli works great dehydrated, which is lucky because it is terrible when canned. Cut into small flowerettes and blanch. Lay out in a single layer and dehydrate to a very crisp texture, like artificial little trees. It works great in cheese and broccoli soup and casseroles.

Fruits are simple to dehydrate, too. You can just slice ripe **bananas** ¼-inch thick onto your tray and dry them to a leathery-hard disc. **Peach** slices are equally easy. Make your own raisins from whole seedless **grapes**. Just stem them, sort and lay out in a single layer. Easy? You bet.

Apples can be peeled (or not) and sliced ¼-inch thick into a bowl of water with a good squeeze of lemon and a teaspoonful of salt in it to prevent discoloration. Then they are drip dried and laid in a single layer on the dehydrator trays. Apples dry to a leathery-crisp texture. I keep about 3 gallons of dehydrated apple slices, as they cook up quickly and easily in recipes from pies to granola. We like them for treats, too.

Strawberries dry nicely when sliced ¼-inch thick. You'll want these dehydrated to a crisp texture. I've used a lot of fresh ones, but have bought frozen strawberries on a great sale and done them up with equal success. I put up as many dehydrated strawberries as I have and am glad for them come winter.

Home dehydrating is easy and the food tastes good. An added bonus is that a bushel of produce can be dehydrated and stored in a couple of jars. Many foods contain up to 90 percent water. Pick up a good book on dehydrating food, and go at it.

Canning foods

While you can buy up a bunch of canned meats, vegetables, fruits, jams, jellies, pickles, and so forth at the store to put in a long-term storage pantry, it's a good idea to learn to home-can foods. Both will have an indefinite shelf life, but home-canned foods will be much more tasty and nutritious. And if a situation develops where you can not buy more storebought food, you can reuse your jars and rings (not lids) and home-can more food to restock your pantry. All it takes is a garden and a little skill.

Nearly anything you see canned in the store can be canned at home, including meat. Here's how:

Equipment needed:

• Water bath canner for high-acid foods, such as fruit, pickles, jelly, jams, preserves, tomatoes and tomato sauce. A "Big blue" canner costs $21-$27 and lasts indefinitely.

• Pressure canner for low-acid foods, such as vegetables and meats. (No, they do not blow up.) This canner has a gauge or weight on top, along with a lock-down heavy lid. Cost new is $89-$139. Lasts indefinitely. (I bought a used one for $5.)

• Canning jars, from half pint upwards, depending on your needs. Cost new is $5.49-$6.49 per dozen, including new rings and lids. Jars last indefinitely, rings 20+ years with care. I've been given boxes and boxes, bought others for less than $1 a dozen at flea markets and auctions. Ask around. Standard canning lids must fit correctly.

• Lids to fit jars, either wide mouth or regular. Cost $.94 to $1.89 per dozen (wide mouth are more expensive). One use only.

• Canning book or manual, such as *Ball Blue Book*. Cost $5.95-$18. Lasts indefinitely (or until a new one comes out with the latest safe canning information).

• Jar funnels, jar lifters, and lid wands to pick up hot lids are all cheap and last forever.

High-acid foods

Fruits, tomatoes, pickles, etc.

High-acid foods are the easiest to can, as they require no pressure canning. High-acid foods do not develop bacteria that cause food poisoning. If they go bad, they mold or ferment instead. Yucky, but not deadly. Canning with a water bath canner processes foods at water-boiling temperature, which seals the jars.

Whenever I begin to can any food, I always get out my canning manual no matter how many hundreds of times I've put up the same exact food. You should do the same. While you are looking through it for the food you are going to water bath can today, take a gander at the altitude chart if you live above 1,000 feet. You will need to adjust the time upwards by 5 minutes for altitudes between 1,001-3,000 feet, adding another five minutes for altitudes between 3,001 and 6,000 feet, another five for altitudes between 6,001 and 8,000 feet, and so on. We live at 4,200 feet, so I add 10 minutes to all processing times.

Okay, let's can peaches to see how to use the water bath canner. The basic process is the same, but there are differences for each food, so read your canning manual before starting.

1. Get out your jars, and check for cracks or nicks in the rim; any damaged jars need to be thrown away because they will not seal and will often break during processing.

2. Wash jars and rings in hot soapy water. Rinse and leave in hot water until needed.

3. Select only sound, ripe peaches (unripe peaches will not peel easily).

4. To peel peaches, dip them in a kettle of boiling water for a minute only, then drain and put into cold water. This loosens the skin, making them easy to slip off.

5. Cut peaches in half. Remove pit. Leave in halves or cut into desired slices. Drop pieces into a large bowl containing cold water and either half a cup of lemon juice or a commercial product to prevent darkening, such as Fruit Fresh.

6. Place jar on dry folded towel and pack peaches, leaving half an inch of head space (head space is just room at the top of the jar).

7. Pick out enough new jar lids for your jars and bring to a boil in enough water to just cover them. Keep them in hot water until you are ready to use them.

8. Cover peaches with boiling hot syrup (see your manual for proportions of this sugar and water solution), leaving half an inch of head space.

9. Slide a wooden spoon or rubber spatula down between the peaches to let air bubbles escape and more syrup contact the fruit.

10. Wipe the jar rim well with a clean damp cloth. Place hot lid on jar and screw down ring firmly tight. Use no force.

11. Place jars on rack of full, hot, water bath canner. Never place hot jars in contact with anything cold or vice versa, as they will break.

12. When the canner is full, the water should cover all of the jars by one inch. If you need to add more water, use a tea kettle of hot water to bring the level up to the necessary point.

13. Bring water to a rolling boil with the top on the canner. When it begins to boil vigorously, begin your timing. For altitudes below 1,000 feet, you'll need to process your peaches for 25 minutes for pints and 30 minutes for quarts.

14. When the time is up, turn off heat and remove the jars from the canner carefully with a jar lifter. Place on a dry folded towel, out of drafts, to cool. Don't tighten any bands that seem loose. The jars will seal. When the jars are cool (over night), inspect seals. A sealed jar will have a tight indentation in the center of the flat lid. It will not give on pressure from a finger in the center. The contents of an unsealed jar should be eaten at once or refrigerated.

15. Remove the bands and wash if necessary. The bands are not necessary to maintain the seal and may cause rust to form. Store the jars in a dark, dry, relatively cool place.

That's all there is to water bath canning. If you can boil water and tell time, you can do it easily.

Low-acid foods

Vegetables, meats, stews, etc.

Remember, none of these foods can be safely canned in a hot water bath canner, no matter what your grandma or auntie used to do. It is simply not safe.

In the water bath canning process we had to adjust the time we processed our foods, according to altitudes above 1,001. In a like manner, we must adjust the pressure we process our foods with for altitudes above 1,001. Check your canning manual for the correct pressure for your altitude.

Before you start, unless your canner is new, have the pressure gauge checked by your extension office to make sure it reads correctly. Most do, but to be safe have it checked.

Some pressure canners have weights over a pressure valve, but for simplicity's sake, we'll assume your pressure canner has a gauge, as most do today.

Let's do up a batch of chili. Most foods are pressure canned in nearly the same way, but, again, check your canning manual for other foods. For recipes with mixed ingredients, simply process the food for the longest length of time required for any single ingredient. In this case, it's meat.

1. Select crack and nick-free jars.

2. Make a large pot of your favorite chili; the beans do not have to be completely tender, but well cooked.

3. Wash jars in hot soapy water, then rinse, keeping hot until needed.

4. Boil enough lids for your jars and keep in hot water until needed.

5. Place jar on dry folded towel and carefully ladle your chili into the jar, leaving one inch head space.

6. Wipe jar rim with damp, clean cloth. Place hot lid on and screw down ring firmly tight. Use no force.

7. Place jars on rack in pressure canner, containing two inches of hot water. (Or the amount recommended by manufacturer.)

8. Fasten pressure canner lid firmly with steam valves open. Turn on heat.

9. Exhaust steam forcefully for 10 minutes.

10. Close petcock or vent, allowing pressure to build.

11. Hold at correct pressure (10 pounds for altitudes below 1,000 feet) for an hour and fifteen minutes (pints), or an hour and a half (quarts). Adjust heat as needed.

12. When time is up, turn off heat. When gauge returns to zero, carefully release any remaining steam and remove lid, taking care to avoid any steam in canner.

13. Lift out jars carefully with jar lifter and place on a dry, folded towel, away from drafts, to cool. Do not tighten any loose bands.

14. When cool, check for seal. Sealed jars dent inward and do not give under the pressure of a finger in the center.

15. Remove rings and wash jars. Store in a dark, cool, dry place.

I told you it was easy.

When opening the jar, again check the seal, then open it and inspect and sniff the product. If any of these raises questions of quality, throw it out where animals and children can not get hold of it. To be safe, always bring low-acid foods to boiling temperature for 15 minutes before eating.

Now, using your home food processing skills, you can effectively and cheaply stock up enough food to last your family through any hard time. Be sure to store goodies, such as fruits, favorite canned recipes, jams, pickles, etc. When one is having worries, nothing helps like a little treat.

Here are some samples of home canned foods you can store and use:

Apples, applesauce, apricots, baby foods, asparagus, barbecue sauces, beans of all types, beef roasts, stew meat, beets, blackberries, cabbage, corn, carrots, celery, cherries, cheese, chicken, chili, clam chowder, clams, conserves, corned beef, crab apple jelly & pickles, cranberry sauce, elderberry jelly, elk, fish, grapefruit, grapes, grape jelly, greens, jams, ground beef, jellies, juices, lamb, maple syrup, mixed vegetables, mincemeat, moose, mushrooms, okra, parsnips, peaches, pears, peppers, pickles, pie fillings, plums, plum jelly and conserve, poke, pork, potatoes, poultry, preserves, pumpkin, rabbit, raspberries, rhubarb, salsa, sauerkraut, sausage, seafoods, soups, taco meat, taco sauce, tomatoes, tomato catsup, tomato sauce, turkey, turnips, venison, watermelon pickles, wild game, fowl, and much more.

Remember though, there are 52 weeks in a year, so if times get tough you will need more food than you first think. There may be no fast food, only homecooked meals. Calculate carefully and err on the bountiful side, rather than have your family go hungry. And can a wide variety. No family likes to eat beans every meal.

Pet foods

Perhaps the easiest foods to store for your dogs and cats are dry foods. Under decent storage conditions, a good quality dog or cat food will remain fresh for at least a year. Store a high quality dry food, not the "cheaper" brands. As with most everything, you get what you pay for. Add up what your pets eat in a week, a month, then multiply it by 12. Store in rodent-proof containers.

It's also a good idea to include a few cans of quality dog and cat food for a treat now and then. I knew a lady who survived the depression with her dear fox terrier. The woman was very poor and could not afford any dog food, whatsoever. And, of course, there were very few table scraps. So to feed her beloved pet, she trapped woodchucks and muskrats, which she skinned for a few dollars and canned the boned meat for her dog. Coupled with a few meager table scraps, her fox terrier came through the hard times fat and sassy.

You and your family can come through hard times in triumph, not merely "survive" them. All it takes is a bit of planning, a lot of hard work, and some ingenuity. Δ

Chapter 8
Seven mistakes of food storage

By Vicki Tate

If you are going to store food, make sure that the food you store is adequate for the need you and your family anticipate. This may not be as easy to achieve as many people think, because the facts are that most people make serious errors when storing food—errors that will come back to haunt them when the food they've stored is the only thing that stands between them and their empty, dissatisfied, bellies.

There are seven common mistakes people make when storing food.

1. Variety

Most people don't have enough variety in their storage. 95% of the people I've worked with have only stored four basic items: wheat, milk, honey, and salt. Statistics show most of us won't survive on such a diet for several reasons. a) Many people are allergic to wheat and may not be aware of it until they are eating it meal after meal. b) Wheat is too harsh for young children. They can tolerate it in small amounts but not as their main staple. c) We get tired of eating the same foods over and over and many times prefer to not eat, then to sample that particular food again. This is called appetite fatigue. Young children and older people are particularly susceptible to it. Store less wheat than is generally suggested and put the difference into a variety of other grains, particularly ones your family likes to eat. Also store a variety of beans, as this will add color, texture, and flavor. Variety is the key to a successful storage program. It is essential that you store flavorings such as tomato, bouillon, cheese, and onion.

Also, include a good supply of the spices you like to cook with. These flavorings and spices allow you to do many creative things with your grains and beans. Without them you are severely limited. One of the best suggestions I can give you is buy a good food storage cookbook, go through it, and see what your family would really eat. Notice the ingredients as you do it. This will help you more than anything else to know what items to store.

2. Extended staples

Never put all your eggs in one basket. Store dehydrated and/or freeze dried foods as well as home canned and "store bought" canned goods. Make sure you add cooking oil, shortening, baking powder, soda, yeast, and powdered eggs. You can't cook even the most basic recipes without these items.

3. Vitamins

Vitamins are important, especially if you have children, since children do not store body reserves of nutrients as adults do. A good quality multi-vitamin and vitamin C are the most vital. Others might be added as your budget permits.

4. Quick and easy and "psychological foods"

Quick and easy foods help you through times when you are psychologically or physically unable to prepare your basic storage items. "No cook" foods such as freeze-dried are wonderful since they require little preparation, MREs (Meals Ready to Eat), such as many preparedness outlets carry, canned goods, etc. are also very good. "Psychological foods" are the goodies—Jello, pudding, candy, etc.—you should add to your storage. These may sound frivolous, but through the years I've talked with many people who have lived entirely on their storage for extended periods of time. Nearly all of them say these were the most helpful items in their storage to "normalize" their situations and make it more bearable. These are especially important if you have children.

5. Balance

Time and time again I've seen families buy all of their wheat, then buy all of another item and so on. Don't do that. It's important to keep well-balanced as you build your storage. Buy several items, rather than a large quantity of one item. If something happens and you have to live on your present storage, you'll fare much better having a one month supply of a variety of items than a year's supply of two or three items.

6. Containers

Always store your bulk foods in food storage containers. I have seen literally tons and tons of food thrown away because they were left in sacks, where they became highly susceptible to moisture, insects, and rodents. If you are using plastic buckets make sure they are lined with a food grade plastic liner available from companies that carry packaging supplies. Never use trash can liners as these are treated with pesticides. Don't stack them too high. In an earthquake they may topple, the lids pop open, or they may crack. A better container is the #10 tin can which most preparedness companies use when they package their foods.

7. Use your storage

In all the years I've worked with preparedness one of the biggest problems I've seen is people storing food and not knowing what to do with it. It's vital that you and your family become familiar with the things you are storing. You need to know how to prepare these foods. This is not something you want to have to learn under stress. Your family needs to be used to eating these foods. A stressful period is not a good time to totally change your diet. Get a good food storage cookbook and learn to use these foods! It's better to find out the mistakes you'll make now while there's still time to make corrections.

It's easy to take basic food storage and add the essentials that make it tasty, and it needs to be done. As I did the research for my cookbook, *Cooking with Home Storage*, I wanted to include recipes that gave help to families no matter what they had stored. As I put the material together it was fascinating to discover what the pioneers ate compared to the types of things we store. If you have stored only the basics, there's very little you can do with it. By adding even just a few things, it greatly increases your options, and the prospect of your family surviving on it. As I studied how the pioneers lived and ate, my whole feeling for food storage changed. I realized our storage is what most of the world has always lived on. If it's put together the right way we are returning to good basic food with a few goodies thrown in. Δ

Chapter 9
Start your food storage on $10 a week

By Alan T. Hagan

If Old Mother Hubbard had had a food storage program before she went to her cupboard her poor dog would have gotten his bone. Given the fact that her cupboard was bare it was probably because she didn't have the wherewithal to fill it. Finding the resources to put food by against troubled times is a common problem, but it is solvable, even for those of us on tight budgets. In fact, over the long term, the food storage program you start now will save you money. It is like starting a savings account. You earn interest through greater savings in your grocery budget.

Despite what many believe, you don't have to spend large amounts of money on specially packaged foods to put away a sizable food store. You certainly can do this if you like, but what you're doing is trading money (and a good deal of it) to save effort and time. Turn that equation around and you can save a lot of money if you're willing to spend a bit more time and effort to get what you want.

Depending on what you decide is important to you, everything you will need for a complete food storage program can be had from your local grocer and, perhaps, some other local businesses.

Preparing for what?

Before buying anything you should sit down at the kitchen table with paper and pencil because you have some decision making to do. Ideally, everyone who'll be depending on the food storage should be at the table as well, but the person who will be responsible for the program can do it alone, if necessary.

Your first decision to make is "what are you storing food for?" What situations and circumstances do you think might occur which would cause you to need your food stores and prevent you from easily being able to get more? Make a list of everything that occurs to you which you think has some significant probability of happening. Just jot them all down as they come to you and then on another sheet reorder them according to how likely you think they are to occur. While you are doing this, make a note beside each one of whether or not you will have some means of cooking or preparing food should it come about. You'd really hate to have stored away hundreds of pounds of food only to find yourself with no way to make it into a meal. This process is called "scenario planning."

Once you have your list, write next to each scenario the length of time you feel it might last. Chances are, the situations that will concern you most are weather related and some of the more common man-made disasters, but may also cover long term unemployment, Y2K (the millennium computer bug), severe economic depression, war or civil insurrection, or threats even more exotic (cometary impacts, anyone?).

Now that you have a list of probable scenarios and the length of time you think each may last, you are ready to plot the course of your program. Plan your food purchases to meet the needs of the shortest duration scenarios on your list first. As you accomplish each goal set your sights on the next longest and work towards covering that one. In this way you are steadily preparing for one scenario after another while making progress towards your ultimate goal of meeting the needs of your longest lasting concerns.

How do I pay for it?

Right off the bat, I want to say where you should not get the money to pay for your food storage and that is by running up debt. This means that you should not put your food purchases on credit cards. The money lost to credit card interest rates is self-defeating in the long run and will just get you further into a problem rather than getting you out of it. If you are the type who can and does pay off their credit card purchases every month when the bill comes due, then using one might be a real convenience; otherwise it's a temptation to be avoided.

Fortunately, the financial outlay need not be so great that you must spend your children's college fund or sacrifice your retirement account. With a little forethought and research it might be so little as to represent the family foregoing one restaurant meal a month or renting a video to watch at home rather than paying full admission to see a first run film at the theater.

As a matter of fact, unless you are compelled by special circumstances to do otherwise, you are better off to not spend a lot of money at first. Like many other long term projects, there is a learning curve involved with building a good food storage program. Your initial purchases will most likely be small while you're learning more about what you need to do. In this way you are less likely to make expensive mistakes that will have to be corrected later.

If you can afford to spare as little as ten dollars a week then you can make a solid beginning in putting food by against time of need. Just today I made a trip to one of my larger local supermarkets, Albertson's, and wrote down a few prices. (See table.)

Rice, flour, beans, milk, sugar, shortening, Tang, canned greens, carrots, pumpkin, and tuna will make for a pretty bland diet, but for only $40 and a month's time it will give you a solid start on a good program. In the second month you can begin to expand the variety of foods in your program.

The specific types and amounts of food I've listed are not meant as rigid rules, but as illustrations of what can be done. Your personal tastes and the circumstances of the scenarios you'll be planning for are what should determine your specific purchases. It is important to only purchase those foods you are presently already eating or are willing to learn to eat starting as soon as you purchase it. Otherwise, there will be the temptation to leave it in its container and not use it. This is bad planning because it leads to failure to rotate the foods out in a timely fashion as they age or lose nutritional content and palatability. By not using the foods in your storage program you also do not get the experience of how to make them into tasty, attractive meals your family will want to eat. This will leave you at a severe disadvantage when the crunch comes and what's in your larder is all you're going to get.

As I cover each purchase I'll give some considerations you should think about such as: If you don't foresee having a way to bake bread, then buying a lot of flour might not make much sense, but you might make flat breads instead or learn to do your baking in a Dutch oven. If some of your short term plans call for removing to another location on short notice, then the food for that part of your planning needs to be of a type that can be eaten with little preparation or cooking being required. If safe water will be in short supply, then foods that require a lot of it to prepare them might not be a good idea.

The foods that I have chosen all have excellent storage characteristics for the short to medium term, up to about two years. Detailed information and instructions on storing foods may be found in my *Prudent Food Storage FAQ.* If you have Internet access you may download a copy free from the Providence Cooperative web site at http://www.providenceco-op.com or from one of the host sites that also carry it. Many of them may be found by searching on the term "prudent food storage" using most any search engine.

The first week

Your first $10 storage food purchase buys 10 pounds of rice, 2 pounds of beans, a jar of Tang, and 5 pounds of vegetable shortening. The 17 cents change is carried over into the next week.

This amount of rice and beans gives a ratio of 5:1, a perfectly acceptable essential amino acid balance (commonly called "making a complete protein") for most healthy adults. An extra $3.45 expenditure will double the amount of rice and another $3.49 will buy five times the amount of beans. Purchasing the rice and beans first means you have food that can be made edible with no other foods having to be added to them and needing no preparation other than boiling. If cooking fuel is short, split peas, lentils, and black eyed peas cook quickly. Pre-soaking and/or pressure cooking is even more economical.

The Tang orange drink provides 100% of the US RDA vitamin C requirement in every 8 oz. glass (6 qts. = 24 8-ounce glasses), lesser amounts of other important nutrients such as vitamin A as well as some sweet taste since we have not yet bought anything else with sugar in it. Vitamins A, C, and D are the major nutrients typically lacking in most storage foods. Don't assume that any drink mix or canned juice has vitamin C in it. Read the nutritional facts label on the side closely to see what the manufacturer claims it contains. An appalling number of juice products, even some canned citrus juices, claim no vitamin C content at all.

The last purchase is the can of vegetable shortening. Fat is actually a necessary nutritional component even if we do tend to eat too much of it in the present day U.S. The shortening allows you to make foods such as biscuits, fry breads, refried beans, pancakes, fried rice and pan breads, and contributes flavor. In a survival diet, fat is an important source of vital calories. This is an important consideration for small children, pregnant women, the elderly, and the ill who might otherwise have trouble eating enough bulky beans, rice, etc., to gain sufficient calories to stave off weight loss and possible malnutrition.

The second week

Your second $10 nets you 20 pounds of all purpose white flour, 5 pounds of granulated white sugar, 3 cans of carrots, and 3 cans of spinach. The 24 cents left over is carried over into the next week.

You now can make bread to give some variety to your rice and bean diet. If you don't have any store-bought yeast to raise your bread, you can do what your pioneer forebearers did and learn to make "sourdoughs" to leaven it. If you have a grain mill or can acquire one then you may be able to find a local source of whole grains at a reasonable price to supplement or replace the white flour. The sugar allows you to make sweet breads, puddings from the flour or rice, adds calories, and greatly contributes to taste.

Of all the canned vegetables to be had from the grocer the dark green and the orange vegetables give the most nutritional value for the money. Canned greens such as turnip, mustard, collards, spinach, and kale range in value from 50-110% of the RDA of the important nutrient vitamin A (in the form of carotene) per half-cup serving. Many of them also include a fair amount

FOODSTUFF	QUANTITY/PRICE	FOODSTUFF	QUANTITY/PRICE
white rice	5 lbs./$1.79 10 lbs./$3.45 20 lbs./$6.90	pinto beans	2 lbs./$1.00 10 lbs./$4.49
Tang (makes six quarts)	21 oz./$2.99	all purpose flour	10 lbs./$2.10 5 lbs./$1.19
white sugar	5 lbs./$1.99	vegetable shortening	5 lbs./$2.39
powdered milk	25.6 ozs./$4.39 (8qts@3.2oz./qt.) 64 ozs./$9.99 (20qts@3.2 oz./qt.)	canned tuna	6 oz. can/50¢
canned carrots	14.5 oz. can/50¢	canned spinach	13.5 oz can/69¢
canned pumpkin	15 oz. can/$1.09	canned turnip, kale, mustard or collard greens	14 oz. can/50¢

of calcium and vitamin C as well. The carrots have 100% RDA of Vitamin A per half-cup.

The third week

The third ten spot buys you the 64 oz. box of dry milk. The slim remaining penny is carried over into the next week.

Sixty-four ounces of non-fat dry milk will make 20 quarts of skim milk to provide essential amino acids, necessary calcium, along with vitamin D (30% of the RDA of calcium and 25% of vitamin D per 8 oz. glass of reconstituted milk). Unlike fresh liquid milk, the dry powder is shelf stable and can be stored for long periods of time. It may be drunk as straight milk or used to enhance dishes made from the ingredients purchased in the other weeks. Dry milk can also be used to make excellent yogurt and even non-fat cheese.

The fourth week

Your last purchase of the first month's cycle brings in 10 cans of tuna, 2 cans of pumpkin, and 5 cans of turnip, mustard, kale or collard greens. The remaining 32 cents is added to the surplus from the prior weeks, now totaling 74 cents.

Although the grain, beans, and milk provide all necessary amino acids, most of us will rebel at a purely vegetarian diet, so at least a little meat three or four days out of a week can go a long way towards making matters tolerable. Other canned meats can be substituted, but as a general rule tuna is leanest and cheapest per ounce. Beware of paying canned meat prices for fillers like pasta, rice, or potatoes. They can be added much more cheaply after the fact rather than buying them already in the can with the meat.

The pumpkin (plain solid pack, not pie filling) can be used like any winter squash, carrots, or sweet potatoes and carries a tremendous amount of vitamin A in the form of carotene (300% of the RDA per half-cup). A friend of mine has developed a pumpkin biscuit that I've grown quite fond of. It makes a good baked dish and is very versatile in casseroles, soufflés, puddings, and as either a sweet or savory vegetable. There's more to pumpkin than pies.

The 74 cents left over seems trivial but it will buy 2 1-pound cartons of iodized table salt, or yeast to make bread with, or baking soda for leavening and other uses, or a small can of pepper to season food. You can also hold it over to combine into the next month's surplus.

The purchasing cycle could be repeated month to month until you reach the amounts you desire, or varied to broaden the selection in your cupboard.

If you can afford to use the economies of scale that making larger bulk purchases gives you, then the price per pound of the foods you buy will drop considerably. By taking advantage of sales, bulk food outlets, warehouse groceries such as Sam's Club and Costco, local restaurant and institutional food suppliers, or ethnic grocers (Asian, Hispanic, etc.) you will do considerably better than what I've outlined above.

If you have the time and resources available to you, much of the fruit and vegetable portion of your storage program can be economically acquired by growing it yourself. Not only do you get wholesome food, but by putting it up yourself you get exactly what you want in the way that you want it. If being frugal is of paramount importance though, growing your own will need some careful analysis to be certain you're not spending more in time, labor, and equipment than the value of the food will make up for. This is especially true when it comes to food preservation, but you can at least partially offset this by choosing appropriate preservation methods. Pressure canning requires quite a bit of expensive startup equipment (canner, jars, lids, rings, etc.) which may make the operation uneconomical. However, if you dry the food instead you can often do this at a much lower cost.

One area of home preservation that generally will be worthwhile to do yourself is canned meats. Beef, pork, and chicken often go on sale and can be had for quite reasonable prices, so even with the price of the jars and equipment necessary to process it, home canned meat will usually be cheaper per pound than any commercially canned meat of equivalent quality.

There are two cardinal rules of successful food storage: The first is store what you eat and eat what you store. The second is to rotate, Rotate, ROTATE! Follow them always, keep a watchful eye on your local grocer's offerings, and be willing to make a moderate investment of time and effort. Do this and you'll have a successful food storage program that your family will look forward to eating in good times or bad without sacrificing your financial well being to get it. Δ

Chapter 10
Cooking from long-term food storage

By Jackie Clay

Y ou should have at least a year's worth of food and essential supplies stored up in a large pantry. Unfortunately, actually eating from long-term food storage conjures up images of consuming endless tedious, tasteless meals of boiled rice and beans. You know—"survival" food.

But this is not how my household works. If I were to serve such meals, there would be total rebellion. After all, we've had at least two years' food stored for 20 years, and we eat daily from this food. We are not martyrs, and we do not eat tasteless food in order to be "healthy." Instead, we eat three meals a day from good tasting, comforting, healthy food, much of it home-raised, home-grown or harvested from the wild.

With a little practice and imagination, any family can quickly learn to produce meals, drawn from your food storage, that draw rave reviews from family members. And you do not need to spend hours in food preparation time either.

Buying for long-term food storage

A lot of problems arise when a family purchases foods they are not used to eating, and are not especially fond of in the first place. During hard times, or in an emergency, are definitely *not* times to begin eating such "survival" food. When you're stressed out, worried, and depressed, you need a lift, not countless meals of boring, tasteless food.

Take stock of the foods your family really likes. Then build your storage pantry on these preferences. Just about anything you regularly eat can be included. One notable exception is hamburgers and cheeseburgers. You can home-can hamburgers, by lightly frying tiny patties, then stacking them into wide mouth jars. I do a few, just for novelty, layered with finely chopped onion. When ready to use, refry them, adding cheese if desired. They're good, but aren't the same as the regular hamburgers the family is used to. And there isn't an alternative to home canned hamburger available for purchase.

Have your family go through the supermarket with you and take notes as to what interests them, even if you have not cooked it before, or recently. You need variety in your long-term storage foods. Meals are like buildings. They need foundation blocks like potatoes, rice or beans, but also windows and doorways like fruits, meats, vegetables, and spices.

Choose the foods carefully, taking into consideration those you use daily or would use, if you had the time....and had no alternatives. Two frequently overlooked items are shortening/margarine and eggs. And make sure there are plenty of opportunities for "goodies," such as cookies, pies, puddings, Jello, etc.

Introducing the family to seldom-used staples

Old-fashioned baked beans

2 cups dry navy beans
¼ cup ham or bacon flavored TVPs or canned ham
½ cup dehydrated chopped onions
8 Tbsp. molasses
4 Tbsp. honey
1 Tbsp. dry mustard
3 Tbsp. vinegar
½ cup tomato sauce
¼ cup catsup

Sort beans, soak overnight in water enough to cover. In the morning, drain beans, discarding water. Place beans in 6-quart or larger heavy pot with 12 cups water and simmer, covered for just long enough to get beans tender (older beans require longer cooking). Drain and discard water. In a 3-quart or larger casserole, mix beans with other ingredients and bake at 350 degrees for 1½ to 2 hours, adding water if necessary to keep beans from drying out. Serve hot with fresh whole wheat bread for a comforting, hearty meal.

There's a definite place in a long-term storage pantry for such staples as dried beans and rice, but instead of buying all navy beans and white rice, consider that there are over a dozen varieties of beans and perhaps six varieties of rice available, each with its own unique taste, texture, appearance, and uses. In our pantry, I have many kinds of beans which we use: navy, red kidney, pinto, Anasazzi, black, and several varieties of Native American beans that we grow at home. You might include a couple of limas (which our family just does not like), cowpeas, Great Northerns, or others.

Then try a few really good recipes and gently ask all family members to try just one small serving with a meal they love.

Work your way into beans. Don't just cook up a huge pot and insist everyone eat them for a meal. You can "sneak" beans into meals by mashing cooked pintos in with taco filling, putting a few mashed beans in a layer of casserole, or into a hearty vegetable stew or soup.

Old-fashioned baked beans, complete with ham or bacon chunks, molasses and catsup will usually do the trick on a cold winter's day.

The same with rice. Few people like a big plate full of steamed white rice. "I don't like rice!" is the usual comment. My answer is get to know rice and all its uses.

Perhaps the easiest way to interest a family member in rice is to serve Oriental fried rice, complete with little chunks of chicken or pork. Spanish rice is another interesting way of introducing rice into a meal. The point is to introduce staples gently into meals, *before* called on to use them every day.

The use of ethnic meals is a great way to introduce a family to basics, as most less-wealthy nations have fabulous recipes, using cheaper staples as the base for meals. You can learn to do wonders with corn flour and corn meal, beans and chiles, rice, vegeta-

Oriental chicken fried rice

2 cups cooked white rice, cooled
½ cup finely diced onions (you may substitute rehydrated dry)
¼ cup rehydrated freeze dried or air dried green peas
1 cup rehydrated shredded carrots (or fresh)
¼ cup oil or shortening
1 Tbsp. peanut butter
½ cup chopped cooked chicken
2 Tbsp. soy sauce
2 eggs, equivalent in dehydrated egg powder
Spices to taste, including garlic, turmeric, hot pepper

In a large, heavy frying pan, heat oil. Add rice, onions, chicken, and carrots. Stir frequently with spatula until rice begins to lightly brown. Add peanut butter (no, it doesn't taste "weird"), soy sauce, peas, and spices. Continue stirring while flavors mix. As rice mixture appears to be done, quickly add beaten egg mixture and continue stirring with spatula until egg is cooked. Serve at once with soy sauce, sweet and sour sauce, or hot mustard sauce.

bles, sauces, and bits of meat, potatoes, and vegetables. I quickly learned that America is one of the few nations in the world where meat is used as the foundation of a meal. (We had adopted two older children from India and three from Korea, as well as sponsoring a family of nine from Vietnam.)

When cooking from a long-term storage pantry, learn to buy or home-can meat in smaller cans and jars. This allows one to use the meat as flavoring and texture to a meal, making a little go a long way, and not give the impression of "making do" or "surviving."

A couple of examples that we regularly use are Oriental Chicken Fried Rice and Tamale Pie. I *never* have leftovers.

Homemade pizza

Crust:
2 cups flour
½ tsp. seasoning salt
¼ cup olive oil
2 tsp. dry yeast
1 cup (plus) warm water

¼ cup chopped olives
¼ cup sausage TVPs
1 tsp. oregano
¼ tsp. garlic powder
½ tsp. basil
1 cup mozzarella or
½ cup dried grated
   parmesan cheese

Mix dry yeast and one cup warm water. While softening, mix other ingredients in medium bowl. Add softened yeast and enough warm water to make a soft, but not tacky, ball of dough. Work dough with hands, greased with a small bit of olive oil until elastic, then set aside in bowl, covered, for half an hour to rise. Oil baking pan with liberal olive oil, press out dough with hands. Prick dough with fork every few inches to avoid bubbles. Bake at 350 degrees until just barely done. It will not be browned but will lift easily from pan when picked up with a fork at corner.

Topping:
1 cup thick tomato sauce
1 tsp. brown sugar
1 Tbsp. rehydrated green
   peppers
1 Tbsp. dry onion

Spread tomato sauce evenly on baked crust and sprinkle brown sugar, green peppers, olives, and spices on top. Top with cheese. Bake until cheese is barely golden brown and bubbly. This is yummy, and it is much in demand at our house. As a bonus, there are many variations including making a double batch of crust, using the second dough to be formed as bread sticks, which can be brushed with tomato sauce, herbs, and sprinkled with cheese and baked at the same time as the pizza. The bread sticks, dipped in a warm herbed tomato sauce, make a great addition to the steaming pizza.

Such goodies as homemade pizza are always hits at home, especially in an emergency or hard-times situation. Key ingredients, such as pepperoni and mozzarella cheese, are in few long-term storage pantries. When one has their own dairy animal, the cheese is a snap, and dry-cured pepperoni lasts for months without refrigeration under cool, dry conditions. I also have canned chunks of pepperoni and am going to try mozzarella cheese too. But without these options, pizza is still a definite "go". Check out recipe above.

But we'll miss fried foods!

I think one of the things a family misses most, living totally from a long-term storage pantry, is simple fried foods. Now this can have an up side, as well as a down. The fewer the fried foods consumed, the better health we enjoy. But, honestly speaking, some fried foods do a lot to boost our morale during rough times.

Now, of course, if a family has their own garden, which a self-reliant family should have anyway, they will have abundant potatoes, fresh or in the cellar. If not, you can fry up a batch of canned potatoes, from time to time, or make potato patties out of leftover mashed potatoes (adding two beaten eggs to hold them together). There are also dehydrated and freeze-dried hashbrowns that are quite good.

One satisfying, simple recipe we enjoy from our pantry is fried tuna patties. This provides meat, as well as satisfying an occasional craving for "fried food."

Roast beef hash is another "alternative" fried food. Unless fresh meat, either home grown or wild, is available, there will be little fried meat available.

One of the home storage pantry's best capabilities is providing quick, nutritious soups and stews at quick notice. These include those using pasta and noodles, as well as the more traditional. One of our favorites is homemade noodles, cooked with chicken broth. You can use store-bought noodles, but there is absolutely no comparison in taste or texture. And noodles are very easy to make, only taking a few minutes once you get the hang of it. Even "mistakes" are very edible.

Fried tuna patties

2 cans light tuna, drained
1 cup crushed dried bread crumbs
¼ cup dehydrated onion flakes
3 eggs, rehydrated equivalent
½ tsp. lemon pepper
flour to coat patties
oil to fry

Mix drained tuna, bread crumbs, egg, onion flakes, and lemon pepper. Divide into golf ball-sized portions, pat into patties, dip both sides in flour. Heat oil to medium heat and gently place patties into frying pan. After one side is done, turn and finish cooking. This is a quick and easy alternative to "fish sticks."

Tamale pie

½ cup cornmeal
½ cup white flour or freshly ground whole wheat flour
¼ cup honey or white sugar
¼ cup shortening
1 egg (equivalent in dry egg powder, rehydrated)
1 cup rehydrated dry milk (+or -)
2 tsp. baking powder
1 tsp. salt
½ cup cooked hamburger (I use home canned) or beef TVP
2 cups tomato sauce
½ cup dry chopped onions
¼ cup dry chopped green peppers or chile peppers
2 tsp. mild chile powder
¼ cup dry sweet corn or ½ cup canned corn

Mix first eight ingredients well, making a medium batter (not runny or not stiff). Then in medium sized cast iron frying pan or 8 x 8 cake pan, mix the last six ingredients well, then top with cornmeal batter. Bake at 350 degrees until top turns golden brown. Serve hot with cold salsa.

Breads

Don't forget the staff of life. Breads provide an endless base to home meals, unlike their tasteless plastic wrapped cousins from the store. On one camping trip, we made an entire meal out of a crispy, fragrant loaf of French bread, without a dab of butter.

Breads can be made of varying flours for entirely different tastes, textures, and appearances. Aside from the "normal" white flour from the store, one can, and should, grind their own grains, producing a wide, wonderful, array of fresh flours. This produces a wholesome taste that most folks have never even dreamed of.

As all grains store much longer as whole grains, it is wise to stock up on these grains and grind the flours as you need them. Some suggestions are red and golden hard wheat for bread, soft wheat for pastries, flour corn for cornmeal, hominy corn for corn flour, buckwheat for pancake flour, rye for rye and pumpernickel bread, and rice for Asian cooking.

You will find that when you are cooking solely from the long-term storage pantry under times of duress, just the milling of the flour and baking of bread will bring peace and contentment to the whole family.

While "plain" bread will probably be most often used, stretch your creativity by expanding to more "exotic" breads such as pitas, tortillas, and sweet rolls, both for taste and variety. Most use about the same simple ingredients, and with just a little variation you can create a whole spectrum of tastes and possibilities.

One of our favorite breads is a versatile quick roll recipe. This recipe makes soft, tender dinner rolls, but also free-form breads, hamburger buns, sweet rolls, and coffee cake with little change.

Tips for cooking from home storage

Cooking from a long-term storage pantry is easy, basic, and very fulfilling. But it is not something one learns to do overnight. It's sort of like gardening. The time to learn to garden is *not* when the trucks stop hauling food to supermarkets and there are acute food shortages. It takes time to get into the rhythm of gardening, learning what works, what does not, and how to do the most work with the least effort.

When a person plunges into cooking solely from home storage, they are quite often frustrated by "all the hard work," the poor results from their cooking, and the lack of enthusiasm from family members. Sort of like when a new young bride begins cooking for her husband for the first time. The results are often ho-hum.

Roast beef hash

1 pint (16 oz) canned roast beef (or wild meat)
½ cup rehydrated onion flakes
1 quart (32 oz) canned potatoes, drained well
oil to fry

Grind meat, potatoes and onion together with hand meat grinder. Heat oil to medium heat in large frying pan. Slide hash into pan, being careful not to spatter. Arrange the hash in a shallow layer, covering the bottom of the frying pan. Allow to cook, turning and stirring with spatula. Add seasonings, finish frying to preference, and serve. Popular condiments include salsa and catsup. Hash makes a satisfying one-dish meal. Leftovers are great for breakfast with scrambled eggs.

Try taking one day a week, at first, to practice cooking out of your storage pantry. Ease into it with a few of these recipes; they are easy and basic. Then expand to others, found in some of the books listed below. Mennonite, Amish, Mormon, and Seventh Day Adventist cookbooks usually provide a good start for comforting, tasty meals with basics, as these religions stress commonsense preparedness and good family eating from basic, healthy ingredients.

It's well to mention at this time that it makes good sense to develop a small garden, at least, and learn to forage for wild foods (which are great tasting, by the way), while learning to cook meals from the food you have stored. Fresh foods are a very welcome change to dehydrated and canned, and they not only taste great, but provide extra nutrition, which could conceivably be lacking in a few long-term storage foods.

Likewise, if it is at all possible, develop your own source of fresh milk, eggs, and meat. Grandmas all over the world raised a small flock of chickens, even in town. It's funny that the U.S. is one of the few countries where this is not common today. Remember that variety is truly the spice of life; cultivate all the variety you can in your family's diet.

Halftime spoon rolls

Dissolve 2 tsp. dry yeast in ½ cup warm water, and set aside. Combine 1/3 cup shortening, ¼ cup of sugar or honey, 1 tsp. salt with ¾ cup hot milk (reconstituted dry or fresh). Cool to lukewarm by adding ½ cup cold water. Add 1 egg (or equivalent reconstituted dry) and softened yeast. Mix in 3½ cups sifted flour. Cover in same bowl, letting rise in a warm place till doubled. Stir dough with greased spoon. With an ice cream scoop (works easiest) dip sticky batter into greased muffin tins, filling half full. Let rise and bake at 375 degrees until golden brown. Remove from oven and brush margarine on top to soften nicely. I promise raves from this one. And you can modify it easily. With the addition of just a little more flour (about ½ cup), the dough will be firm enough to handle lightly, which makes forming hamburger buns on a greased cookie sheet easy, or forming into caramel rolls, cinnamon rolls, or coffee cake.

Basic whole wheat bread

Heat 4 cups milk (rehydrated dry or fresh). Soften 4 Tbsp. dry yeast in ¾ cup warm water. Add ¼ c. honey to warm milk, along with 1/3 cup oil or melted shortening, 2 tsp. salt, and 2 eggs.

Beat well, then as milk cools to luke warm, gently add yeast. Add about 14 c. fresh whole wheat flour, one cup at a time, mixing after each. When nearly stiff, mix with hands, incorporating just enough flour to make an elastic, workable ball of dough. Don't stop if it's sticky, and don't get it too stiff. Knead on a floured board for 10 minutes. Grease a large mixing bowl, place ball into bowl, and grease top. Pull ball out and put back in, greased top up. Cover with a warm, damp kitchen towel and let rise in warm place until about double. Knock down and let rise again. Divide into two or three loaves and place into greased bread pans. Preheat oven to 350 degrees. When loaves are nearly doubled in size, place in oven and bake for about 35 minutes until tops are golden brown. Grease tops with margarine to soften. Enjoy the best bread you've ever tasted.

Homemade noodles in chicken broth

1½ cup flour (either freshly ground whole wheat or white
¼ tsp. salt
2 eggs, reconstituted or fresh

Place flour in mound on board, making a nest or well in the center of the mound. Pour eggs into nest. Beat the eggs with a fork, gradually bringing the flour into the mix. Work the dough into a ball with your hands, picking up only as much flour as it takes to make a stiff, but workable ball. Knead the dough for about five minutes. It should not stick to the board. If it seems too moist, add a little more flour; if too dry, dampen your hands and knead longer.

Divide the ball into quarters. Cover three and reserve one to work with immediately. Lightly sprinkle board with flour and roll out dough, pulling it into a uniform thickness oval. Make it as thin as workable and let rest in a warm, dry place. Repeat with other three quarters.

When all dough is dry, but not stiff and brittle, roll like a jelly roll, cutting into desired thickness with a sharp knife. You can then either fluff out to separate and then carefully hang to dry or lay it flat to air dry for an hour.

Pour a quart of chicken broth (or use dry chicken granules to make a broth) into a large pot. Add diced, canned, or freeze dried chicken meat, if desired, as well as onion, carrots, and spices as wanted. Bring to a medium boil, then carefully add noodles, simmering just long enough to make them tender. The flour on the noodles provides natural thickening. You'll get raves for this simple, yet satisfying meal.

You'll find you get into the rhythm of this type of cooking easily. And you'll quickly develop time-saving ways of doing things. For instance, it didn't take me long to decide that if I ground a week's worth of grains I truly saved time, and cleaning of the grain mill, and I always had the grain I needed on hand conveniently.

I can honestly say that it takes only minutes longer per meal to prepare a great dining experience from my pantry than it does to rip and pry plastic wrap from something that appears to be food. And it makes the whole family feel great. We believe in *living*, not just surviving! Δ

Chapter 11
Storing water for an emergency

By Vicki Tate

Any of us who've thought much about emergency preparedness realize that one of the most critical items to store is water. Without sufficient water to see you through an emergency that lasts more than a few days, you and your family are at great risk. You simply can't live without water.

Fourteen gallons of water per person is the suggested amount to store for a two-week emergency situation. This amount is enough for subsistence purposes only: two quarts for drinking and two quarts for cleaning and bathing purposes a day. When you consider that a person normally uses in excess of 140 gallons of water per day for drinking, bathing, laundry, dishes, watering lawns, etc., this isn't a lot of water. If you have the room to store more you will want to do so.

The easiest way to store the bulk of your water is in 55-gallon polyethylene (plastic) water drums. These can be obtained from most food storage companies or from local container companies found in the yellow pages. It is important that you use only *food grade*, good quality containers. Many times you can get food grade containers from companies that distribute beverages or syrups. If you clean them well, they can provide a good container that costs considerably less.

One word of caution: often the taste or odor of the previous contents has leached into the plastic and over time may be reintroduced to your water. If you plan to use previously used containers, make sure that what it had in it before is something you wouldn't mind tasting or smelling in your water.

Most water containers come in 5-gallon, 15-gallon, or 55-gallon sizes. I always suggest that a family stores between two and six of these smaller containers, along with their 55-gallon drums. This is a prudent suggestion in situations where you might need to transport water in the normal course of events or in a situation where your normal water source might be disrupted, such as after an earthquake, hurricane, etc., and you might have to go to a secondary water source such as a water truck, stream, etc. to refill.

Water weighs approximately 8 pounds per gallon, so 55-gallon drums are much too heavy to handle (440 pounds), plus they are awkward. Smaller containers don't hold enough water and would require too many trips, especially if you have to go to a source on foot. Five to fifteen-gallon containers are more practical and can easily be put into a wheelbarrow or child's wagon and wheeled to and from an area.

Two-liter pop bottles make a good container for additional water storage and cost nothing if you save them and fill them with water as you empty them. To economize many people are tempted to use empty milk jugs, but don't plan to store water in these for more than three to four months. They are biodegradable and will break down within six months. Not only may you lose your water, but if they are stored near food or other items they may damage them. Heavy containers should always be stored close to ground level and secured to prevent breakage or possible injury in the event of earthquake, etc. Be sure to store your water away from any harmful chemicals or objectionable-smelling products.

Culinary water (tap water) is what is usually stored for long term storage. If you have a clean, opaque container where the light cannot get through and your water is bacteria-free when you store it you probably don't need to treat it further. Under these conditions the water actually gets more pure as it is stored. However, for most of us there is no guarantee that our culinary water is bacteria-free, so most of us prefer to treat our water in some way as a precaution as we store it. Several methods have traditionally been used to purify water for long term water storage.

2% Tincture of iodine—To use this add 12 drops per gallon of water. Note: pregnant or nursing women or people with thyroid problems should not drink water with iodine.

Chlorine bleach—Household bleach can also be used. This should contain a 5.25% solution of sodium hypochlorite without soap additives or phosphates. Use 1/8 teaspoon (about 5-8 drops) per gallon of water.

Most of us have used one of these methods to treat our water over the years. Both are inexpensive and are effective methods of killing bacteria. I have always preferred the iodine method myself. The one drawback, however, is that both may have negative health effects if used for long periods of time.

I was introduced to a product a couple of years ago that I now prefer to use instead because it is an excellent water purifier, but it also has many medicinal properties. It is a stabilized oxygen called Ion that is effective in killing all harmful bacteria without any of the harmful health effects associated with chlorine or iodine. For long term storage add 20 drops of Ion per gallon of water. One bottle will purify two 55-gallon drums. It is also excellent for your emergency packs (72-hour kits). It is small and light weight (2.33 oz.) but extremely effective.

Studies show that if water is bacteria-free and is stored in clean containers it will stay safe for several years. It is a good idea, however, to periodically check your water for purity and taste. And every few years it's a good idea to change it. One of the things that affects the taste of water is it "going flat." This occurs because of the oxidation that takes place as it sits. You can improve the taste by pouring the water back and forth between containers to aerate it or by beating it with a hand egg beater. You also may want to store some flavorings such as fruit drink powders, kool-aid, etc. to add to your water if you find the taste objectionable. One of the other benefits of Ion is the oxygen remains suspended, maintaining its good taste for much longer periods of time.

Remember also that you have several sources of water already in your home that can be tapped in an emergency, such as your hot water heater, toilet tanks (don't use water from a tank that contains colored disinfectant, as it is poisonous), water pipes, ice in the freezer, etc.

Water is relatively inexpensive to store and certainly not difficult to do, but certainly the time to store it is now. We take water for granted when things are normal, but in an emergency it becomes absolutely critical. This is an item you can't afford to overlook in your preparedness preparations. Δ

Chapter 12
Stay warm in emergencies, at home, outdoors, & in your car

By Don Fallick

D isruptions in services during a disaster can be deadly to those who are not prepared for them. If the disaster occurs in winter, staying warm is likely the most urgent non-medical problem we may face.

Ten years ago, I watched a winter storm dump two feet of snow on Seattle, a city which almost never gets snow. Tens of thousands filled the city shelters. Their all-electric homes had frozen when the power lines went down. Even those with gas furnaces were without heat. Their thermostats quit, or their pilot lights turned themselves off when the furnace fans failed. Virtually the only people left at home were those with fireplaces or woodstoves.

With a little preparation and knowledge of cold weather survival techniques, they could have stayed home in safety, if not in comfort.

General principles

Stay dry and out of the wind. Water and moving air are the two fastest ways to carry heat energy away from the body. In a winter disaster, nothing is as important as getting into good shelter and staying there as much as possible. You can survive for a month without food, for a week without water, but even hours without shelter can kill in severe cold. It's often safer to stay in an unheated house than to go looking for better shelter.

Insulate the smallest volume unit. If you have only a small heat source, close your house down to one room, and insulate that room tightly. The absolute smallest unit of volume is your body and your body is an excellent heat source. Capture as much of its output as you can by staying under wraps. Two or more people together can create a lot of heat.

Conserve energy. You don't know how long the emergency will last. Don't heat the house one degree warmer than necessary. Reduce trips outside to a minimum. Every time you open the door, you throw away several hundred BTUs.

If your toilet is not working, keep a "honey bucket" with a tight fitting lid inside the house. Line your "honey bucket" with strong plastic bags. Tie off full ones and stack them outdoors to freeze. You can dispose of them later, when services resume, or bury them when the ground thaws. Conserve your own energy, too. Plan for a minimum work schedule. You will tire quickly; fighting off the cold takes energy.

House heating

Do not depend on any central heater or furnace that uses power company electricity. Power is the first utility to go in any disaster, natural or man-made. All furnaces and most gas or propane heaters depend on electric fans or thermostats. But even if you make your own electricity, disruption of services may affect your ability to provide heat. Will you be able to refill your propane tank or buy generator fuel?

Plan ahead to keep your house livable in a cold weather disaster. Pick a room to heat. If you have a functioning heater, fireplace, or woodstove, that is the room where your entire family will live throughout the emergency. If you have a portable heat source, weigh the following factors: the ideal room is protected from wind and air leaks, well-insulated, low-ceilinged, small in area, on the top floor beneath an insulated ceiling, and it has good natural light.

You will never find this ideal room. In fact, some of these factors are mutually exclusive. Make the best compromise you can, then plan to make up for deficiencies. If the living room has a woodstove, but there's a bad air leak under the door and lots of windows, you can make a fabric "door snake" and improvise storm windows.

For the door snake, cut a piece of sturdy fabric four inches wide and two or three inches longer than the door's width. Sew it lengthwise into a tube, sew one end closed, and turn it right side out. Fill the snake with dry sand and sew the other end closed by hand. Place it against the door to stop drafts. You'll have to replace it every time someone opens the door, but it will save an amazing amount of heat.

For the improvised storm windows, cut plastic sheeting three or four inches bigger than you need, roll the edges, and staple to the wall with a staple gun. Stretch the plastic tight, leaving a 3/8-inch gap between the glass and the plastic. A larger gap will allow air to circulate between them, transferring heat out of the house by convection.

Woodstove. Lay in a supply of good, dry oak, maple, ash, or other hard wood for emergencies, plus some lighter woods for kindling. Be sure to have an extra axe handle in case yours breaks. With a good woodstove and plenty of wood, you'll have no warmth problems for your home.

Fireplaces are notoriously inefficient as room heaters. Most of their heat goes up the chimney, carrying warm house air with it. The rising air draws in cold air from outside the house. It may be warm right in front of the fire, but the total amount of heat in the house is reduced. There's a fairly simple fix for this: install an air pipe from the outdoors, directly under the fire. Cold air is then drawn from the outdoors directly into the fireplace, where the fire heats it. Some heated air goes up the chimney, and some goes into the room, for a net gain in heat. It works pretty well, but it has to be done before the cold weather disaster strikes.

Kerosene space heaters work much better than fireplaces. They are cheap, portable, fuel efficient, and easy to store. Discount stores sell them for less than $150. Even a small one will heat a 16 by 20 foot room for a gallon a day or less. Kerosene will keep for years if you just add an algae inhibitor, and it is not explosive. Good quality kerosene costs three to five dollars a gallon or more, so it is a bit pricey for the long haul.

If you don't have a woodstove or fireplace in a downstairs room, your best bet to stay warm may be an upstairs bedroom. Upstairs rooms are much better insulated than ground floor rooms. Heat rises, so the most important side of any room to insulate is the ceiling. Nobody insulates between the floors, but upstairs rooms usually have lots of insulation in the ceiling or attic. When the disaster strikes, it wouldn't hurt to move extra insulation from above other parts of the house to the area directly above your chosen room.

Bedrooms rarely have more window area than is absolutely necessary, seldom have leaky exterior doors, and are usually carpeted—another source of insulation from the cold air below. If your house is already pretty tight, and you have another source of light, you may be able to make an upstairs bedroom really cozy by insulating over the windows. An inch or two of foam insulation, cut to fit the inside of each window opening, can work wonders. Use duct tape to seal any cracks. Even ordinary, fiberglass batting will help a great deal. You can remove some of the insulation during the day for light.

Don't run any space heater with open flames in a tightly insulated room without adequate ventilation. At night, you can button up tight with the heater off. Just snuggle up with another warm body under blankets, or climb into a good sleeping bag such as an old Army down-filled bag. In the day time, people going in and out of the room provide adequate ventilation. If it starts to feel stuffy, pull the door snake away from the door, or even briefly open it a crack. Moderate, controlled ventilation causes much less heat loss than a small, uncontrolled leak that continues around the clock.

You will feel much more comfortable if you can eat at least one hot meal per day, or at least drink a hot drink in the morning. Contrary to manufacturers' instructions, you can safely use a propane camp stove or barbeque indoors. Millions of homes already have natural gas stoves and ovens that run on the same principle as propane campstoves and barbeque grills. The actual danger is that propane is heavier than air, so it can collect in basements, where furnace or water heater pilot lights can ignite it. If you have a propane leak, you will smell it. If you suspect one, brush a solution of one part water to one part detergent on all connections and joints. Even tiny leaks will blow lots of bubbles. A small amount of propane will dissipate harmlessly in the air. The real danger is from a leaking tank that does not shut off completely. Store your propane tank out of doors when not in use to avoid these problems.

You and your family are not the only things in your houses that need to keep warm. Pipes will freeze and burst unless you leave the water running. Moving water resists freezing at temperatures as low as 20 degrees Fahrenheit. Adjust every faucet to provide a constant, steady drip. Set "one control" faucets to provide a mix of hot and cold water to prevent the hot water pipes from freezing too. Adjust toilet float valves so the water level is above the top of the overflow tube. Disconnect washing machine hoses at the machine end, and let them drip directly into the drain. Do the same thing with the refrigerator ice maker or any other machine directly connected to water pipes.

Check faucets a couple of times a day to make sure they are still dripping. If they are not, or if temperatures are in the low twenties, you may want to turn off the water service to your house and drain all the water lines. Fill the biggest containers you've got with drinking water first.

Drain pipes can freeze too. This can be a worse problem than frozen water pipes, as they are often embedded in concrete and very hard to replace. Pour automotive antifreeze into floor drains, toilets, and sink or tub traps. Pour in enough pure antifreeze to completely fill the trap. The dripping faucets will dilute it. Use the recommended dilution chart on the antifreeze container for any drains that will not be used. Any drain that is being used regularly, such as a toilet, will need to be topped off with antifreeze after each use. Where water is dripping into drains, refill with antifreeze daily.

WARNING: do not use antifreeze where there is *any* possibility that someone may drink the water, even years later. For example, do not add antifreeze to a water heater tank. Even if you drain it later and wash it out, it can still contain enough residual poison to kill someone. Depending on your plumbing system, it may be possible to shut off the water heater, then drain it. Use a hose to run the water into a floor drain or outside. Leave the drain at the bottom of the water heater open, with the hose attached, then open the supply valve just enough to drip water into the heater tank.

Roughing it

Excessive snow loads can collapse a roof, though most winter storms are not likely to destroy houses. But other disasters can still occur in winter, including fires, floods, earthquakes, toxic spills, and acts of war or terrorism. It's been 20 years since I did damage assessments for American Red Cross

Disaster Services, but some things don't change. If your house is in danger of collapse, has already been destroyed or rendered uninhabitable, or if you are caught in transit, you will need to seek other shelter quickly.

Permanent buildings usually offer better shelter from the elements than tents, and are safer to heat, but can be very hard to insulate. Consider erecting a tent inside a garage or shed. Seal overhead doors with duct tape, and improvise insulation from loose hay or straw, crumpled up newspapers or rags, etc.

Baled hay or straw is good for building a quick, temporary shelter, but has a lower R-value than loose hay. A hay bale igloo can keep you plenty warm. Build up the floor of the igloo with bales, covered with a tarp, blanket, sheets of plywood or drywall, etc. Leave a crawl hole in the floor for the entrance. Cold air sinks, so you can keep your entrance open for light and ventilation, if it's lower than the floor. Stuff loose hay between bales, and cover the igloo with plastic tarps, to keep out wind and water. Then bury the whole thing in snow. Snow makes a very good insulator. If you've got enough bales, make double walls and dump loose hay between them.

Don't bother providing for fires or heaters. Your own body heat will keep you warm, and you don't want to build a fire in the center of a tinder-box. For light, improvise a lamp from a car taillight bulb, some wire, and an automotive battery. You can use electricians' tape, or even duct tape, to connect the wires to the bulb and the battery terminals, but hose clamps work better. Such an improvised lamp with a fully-charged battery should be good for a hundred hours of illumination or more. Stretch your time by using flashlights briefly at night, with the "main" light off. Keep the battery inside the igloo with you. Just like you, batteries lose energy when they get cold.

Cars

What if a disaster or emergency renders the whole area uninhabitable, or you get stuck in a blizzard? Your car can provide temporary shelter. It's best not to run the engine for heat at all, if you have warm clothes and blankets in the car and there's any chance you could have knocked part of the exhaust system loose. Running the engine could fill the car with deadly carbon monoxide. You'd never even know it.

If there is more than one person in the car, huddle together for warmth. One "space blanket" can keep two people warm enough to survive this way. If you absolutely must run the engine for heat, run it just long enough to warm up the car, then shut it off. There won't be enough gas to run it all night anyway. You might as well conserve gas and minimize the carbon monoxide danger, too. Don't play the radio more than a few minutes when the engine is not running. You want to be able to start the motor after the blizzard quits.

Melt snow to drink by putting it in a cup or other container inside the car. Eating snow will make you lose precious body heat. You'll do much better if you have some hard candy or other source of energy on hand. Beef jerky is not good for winter survival. It makes you thirsty. Even if you have plenty of water handy, you will have to pee a lot, losing body heat in the process. If you don't have food, plan to sleep a lot. Eskimos have a saying, "Sleep is food." The more you sleep, the less food you'll need.

The worst danger in winter survival camping is not snow, but wind. Snow is actually a pretty good insulator. Stay inside the car and out of the wind as much as possible. Nevertheless, you do not want to get buried. Preserve air circulation by checking every two or three hours, to make sure you are not completely covered, and can get the door open. Let someone know where you are. If you have a cell phone, call 911. If you do get buried, at least they will know where to look.

You may have to abandon your car. Some friends of mine were stationed in the Philippines when Mt. Pinatubo erupted. They had less than an hour to evacuate, but they were prepared. The trunk of their car was stuffed with sleeping bags, a tent, a camp stove, and clothes, and each family member had a backpack with food for three days. Those backpacks served them well. The road was blocked by debris, so they had to abandon everything they couldn't carry, and walk to the sea. Rescue ships were held up for a week by a hurricane, and for another week, crossing the Pacific. The tent, hot food, and hot drinks helped them survive for two weeks. Do not depend on your car for shelter. Be sure any tents, sleeping bags, and other emergency equipment in your car are easily portable.

Improvised shelter

If you are caught in the open in cold weather with no "real" shelter available, you have a true emergency. Two cardinal rules apply: stay dry and out of the wind. Use any available shelter from the wind—rocks, trees, etc. Cut or break branches from brush and trees to make an emergency "wikiup," or rude shelter. Pile up brush to create a sleeping platform or mattress, to keep you off the cold ground. Insulate a wikiup with leaves, snow, clay, or dirt— the thicker the better. Keep door openings small and low.

Sleeping in unsupported snow caves is dangerous. If the snow collapses, you could be buried alive. It's better to build an igloo. My Eskimo friend Nanook taught me how. Eskimos recognize seventeen different kinds of snow; only one is considered right for igloos. It's the hard, stiff kind that doesn't compress easily. If the snow is not hard enough to walk on without snow shoes, it's not the right kind. Dig a five foot diameter pit in the snow, down to within two feet of the ground. Carve out blocks of snow with your shovel, and stack them in a circle on the edge of the pit. Lay each course of blocks in a slightly smaller circle than the last, and tipping each course further inward. The last block, or "keystone", must be slightly tapered, and cut to fit exactly. Dig the entrance tunnel under the wall. Excavate the floor, inside the entrance, so it's possible to crawl in and out. Fill cracks and smooth the igloo, inside and out, with hand-packed snow. A candle or small lamp will be adequate for light, and its heat will help pack and smooth the inside walls and ceiling.

If you are not an experienced snow-builder, or the temperature is not cold enough to prevent melting, it's best to avoid igloos altogether. Instead, build walls of hard-packed snow, with brush or wood "rafters" to support a packed-snow roof. Not as elegant as a real igloo, but a whole lot safer than a badly built igloo.

Personal warmth

For most of us who live in cold weather climates, keeping warm in good shelter, without a functioning furnace, may simply mean dressing indoors the way we would normally dress outdoors. Because there is no wind indoors, it may even be simpler. A couple of sweaters can keep you quite warm, out of the wind and wet. I had a neighbor in eastern Washington State, where the winters are quite cold, who never heated his house at all. He had no pipes to freeze, so he and his family just wore lots of sweaters.

The basic principles of dressing for cold weather are dressing in layers, keeping out wind and water, and fitness for intended use. Wear thermal underwear indoors and out. When doing the laundry is difficult or impossible, wear regular underwear beneath the long johns to keep them clean longer.

Keep the layers loose. Still air is the best insulator. Thermals covered by pajamas and/or sweats make a comfortable indoor combination. Wool or flannel shirts, plus sweaters and sweat shirts, will keep you toasty warm in all but the most bitter weather. Layering also provides different levels of insulation for different activities. If you frequently change from sedentary to active roles, dress for the most active, and cover up with a robe or blanket when inactive.

Exercise can certainly keep you warm, but don't work up a sweat. Sweating is supposed to cool the body, and it works all too well in cold weather. Exercise also uses up energy, which must be replaced with food. The best foods for cold weather are hot and high in fats and sugars.

American Red Cross Disaster Services recommends hot coffee (not decaf) brewed strong, with plenty of sugar and cream. Caffeine helps the body release stored energy, while sugar and cream are good energy sources themselves. Unfortunately, most strong coffee contains acid. This stimulates increased urination, causing loss of water and body heat. Low acid coffee is best, if you can find some that is not also low in caffeine. Do not use alcoholic beverages in cold weather. They may make you feel warmer, but at the expense of diminished circulation in the extremities, where you need it the most.

Retire early. There's not much to do after dark in the cold, so you might as well be sleeping. Bedtime can be the best time of the day, with story-telling by Mom and Dad. Children should never sleep alone in cold emergencies. Another warm body can make a bed really comfy. If you have a stove or fireplace, heat bricks up just before bedtime, wrap them in a towel to prevent burns, and place in the foot of the bed, to keep little feet warm. It works for big feet, too. Many a cold, winter night, my whole family has piled in together, with seven people (and half a dozen hot bricks) in one big bed. I won't say it's comfortable, but it is warm.

Don't put on too many clothes in bed. Loose, cotton pajamas or night gowns are about perfect. Many campers have learned that it's warmer to sleep nearly naked than with lots of layers of clothing, if you have plenty of warm bedding. I've never heard a satisfactory explanation for this, but have verified it many times.

Frostbite & hypothermia

Frostbite is not usually life-threatening. It is caused by the freezing of skin and muscle cells, usually in extremities, nose, and ears. Frostbitten skin is grayish-white and has no feeling in it. Never pour hot water on a frostbite or rub it with snow. Because of the lack of sensation, you can tear or scald skin without the victim even knowing it.

Body heat is best. Place hands over frostbitten nose or ears. Place frostbitten hands or feet in underarms or between legs. If all else fails, briefly immerse the frozen part in lukewarm water. It hurts like fire as the feeling returns. Have the victim exercise frostbitten fingers and toes to increase circulation, and drink hot water or coffee. If feeling does not return, the body part is frozen. Seek qualified medical help immediately to prevent gangrene.

Hypothermia occurs when the core body temperature begins to drop. If someone is turning blue, or their teeth are chattering, they are in the initial stages of hypothermia. Get them warm right away. Get them out of cold clothes and under covers. If you can sandwich them between a couple of warm bodies, so much the better. Skin to skin contact helps. Give hot, sweet coffee or soup to drink.

In the final stages of hypothermia, people stop shivering, and become physically and mentally sluggish as body systems shut down. They may lose consciousness or stop breathing. Do not give up hope. Hypothermia victims, especially children, have been revived after hours without an apparent pulse or breath.

Nevertheless, get the victim warmed up as fast as possible. A warm bath (not hot) is the best way to do this, if you can arrange it under the circumstances. Do not leave him alone in the tub. He may lose consciousness again and drown. Give him hot but not scalding liquids when he begins to notice his surroundings. When he's able to get out of the tub, pat his skin dry with the softest towel available. Rubbing may tear the skin if it has been frozen. Get him into a warm bed and keep him there until medical help arrives.

Resources

First Aid, American Red Cross—the classic first aid manual. Covers just about everything. Be sure to get the most current edition. Every home needs one.

What's That Noise?! by Don Fallick, Holiday House Publishing, PO Box 27153, Salt Lake City, UT 84127. Comfort and advice for the first-time car owner.

Wood Heat by John Vivian, Rodale Press. Everything you ever wanted to know about the subject. Out of print.

Disaster Services Training Manuals, American Red Cross. Take the course. You have to volunteer for Red Cross Disaster Services, which is also not a bad idea. Δ

Chapter 13
The return of home emergency shelters takes on a dual-purpose approach

By Jeffrey R. Yago, P. E., CEM

After September 11, 2001, all of us became much more concerned with protecting our families from biological, nuclear, and terrorist attacks. However, if you followed up by trying to learn more about civil defense in the United States you soon found out the dirty little secret—there isn't a national civil defense program in the United States today.

After our National Civil Defense Program died a quiet death in the 1970s, the Federal Emergency Management Agency (FEMA) took its place, but with an entirely different set of goals. FEMA is not in the business of promoting self-preservation or shelter construction. Our government has taken the position that it would be impossible to construct enough government-funded shelters to protect all United States citizens, and even if it did there is the belief that most of these shelters could not provide enough protection and would not be properly maintained.

It is the public's attitude that survival preparation is somehow a waste of time because life would not be worth living after a nuclear attack. This is not only untrue, but borders on a premeditated form of national suicide. This is not the attitude of most other governments. Their view is that with minimum civil defense training and some basic advance preparation, most people can survive almost any calamity, including a nuclear attack, and go on to rebuild a new life.

A fatalistic federal response

FEMA views its role as a facilitator of emergency response *after* a natural catastrophe has happened. Many feel there is nothing that can be done to protect our large population in advance of an unknown threat, so better to organize for handling mass casualties and mass evacuation after it happens. Although our government does not currently promote any form of self-protection for its citizens, it does provide well-supplied underground shelters for "critical" Federal government employees and elected officials. As of this writing, there is no Federal agency providing shelter designs that have been tested and approved. Most of the shelter designs available are reprints from

testing that was done as part of
atomic bomb testing during the early
1950s, and they do not reflect the
more advanced construction materials and survival equipment available
today.

To fill this lack of up-to-date information at the Federal level, the
Internet has become the primary
source of design and product information related to emergency shelter
construction. But how is the average
homeowner going to know what
designs work best and what should

*Family size underground
survival shelter (Courtesy
of Utah Shelter Systems)*

be done since there isn't a "government seal of approval" technical review or
standardized rating system?

Also now missing, but originally included in the Federal civil defense program, is civilian training. Just what would you do if you actually heard an
emergency warning? Should you go to the lowest point, highest point, jump
in the car and evacuate, lay down in a ditch, put on a gas mask, get under a
doorway, or stay where you are? Each of these answers could be right or
wrong depending on the threat, but without any training or guidance most
citizens will just follow the herd—even if it's over the cliff.

The starting point for taking control of your own protection starts with
identifying what are the most likely threats you face, and what type of shelter
will offer the best protection from these threats.

Types of shelters

There are many potential life threatening events facing a typical family
today. Depending on where you live, some threats are more likely than others, but in almost all cases there is an emergency shelter design that can
reduce your risks and lesson your discomfort. Before going into more specific details on shelter designs, let us first review the many uses for a shelter
and the different types of shelters that can be built.

An underground storm-type shelter could protect your family from weather related threats including tornadoes and hurricanes. A well-stocked basement with emergency lighting and heat could provide comfort during an
extended power outage or snowstorm. A fireproof type shelter could provide
life saving protection for family members in the event of a fast moving forest
fire or home fire. A bulletproof type shelter hidden in a bedroom closet can
save the lives of family members during break-ins by lawless vandals.

Prefabricated safe room
(Courtesy F-5 Storm Shelters)

Many homeowners are now installing bulletproof safe rooms inside existing homes. These shelters are usually prefabricated metal enclosures with heavy metal doors, and they are designed to fit inside a bedroom closet or add-on room. These shelters are primarily for temporary personal protection from intruders or vandals, and are not intended to provide protection from radiation or biological type threats.

If you live near a nuclear power plant or military target, a fallout type shelter could improve your chance of surviving a biological or nuclear attack or accident. Most people today believe it is not possible or desirable to survive a nuclear explosion. However, unless you are located near the point of the actual impact, it is fairly easy to survive the blast by knowing what to do and seeking the safety of a properly designed fallout shelter. The greatest danger from a nuclear explosion comes in the form of radioactive vaporized dirt that is sucked up into the sky and soon starts to fall back to earth and cover the ground like a deep snow. Most of this material will loose most of its life threatening radioactivity in as little as two weeks. It is not unrealistic for a family to live comfortably inside a properly furnished shelter for this brief period until the exterior radiation levels reach safe limits.

Dual use shelter

Many people consider installing an emergency shelter a waste of space and money, especially if it is never used, but what if it has another function? What if your emergency shelter is also that big food pantry you always wanted, or a cool wine cellar, or a hobby room? In other words, the shelter function is in the design, but this will not necessarily interfere with the everyday use for this room or space. The following shelter selection guidelines will provide a good place to start.

Basic shelter guidelines

If you have viewed pictures of the flat concrete slabs remaining after a tornado or hurricane with the rest of the house missing, you will see why a storm shelter will probably need to be underground to provide suitable protection from high winds. If located within a house, the shelter should be constructed of strong nonflammable building materials like steel reinforced block and concrete. Since flooding can accompany many

6'x6'x10' steel tornado shelter
prior to backfill
(Courtesy of F-5 Storm Shelter)

storms, the danger of high water needs to be considered when designing a below grade storm shelter. Basements can be used for some types of shelters, but they should not rely on the wood floor above for a secure roof. A basement shelter should have its own concrete roof just below the wood framing above.

If you want protection from radiation, you will need at least 12 inches of concrete to provide even a basic level of radiation shielding. If this is not practical for your basement, a 24 to 36-inch layer of sandbags will provide a suitable substitute, and be much cheaper to build. Any shelter should provide a minimum of 20 square feet of floor area per occupant. Most underground radiation shelters have at least three feet of earth cover, and use an entry having one or more 90-degree turns to block radiation which travels in a straight line.

Many do-it-yourself type underground shelters can be made from large diameter galvanized corrugated steel culverts or concrete storm pipe, or fabricated rectangular steel tubes in 10 to 40-foot lengths. Some people are even burying metal containerized cargo trailers to make their own low cost shelters. Although these have very strong corners to allow stacking several high, their thin metal sides and roofs are weak and require extensive reinforcement to prevent buckling when backfilled. Several manufacturers now offer fully assembled steel and fiberglass underground shelters that can be shipped by trailer to the site and buried, leaving only an access door and vent pipe exposed above ground.

Site-built underground shelters usually follow the same construction techniques used to build home basements, but roof span widths should be minimized due to the extremely heavy column loading for an earth covered concrete roof deck. The potential for moisture condensation on cool interior shelter walls and ceilings, and a higher potential for water leaks must be

Corrugated steel pipe shelter ready to bury. Note substantial waterproofing. (Courtesy of Utah Shelter Systems)

addressed in any underground structure. Many shelters will use the same type of exterior wall waterproofing and interior wall damp-proofing as used to protect basements in areas having a high water table.

A shelter should have a fire resistant and gasketed hatch or door. Although a custom-made door and door frame fabricated from heavy-gauge steel is usually required to resist high-pressure shock waves from a nuclear blast, a more practical solution for non-nuclear shelters may be a commercial metal fire rated exterior door sold by building supply outlets. Be sure to include a good fireproof gasket seal around the sides, top, and bottom of any exterior hatch or door, and locate all doors to minimize the potential for egress blockage. Mounting a door that swings out increases the perimeter frame resistance to high pressures, but also increases the risk of being blocked in by wind-blown refuse. Multiple dead bolt locks should be added since a residential style lock will not hold. One of the biggest problems with the underground tornado shelters common across many western states is insect infestation. Without good door seals and insert screening on all vents, you may find that your shelter is already occupied when you really need it.

If your shelter is intended to provide survival protection for weeks, not hours, you will need to think about interior ventilation, emergency lighting, sanitation needs, and basic food, medical, and water supplies. Since any event serious enough to require the use of a shelter will almost always include the loss of utilities, you should have several low energy battery powered lights and a battery powered exhaust fan. The January/February issue of this magazine (Issue No. 73) included an article describing how to make a solar powered lighting system that will easily meet all shelter lighting needs.

Shelter ventilation

Outside air ventilation is a very critical requirement for all shelters. Any extended use of a sealed shelter will require constant air changes. There have been numerous medical problems related to fallout shelters that were traced to stale air, not radiation poisoning. Older Department of Defense shelter design guidelines recommended 4 cubic feet per minute (CFM) of outside air ventilation per shelter occupant, but most shelter designers today feel this is the threshold for carbon dioxide sickness and much higher ventilation rates are needed. Since outside ventilation air is also necessary to reduce high humidity levels and overheating in any confined area, a more realistic value of 10 CFM per person in colder climates and 30 to 40 CFM per person in hotter climates is more realistic.

Several manufacturers offer a rotary hand operated blower designed to ventilate underground shelters continuously, but these can be ineffective in larger shelters due to their low flow rates and the need for manual cranking 24 hours per day. There are several homemade manual ventilator designs similar to the old blacksmith forge bellows available on the Internet.

All shelter air intakes, exhaust vents, and piping should include a manual internal shut-off valve or gate. You should also understand that a typical tornado or hurricane can tear off or bend over all pipes and vents sticking up out of the ground or through a concrete floor slab. Locate all vents to minimize the potential for wind damage and provide good structural support. Wind speeds and air pressures related to a nuclear explosion can be multiple times higher than the most severe hurricane. A turned-down steel pipe intake vent will minimize the risk of vandalism or rainwater flooding a below grade shelter. In general, a properly designed air intake will keep air velocities low to avoid pulling in any falling radioactive dust particles. Air intakes should be turned-down steel pipes located high enough above any radioactive dust that has settled out and covered the ground.

A combination HEPA filter and an activated charcoal filter are needed to make ventilation air totally safe from biological and radioactive contaminates. All outside air intake and exhaust vents should be manually closed off during the initial threat of any attack, then reopened when the threat is reduced. Many of the automatic spring loaded blast valves manufactured to protect the external openings of military shelters will no longer operate when required after providing a home for birds, rodents, and insects for years.

Shelter sanitation

A conventional commode may not have a domestic water supply for flushing after a major catastrophe or may be located below the existing sewer line, but there are two types of low cost sanitation systems that will

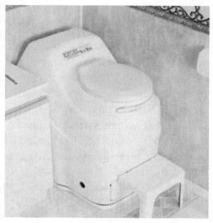

Composting toilet (Courtesy of Sun-Mar Corporation)

work with most underground shelters. The commode seat and disposable bag system sold for camping trips can meet short-term sanitation needs for one or two shelter occupants. For longer shelter stays, several manufacturers offer a self-contained water-less composting toilet. Using a manually rotated drum containing a biodegradable material, all wastes are converted to safe composting material, and any remaining liquids are converted to drainable non-potable water. Due to a higher risk of illness during longer shelter stays, you should also have several sizes of plastic trash bags for other biological and medical waste storage.

After major floods, hurricanes, and tornadoes there is always a major fly infestation due to thousands of animal carcasses that may remain out in the open for weeks. Since using insect sprays in a confined air space can be a ventilation air problem, quality insect screening on all openings is critical.

Shelter food and water needs

There are many books available that describe emergency food and water supplies. This magazine's big anthologies are filled with such information. All shelters should include at least a basic quantity of food, medications, and drinking water for all occupants for up to two weeks. FEMA recommends a minimum of one-gallon of water per person per day. Keep in mind that all emergency food and water supplies have a limited shelf life and should be rotated every six months. Pre-packaged dehydrated survival foods are available that require minimum storage space and have a shelf life of several years. If your dual use shelter will be used as a pantry, be sure to also store foods that can be eaten without cooking or further preparation. You will also need disposable eating utensils, paper plates, and garbage bags.

Shelter furnishings

Since your dual-use shelter will be used for its alternate purpose throughout most of its useful life, you will want to minimize the floor space required for "shelter only" items. Although you can sit on the floor for a few hours during a serious storm, you will want a comfortable place to sleep and sit for extended shelter stays. Most camping supply stores offer excellent cots, sleeping bags, camp chairs, and tables that fold up into easy to store bags. A reinforced plywood bed foundation can fold completely up against a wall or be used as a table during the day. You can stack beds up to three high along each wall for higher occupancy needs or use hanging rope hammocks. Do not forget to include books to read, a quality battery powered radio, several flashlights, and extra batteries.

Shelter medical issues

When a shelter is only used to wait out a fast moving storm, there will be little need to store food and medical supplies. However, events that require a shelter stay of several days can increase the risk for medical conditions that most people do not normally deal with. When several people are confined together in a small windowless enclosure that has minimum fresh air, no sunlight, higher than normal temperatures and humidities, little or no bathing or personal hygiene, and a major change in daily diet, there will be a much higher risk for headaches, diarrhea, skin rashes, fungus infections, and insect bites. Fortunately, there is an endless choice of low cost over-the-counter medications to treat each of these problems. Any extended-stay shelter should include these basic medical supplies, along with personal hygiene and eye, ear, tooth and hair care products. A good supply of waterless wipes, skin lotions, toilet tissue, paper towels, Vaseline, no-pest strips, disinfectant, Clorox, bacteriological soap, disposable medical gloves, water purification tablets, canned heat, matches, and several face cloths will also make confined life much easier. Again, this magazine's anthologies have articles addressing emergency medical kits.

Shelters can be above ground, below ground, or installed in existing basements or closets. Shelters can be homemade or purchased premanufactured. A single shelter can be large enough to protect an entire retirement community or just a single person safe room. All shelters can serve multiple purposes to make them more cost effective and to provide extra space during non-emergencies. It is hoped this introduction will allow you an opportunity to review your own shelter needs. For more detailed shelter design and construction information, please refer to the following texts and web sites.

Resources

Shelter design and survival books:

Principles of Protection—U. S. Handbook of Shelter Engineering Design Standards—5th Edition, by Walton McCarthy

Making the Best of the Basics by James Stevens

No Such Thing as Doomsday by Philip Hoog

How to Implement a High Security Shelter in the Home by Joel Skovsen

Nuclear War Survival Skills by Cresson Kearny

Fallout Shelter Design Collection (Second Edition) by FEMA

Emergency Preparedness and Survival Guide by Backwoods Home Magazine (See ad on page 19.)

All of the *Backwoods Home Magazine* anthologies (See ad on page 91.)

Nongovernment civil defense groups:

Survival Ring Newsletter by Richard Fleetwood, www.survivalring.org

The American Civil Defense Association (TACDA), www.tacda.org
*Dominion Group Survival Preparedness,*www.cpn.freeyel-low.com

Shelter-related websites:

Underground shelter resources and survival database, www.earthmountain.com

Solar and battery powered lighting systems for shelters, www.dunimis.com

How to build a bomb shelter, www.plansfordummies.com

Permanent family size fallout shelters, www.oism.org/nwss

Shelter composting toilets, www.sun-mar.com

Pre-built shelter manufacturers:

Fiberglass underground radiation shelters, Radius Defense and Engineering, Inc., 603-942-5040, www.undergroundshelters.com

Underground storm shelters, Blue Sky Contracting,
www.groundsafe.com

Underground corrugated pipe shelters, Utah Shelter Systems, 435-657-2641, www.disastershelters.net

Underground and above ground fabricated steel shelters, F-5 Storm Shelters, 318-248-2994, www.f-5stormshelters.com Δ

Chapter 14
Storing LP gas, gasoline, diesel, and kerosene

By Emory Warner

Home storage of fuel is a good idea, but it must be done properly. Your car, truck, tractor, and standby generator require fuel. So do your propane refrigerator and kerosene lanterns. Here are appropriate methods of storage for LP gas, gasoline, diesel fuel, and kerosene, as well as some tips on safe fuel handling.

Fuel types

LP gas is one of the easiest fuels to store and also one of the most dangerous. It is a highly versatile fuel which can be used to power internal combustion stationary engines, tractors, and other motor vehicles, as well as for cooking and heating. LP has two serious drawbacks: First, it must be stored under pressure to remain a liquid; any leak (which may not be visible) could leak away all of your fuel without your knowledge. Second, LP is only slightly heavier than air, and will disperse at the exact ratio to produce an explosion. It will also "puddle" in low spots, waiting for an ignition source.

Gasoline has the advantage of being a liquid at room temperature. But it is probably the hardest fuel to store for any length of time. It has a high vapor pressure (which means it evaporates quickly) and will go stale in a few weeks if not chemically treated. It does have a fairly high ignition temperature (about 500-800° F) even though it does not need a large volume of heat to ignite. Stored gasoline must be treated with a BHT additive like *Sta-Bil* and protected from moisture if it is to be stored for any length of time.

Large quantities of gasoline make me nervous. I used to live on the water in southern Maryland, and was witness to several boat explosions and fires due to gasoline vapor in the bilges.

Kerosene is one of the easiest fuels to store, and is more versatile than most people think. It does not evaporate as readily as gasoline and will remain stable in storage with no special treatment. Many pre-1950 farm tractor engines were designed to run on kerosene, and diesels will run on kerosene if necessary. Kerosene stoves and refrigerators are also available and would definitely be preferable to LP models from the safety standpoint.

145

*Salvaged 275 gallon horizontal fuel tank with hand fuel pump and filter.
This type of pump is suited for all fuels; current use is for diesel fuel.*

Diesel fuel stores almost as easily as kerosene and is becoming more and more popular among the self sufficient. It is difficult to ignite intentionally and almost impossible to ignite by accident. Two grades are available: #1 diesel which is old-fashioned yellow kerosene, and #2 diesel which is the same thing as #2 home heating oil. (You may see literature to the contrary, but #2 diesel is #2 heating oil. Period.) Diesel fuel presents its own unique storage problems: The first is that it is somewhat hygroscopic; that is, it will absorb moisture from the air. The second and related problem is sludge formation. Sludge is the result of anaerobic bacteria living in the trapped water and eating the sulfur in the fuel. Left untreated, the sludge will grow until it fills the entire tank, ruining the fuel. Stored diesel fuel should be treated with a biocide like methanol or diesel *Sta-Bil* as soon as it is delivered. Unique to #2 is the fact that some paraffin wax is dissolved in the fuel and will settle out at about 20° F, clogging the fuel filter. This "fuel freezing" may be eliminated by adding 10% gasoline or 20% kerosene to the diesel fuel. Commercial diesel fuel supplements are also available to solve the same problem. Diesel should be filtered before use.

Alcohol (ethanol) is not commonly considered a storage fuel, but here is the data on it for those who distill their own. Alcohol is as hygroscopic as it gets, and must be stored in a sealed container to prevent moisture contamination. It is about as volatile as kerosene and presents the unique problem, when ignited, of burning with an almost invisible blue flame. It may be best to store the raw material for stilling the alcohol and producing the fuel as needed, rather than producing a large quantity and storing it.

Whatever fuel you store, it would be a good idea to monitor your fuel usage and plan your storage around a 90-day supply.

Safe fuel handling

Regardless of the fuel in question, all liquid fuels should be handled in the same matter as the most volatile, which is either gasoline or LP gas. Fuel should be stored in an isolated area, downhill and downwind from any other buildings. Fuel vapors are

One type of approved and properly marked portable fuel cans.

heavier than air, and will flow downhill. LP tanks should be left in the open and not enclosed in any way. Liquid fuel tanks can and should be stored in a well-ventilated building or open lean-to to prevent solar heating from evaporating the fuel. If the storage location is permanent, consider using a buried tank. If set below the frost line, temperatures are stable at 55° F or so, which will inhibit evaporation. The tanks will be safe from everything, including stray (or aimed!) gunfire, brushfires, and just about everything else except the EPA. If buried fuel tanks offend your sense of environmental responsibility, then consider an underground vault. This has the added advantage of being able to inspect the tanks from time to time.

Regardless of the tank location, a dry chemical or CO_2 fire extinguisher should be hung on the outside of the building or near the pump. Any electrical fixtures should be "explosion proof" (sealed) and wired in sealed conduit to prevent fuel vapors from coming into contact with electrical sparks. Prohibit smoking or carrying of smoking materials within 50 feet of the fuel pumps. Electrical fuel pumps should have a heat sensitive shutoff to stop the pump in the event of fire. Always shut down the engine of the machine being fueled. Promptly clean up any spills. Last of all, be certain to use only the equipment that is approved for the fuel in question. (Some fuel pumps are approved for diesel only, and are unsafe to use for gasoline.)

Fuel storage methods

Liquid fuels use the same storage systems and will be covered as a group. LP gas is normally stored in pressurized tanks supplied by the LP dealer, and will be only briefly covered.

The most basic fuel storage system is the common portable fuel can. If you are still on the grid and have a job "off the property," then this is a workable

Thirty dollar drum pump mounted on a 55-gallon drum of kerosene. This type of piston pump is not suitable for gasoline.

and economical method of fuel storage. A minimum of three cans will be required: one full at all times, one for use as needed, and one to be refilled at the first opportunity. Rotation of the cans will ensure some amount of reasonably fresh fuel at all times. This storage system has the added advantage of portability in the event that the storage site must be abandoned. Use only approved containers, and use caution not to mix up containers. The standard color code for portable cans is blue for kerosene, red for gasoline, and yellow for diesel fuel. This is not cast in stone. Use whatever color scheme you like, but be consistent with it. Gasoline introduced into a diesel tank will make the diesel engine hard to start when hot. Gasoline in a kerosene heater will explode like a Molotov cocktail. Diesel #2 in a kerosene lamp will smoke and stink and soot up the globe. If you use all three fuels like we do, it seems that you will be filling a fuel can every time that you go out. Delivered fuel is much more convenient, and usually cheaper.

The next storage system is the 55-gallon drum used with a hand pump or horizontally on a rack. This is a highly flexible storage system, as drums may be added as needed to suit individual requirements. Most fuel dealers have a 100-gallon minimum delivery, so at least two drums will be needed. You can even load one drum in your truck, drive to the service station and fill it, then bring it home and pump the fuel into your storage drum. Drums are also portable enough in the event that the storage site must be abandoned. The only disadvantages are the negligible cost of the drums and that the drums will eventually rust and leak. We use drums for our kerosene and gasoline storage. Label each drum clearly if you are storing more than one type of fuel.

If you wish to store large quantities of fuel, then the built-for-the-purpose fuel tank is the system of choice. Tanks are available new in capacities from 100 to 10,000 gallons in above ground and underground types. Most commonly used here in the Northeast is the standard residential 275-gallon fuel tank. These are available new at plumbing and heating suppliers for about $150. Used tanks are usually available free for the hauling, including whatever fuel is in them. As a side note, an individual with a pickup truck and a reciprocating saw could make a fairly decent living removing old fuel tanks

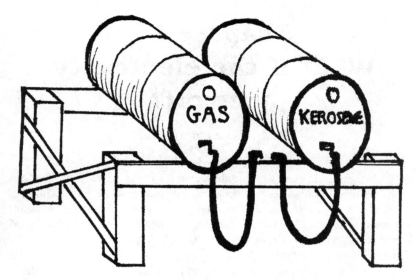

A horizontal drum storage system. Front and rear 2x6s are notched to hold drums and are bolted to 4x4 posts. Braces are 2x4s. This would be nice to have under a lean-to beside the tractor shed.

as homeowners change away from fuel oil to natural gas. This is about the dirtiest work available, and pays about $100 per tank. The removed tanks could be cleaned up, painted, and resold for $50 or more. I have accumulated about five or six tanks in the last few years without really looking for them.

Fuel dispensing is a matter of choice. An elevated tank needs only a valve and filter; gravity will do the rest. We prefer to use hand pumps for our kerosene and diesel tanks. Valves have been known to leak, and vandalism is an unfortunate reality of modern life-especially if the vandal elects to open the valve on a tank of gasoline and follow it up with a lit match. Hand pumps are safer, and they are more easily secured if the tank must be left unattended.

The author's system

My personal fuel storage system is a salvaged 275-gallon fuel tank with a hand pump and filter for our diesel fuel storage. Our principal tractor is diesel powered. We also use it to operate a PTO (power takeoff) generator for standby use. We use two or three 55-gallon drums for kerosene storage, with a lift pump for dispensing. (We rely on kerosene heaters to supplement our woodstove.) But, as I have a job "off the property," and we have two old gasoline engine tractors, as well as a chainsaw, lawnmower, etc., the fuel can system works well for our gasoline supply. This is particularly suitable for us, as I feel uncomfortable about storing large quantities of gasoline. Δ

Chapter 15
What if the electricity goes off?

By Michael Hackleman

T he name changes, the date shifts, but it's the same question: Are you ready? Earthquake, fire, flood, plague, meteor strike, nuclear attack, hurricane, tornado, and terrorist attack—all strike in the moment. Economic collapse, crop failure, famine, and nuclear winter are forces of siege that could last months or years.

From a distance, the first evidence may be a blackout or a news report. The area affected by the disaster will dictate the probability, frequency, and durations of blackouts. If the scope of the disaster is large, other services—water, natural gas, gasoline, fuels, food, and goods—will fail. Following that will be the loss of phones, police, fire, rescue, utility, Red Cross, and government services.

It is said that crisis has two components: danger and opportunity. There is danger in a crisis—catastrophe, collapse, and chaos. There is opportunity in crisis—restoration, renewal, and revival. Preparedness doesn't mean you'll survive, but it won't contribute to your demise.

There are issues that are specific to living in a city or in the country, so I will treat each as distinct scenarios. As you discover issues that approximate ones you may experience, you will likely be drawn to research these topics in more detail.

A blackout is a likely scenario in either a short-term or long-term crisis, so that is a good place to begin.

Blackout ready

The pressing question when a blackout occurs is: When will it end? Virtually anyone can put up with a few hours of interruption. Just break out the candles, don warmer clothes, and read a book or enjoy the company of a friend. The average blackout is a pop quiz. "Are you ready?" it asks. When the blackout continues, with no end in sight, the need for light, heat, water, and food grows.

There are four critical loads in a home affected by a blackout: lighting, heating, refrigeration, and the water system. More specifically:

• **Lighting**. Lighting is essential for overall safety, particularly at night. Fortunately, it need not be electric. Candles, flashlights, and kerosene lanterns are traditional lighting sources for blackouts. Preparation for a blackout requires stockpiling matches, candles, batteries, or fuel for lanterns. Don't forget to put this stuff where you can find it in the dark!

• **Heating**. Central air heating systems, even if they use natural gas or propane, depend on electricity for the blower that will circulate the heated air. During a blackout, this system will not work. Areas with temperate climates allow most users to compensate with warmer clothing and the use of small propane or kerosene heaters. Wood stoves are also a popular alternative to central heating systems.

• **Refrigeration**. A refrigerator will keep things cool for a long time after power is interrupted. From the beginning, minimize the frequency and duration of opening its door to preserve its cool! As the blackout continues, consume the more perishable items first. Even a small stockpile of canned or freeze-dried foods will prove helpful during a blackout. Unless you've arranged for a way to heat and cook food, ensure that your supply is edible "as is," or with simple re-hydrating with water.

• **Water system**. Most community water systems are designed to work for some time following a blackout, powered with huge standby generators. Private water systems built around streams, springs, and wells that use electric pumps will quit working as soon as the electricity goes off. The pressure tank will still deliver some water, so immediately fill handy containers (bottles, buckets, bowls, bathtub, etc.) before this supply is depleted. The standard household water heater is another source of 30-50 gallons of water. How will you handle toilet, shower, and sink during a blackout? Some forethought and planning will help with these processes during an extended blackout.

Other sources of electricity

Utility electricity available at the wall socket in a home or business is rated 120 Volts and 60-cycle AC. There are two ways to supply this same specialized power in a blackout: a standby generator and a battery-powered inverter.

The standby generator:

Where the interruption of utility power even for a few hours is critical—i.e., emergency equipment and services in businesses and hospitals—a standby generator may be used to supply power. A standby generator is an engine combined with a generator. This unit may be started manually or automatically and requires only fuel (gasoline, diesel, or propane) to operate until grid power is restored.

Dual meters are common when renewable energy systems put power back down the utility line.

Homes may also use a standby generator to supply electricity during a blackout. A common arrangement is to start the backup generator from a remote control panel in the house. Some or all of the household circuitry is transferred from the utility line to the standby generator. This process is reversed when utility service is restored.

A standby generator for homes, businesses, or hospitals is usually rated to handle only some of the existing loads. A generator large enough to handle *all* of the loads is big and expensive to buy, maintain, and operate. A detailed analysis of existing loads should precede the installation of any standby generator. Make a load list. This is a good place to rate loads as essential or non-essential. Later, this helps identify circuits that will be left ON or shut OFF during generator operation.

In theory, the standby generator seems like the best way to handle blackouts. However, there are five reasons why it is less than an ideal solution: expense, fuel supply, peripherals, efficiency, and sound.

• It is a fairly expensive system for only occasional use. For a big chunk of time, the generator is not doing anything for you at all. Standby generators designed for long life and minimal noise are more expensive than ones operating at higher rpm (3600 rpm).

• Requires fuel to run. Either you must install a large fuel tank nearby or you'll be transporting fuel cans to and from town to feed a rather thirsty beast. Weather severe enough to require generator operation is rarely the best time to travel to refill empty gas cans.

• Needs peripheral hardware to work. Remote startup. Transfer switch. Monitoring gauges. Fuel supply. A firesafe, weatherproof installation (shed?). A battery that is ready to start the generator. Add these costs to that of the generator itself.

• It is needed for even small loads. A generator powering a few loads has a much lighter load, but gobbles (inefficiently) fuel as though it's doing more work than it is. Either way, it experiences wear.

• It is noisy. This is a security issue. A standby generator lets everyone in the area know where you are. At the same time, proximity to the generator impairs one's own hearing. Bad combination.

Despite these limitations, standby generators have their place. There is 100 times more available energy stored in a pound of gasoline than a pound of battery. In the short term and for big loads, the generator gives the biggest bang for the buck. The questions are: how big is your need and what's the duration of the blackout?

The battery-powered inverter:

Another way to make electricity like that supplied by a utility is through an inverter. An inverter is an electronic device that converts DC electricity into AC electricity. (DC is direct current. AC is alternating current.) The result is identical to the stuff from the utilities, even cleaner.

One source of DC electricity is a battery. Thus, an inverter can transform the DC electricity from a battery into 120V, 60-cycle AC power. A battery is not truly a source of electricity. Rather, it is a means of storing the energy (in a chemical form) of the DC electricity supplied to it. The best sources of DC elec-

A solar-powered food dehydrator lessens the need for refrigeration.

tricity are PV (Photo-Voltaic, or solar) modules, wind-electric machines, and small hydro-electric systems. More on this later.

A battery charger plugged into the utility line will also supply DC electricity to a battery. This is a popular idea. The batteries are charged and maintained at full readiness, and ready to substitute their energy for that of the utility for as long as they're able. The bigger the battery (bank of batteries), the longer the system can bridge the blackout.

These systems are common. Have you ever wondered why your phone works when a blackout occurs? Phones run on electricity, too. The phone company has a "standby" or backup system which switches ON automatically when utility power is interrupted. This is called an uninterruptible power system, or UPS. At the heart of the UPS system is a bank of batteries that are much like the battery in your car, except bigger and heavier. Those batteries store enough energy to run an entire complex of telephone-related equipment for many hours during a blackout. When a blackout lasts longer than that, an engine-driven generator (fueled by gasoline, diesel, or propane) is started up to handle the entire load and recharge the batteries.

Until a few years ago, a small UPS system was the primary way to avoid the loss of power to a computer during a blackout. A critical period is the time it takes to switch between utility and battery power. To avoid any glitch, early UPS systems would run the computer's inverter from the batteries full time, while utility electricity only maintained the battery pack's charge. Better electronics have improved the purity and speed of the transition time. Today, many computers are unaffected by the transition as newer "line-tie" inverters switch from utility to battery, or back, in milliseconds.

There are many applications where a split-second transition between utility and battery power is not an issue. Or where more modest loads are dictated. Here, a simple and less expensive system—a small inverter, battery, and transfer switch—works well. The system I installed when I lived in the city was sized to power a furnace blower (and its controls), refrigerator, stereo, and four lights during an emergency. The system was installed near the main distribution box (where the fuses or breakers are located). It involved moving the wires and breakers (to which the wires are connected) into a service box I added. With a transfer switch added between the two boxes, I could shift these three circuits between utility power or the inverter's output. This is basic electrical wiring, easy for a DIY (Do-It-Yourself) homeowner or a local electrician.

How did it work? I'd give the blackout 10 minutes before I looked for the load list. It's a map that lets me move about the house, shutting off unneeded loads on the few circuits that will be switched to the inverter. (The energy stored in the battery is the lifeblood of the backup system. Don't let it bleed away needlessly!) Next, I'd shut off the main utility switch, flip the transfer switch to inverter, and turn the inverter ON.

A home UPS system

The simplest backup system is composed of two major components—a battery and an inverter. Batteries and inverters come in all shapes and sizes. Select carefully and they will serve you well.

The important characteristics of a battery are voltage (V), capacity (Ah), and design cycle.

1. Voltage. Common battery voltages are 6-Volt and 12-volt (hereafter, 6V and 12V). Large battery banks will employ individual 2V cells with massive capacities.

2. Battery capacity. Battery capacity is rated in Ah (Amp-hours) or cold-cranking amps (useless for our purposes). The Ah rating is helpful in describing the amount of energy the battery can hold.

3. Design cycle. Batteries are of two types: SLI and deep cycle. (A cycle is a discharge and full recharge.) A SLI (starting-lighting-ignition) battery is used in a car to start the engine—a fairly shallow cycle—and is immediately recharged by the engine's generator. Deep cycle batteries are used in applications where the battery's energy may be nearly depleted—a deep cycle—in use. This process will damage a SLI battery internally and eventually result in its failure.

12V vs 6V batteries

The smallest deep-cycle battery you might use for an inverter is rated 12V and 110Ah. These are used in boats, trolling motors, and RVs. At 50-70 pounds, this battery is about as much as a healthy person can carry and maneuver in a confined space. To increase the capacity of this system, you "parallel" a second battery with the first (Fig. 1). To parallel a battery (same voltage only, please!), make connections positive-to-positive and negative-to-negative for both batteries and load. The voltage will stay the same; in this case, 12V. At any time later, you can increase the system's capacity (the rate or duration of power delivery) by adding batteries of the same voltage, even if they have different capacities.

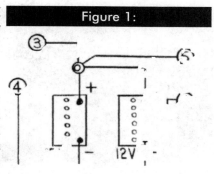

Batteries may be wired in parallel to increase capacity.

A better building block in a battery bank for inverter operation is the 6V, 220Ah battery used in golf cars. It has half the voltage, yet twice the Ah of a 12V battery of the same size and weight. So, they have the same "energy density."

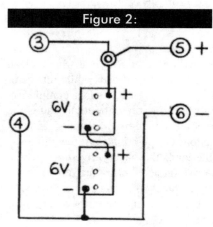

Batteries are wired in series to increase voltage.

To supply the 12V electricity our inverter needs, two 6V batteries are connected in series (Fig. 2) like dry cells in a flashlight, with ONE wire connecting the positive of one battery to the negative of the other. (A novice may try to connect the other two posts together, which results in a very hazardous short-circuit.) The result of the series wiring is a new, bigger battery of 12V with the remaining posts, positive and negative, connected to the system in the same way as would be any 12V battery.

Theoretically, pound for pound, two 12V batteries in parallel will

Solar cookers achieve 250-350 degrees during operation.

equal the capacity of two 6V batteries in series. In reality, a 6V battery is tougher— thicker plates, fewer cells to water, and greater tolerance to deep cycling and cold weather—than a 12V battery, resulting in a longer service life for almost any application.

Expect to pay $70-85 for a 6V, deep-cycle golf car battery (or equivalent). You'll need them in pairs for inverter operation at 12V.

Inverter features and ratings

Today's inverters serve two critical functions. First and primary, they convert the battery's output (low-voltage DC) to a form that your household can use (120 or 240 volts AC, 60 cycles). Second—and most desirable for standby generator or utility interaction—is the internal battery charger option. A battery charger's operation (DC-to-AC) is simply the reverse of an inverter's operation (AC-to-DC). When combined in one box, the inverter and battery charger share (use) the same electronic hardware. In this way, utility electricity stores itself in a battery which, in a blackout, will release the energy, powering an inverter to make 120V, 60-cycle AC.

The battery and inverter must be "matched" to each other and to the loads you expect them to power. Appliances, lights, and tools are referred to as "loads." Each "load" has its own power (consumption) rating. You may have heard the term "wattage." This is an expression of the RATE at which a load uses electricity. Generally, lights and radios are small loads while refrigerators, motors, and toasters are big loads. The effect of loads is accumulative. That is, if you operate more than one load at one time, the total load is the addition of all those wattages. The power consumed by even one small light all night might be greater than that of a toaster operating for a few minutes.

In an emergency, you must reduce the loads the battery/inverter unit will power. The faster you use the energy stored in the batteries, the sooner you'll have a "second" blackout! Make sense? In a blackout, you become the power company, responsible for rationing both the rate and quantity of expected household needs for a specific time period.

Inverters have voltage and wattage ratings.

1. Voltage. The voltage ratings are divided into input and output. The input voltage is the DC voltage of the battery bank. Inverters exist to handle DC voltages of 12V, 24V, 32V, 48V, or 120V.

The output voltage of the inverter is the 60-cycle AC voltage. It may be 120V (commercial) or 220V (industrial), or both.

2. Wattage. Wattage ratings of inverters range from 50-4,000 Watts (4kW) or larger. What wattage works for you? Here's a handy rule-of-thumb.

a. The *minimum* wattage rating of the inverter is determined by the largest single load you expect it to power.

b. The *maximum* wattage rating of the inverter is the largest combination of loads you want it to power simultaneously.

For example, if you had loads of 50 watts, 120 watts, 220 watts, 1200 watts, and 1400 watts, the inverter rating could be as low as 1400 watts (for the biggest single load) or as high as 2940 watts (for *all* of these loads.)

High-power inverters are expensive and require more battery capacity. Smart owners balance this situation by avoiding simultaneous use of heavy loads. In this example, then, selecting a 2000-watt inverter would handle everything else if the operator avoids using the two biggest loads simultaneously.

The price tag of a small UPS system is well within the reach of many homeowners. Inverters average a dollar a watt and batteries (lead-acid type) about a dollar a pound. A battery/inverter system is virtually maintenance-free and tucks away on a shelf in the garage or carport, ready to work when the blackout comes. Fortunately, your investment in this system has a second success. It is the core of a system that enables you, when you're ready and able, to tap the renewable energy sources—solar, wind, and hydro—all around you.

A no-inverter DC system

Utility power, in the form of 120VAC, 60Hz, is very specialized power. In a blackout, you may have less need for it than you might think. It is well known that a car or truck is useful in emergencies for the radio, light, heat, and shelter it offers. Without the engine running, there is enough capacity in a vehicle's 12V battery to power lights, radio, and the horn for some time. Periodic engine startup adds heat to the equation and recharges the battery, too!

Similarly, a stand-alone 12V battery pack located in the garage or home may be kept on charge (with a battery charger) until utility power fails and its stored energy is needed "as is," at 12V. This does not mean that you can power the same 120V loads as an inverter will. The RV (recreational vehicle), automotive, and marine markets offer almost any type of appliance, motor, tool, pump, and light that will work directly from 12 volts DC. For example, several high-efficiency 12V fluorescent lights will provide 20-40 hours of welcome light from one automotive-size battery. I can think of nothing more reassuring in the darkness, particularly when a storm is raging, than the steady glow of a lamp.

How do you wire up a 12V system to be blackout-ready? For occasional use, clamp-type lamps and several lengths of extension cords may be connected together to distribute light through a dwelling. This assembly can be coiled up and put away until a blackout occurs. A more permanent solution is to dedicate an electric circuit to 12V use. Existing household circuitry rarely adapts easily to a dedicated usage (unless one is still building one's home). Here, a well-planned layout and one standard roll of Romex wire will add a 12V circuit to any home, shop, or building for lights and a radio.

Living beyond the grid

Most RE (renewable energy) systems are based around 6V and 12V storage batteries. The simplest RE systems use a solar module, one or two batteries, a few 12V lights, and a 12V radio. Except for the PV module, this is identical to the system (described above) to supply power during a blackout. Becoming blackout-ready, then, is a step in the direction of becoming energy-independent.

RE systems are generally located "beyond the grid." The cost of bringing in utility service even a mile is often more expensive than investing in a system that is utility-free. RE technology has focused on being modular. This makes it simple to add more capacity, and to move and re-install the system.

There are energy sources other than PV modules worthy of your attention: wind and water. Wind-electric machines and small hydro-electric turbines are also viable energy producers. A multi-source system is smart for three reasons:

1. Seasonally, wind and water sources of energy are complementary with solar-generated power.

2. Solar, wind, and water system hardware is designed to supply low-voltage DC, particularly 12V and 24V.

3. A system designed around one source readily accommodates additional sources. The systems are more similar than different. Therefore, the battery bank, distribution and fusing panels, and monitoring equipment are virtually the same and are shared by the different sources.

Putting together a backup or RE system is also a good way to learn the basics of electricity itself (i.e., volts, amps, watts, and amp-hours). I believe this is essential if one is going to rely on electricity for anything. With this knowledge comes an appreciation for how energy moves and changes, and how it can be harnessed to fill your needs.

Beyond a blackout

Preparing for something worse or longer than a normal blackout is a frightening prospect. I avoid being overwhelmed by the sheer immensity of the topic by dividing the issues into two phases: basics and preparation.

Basics:

Basics represent the checklist of life. What does a human being need to survive, short and long term? Air, water, shelter, and food.

Air: Few think much about breathing until they can't. Remedies that take longer than three minutes are of little value. Shelters must remain tied to the atmosphere directly. If there are airborne pollutants (smoke, ash, etc.), filters will be needed to breathe without risk of injury.

Water: Humans can live only three days without water. See that you store some or have access to it. Water is easily contaminated. Figure out a way to purify it. Drink and cook with pure water or risk illness.

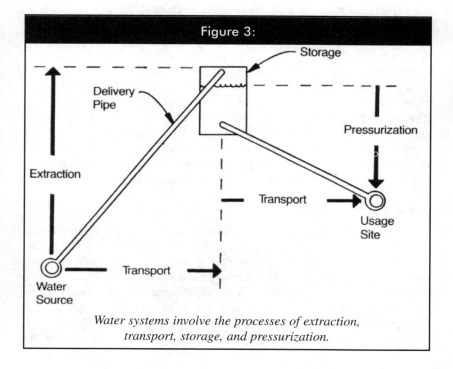

Figure 3:

Storage

Delivery Pipe

Pressurization

Extraction

Transport

Usage Site

Water Source

Transport

Water systems involve the processes of extraction, transport, storage, and pressurization.

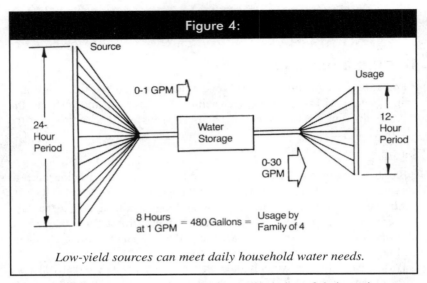

Figure 4:

Low-yield sources can meet daily household water needs.

Shelter: Human beings are amazingly manipulative of their environment, yet remain vulnerable to it in crisis. Shelter holds back the extremes of heat and cold, offers dryness, and feels safer for sleeping.

Energy: While we manipulate energy in our home, workplace, and car on many levels every day, it is all artificially generated. When that source is lost, the first job is to conserve it, in whatever form it is available. With any prolonged interruption of transportation or utility services in crisis, stockpiles of fuels like gasoline, diesel, and kerosene will be depleted or prohibitively expensive.

Food: Humans can live about a week without food, less in cold weather and limited water. In a mild emergency, stockpiling food, even enough for 5-7 days, saves having to forage, hunt, buy, barter, or trade for it. Or worse. Hunger strips away the resolve of people unaccustomed to its grip. Foodstuffs in most cities would disappear in a few days during a real crisis.

Preparation:

As one becomes more self-reliant, there is less dependence on (or need to buy) water, electricity, food, and fuels. Transportation needs also decline, allowing you more time to live and work at home. Coincidentally, this process prepares oneself for short and long-term disasters.

Here are some additional thoughts on preparations for water, food, energy, heat, lighting, motors, electronics, communication, and transportation.

Water: In a crisis, life is water. If your shelter—home, building, garage, cabin, RV, camper, tent, tipi, tarp, or cave—is connected to the town or city

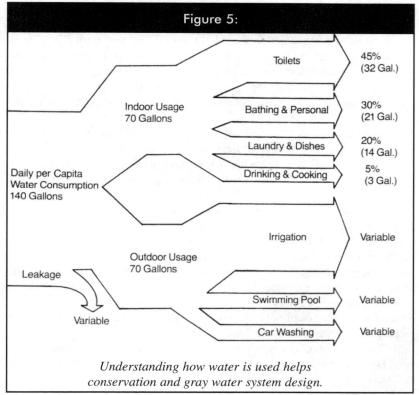

Figure 5:

Daily per Capita Water Consumption 140 Gallons

Indoor Usage 70 Gallons

Toilets — 45% (32 Gal.)
Bathing & Personal — 30% (21 Gal.)
Laundry & Dishes — 20% (14 Gal.)
Drinking & Cooking — 5% (3 Gal.)

Outdoor Usage 70 Gallons

Irrigation — Variable
Swimming Pool — Variable
Car Washing — Variable

Leakage — Variable

Understanding how water is used helps conservation and gray water system design.

supply, your backup plan is to fill everything you can as soon as you can. If you can't develop your own source, prepare some way to store water in 5-55 gallon plastic containers, or plastic, wood, or steel tanks.

If you plan to develop a water source, or already have, make certain that your system is not completely dependent on utility or generator power. The process of water usage can be broken down into four areas: extraction, transport, storage, and pressurization (Fig. 3). Treat them as separate issues to maximize the versatility of the system. A low-yield water source quickly accumulates enough water to handle a standard household (Fig. 4).

There are low-power, low-voltage, and energy-efficient alternatives to the standard submersible pump. These can be piggybacked onto existing systems or work alone. PV modules powering a 12V or 24V pump (no battery) have seriously challenged wind-powered pumps in unattended operation, like livestock watering, in the past decade. Most renewable energy systems use something similar.

Water you waste also wastes the energy invested to get the water to you. A more active conservation method makes multiple use of the water. A "gray-water" system often doubles the usefulness of the water supply (Fig 5). Cooking, drinking and rinsing are the purest uses. Garden, clothes washing, and toilet are secondary uses. A plan and a bit of plumbing will help with this. There are several books on gray-water systems.

Look at rainfall collection, cisterns, and pools as additional sources and storage methods.

Food: Food is one of the first concerns anyone will have in a crisis. Food issues revolve around supply, preservation, and cooking.

1. Supply is what you start with, if you don't grow your own. A stockpile, however small, is a good idea. Trading work or goods with people who farm and garden also works.

2. Preservation recognizes that food must be preserved against spoilage and infestation. Standard refrigerators and freezers work when there is abundant electricity. In an RE system, they hog energy. A high-efficiency, low-voltage refrigerator is expensive, yet rugged. More importantly, it frees up an appreciable chunk of energy that would be otherwise generated, stored, and inverted—only to be wasted. There are alternatives to refrigerators—canning and dehydrating, selective harvesting, and earth storage (i.e., a root cellar). Several good designs of solar dehydrators exist. Using one or more of these techniques further reduces the load on, or the need for, a refrigerator.

3. Cooking. It takes energy to cook food, particularly grains and vegetables. How much? Of what type? Solar cookers are a good bet if you're home. A 24-hour solar-powered oven is possible. A parabolic tray of less than 100 square feet can heat natural oils in excess of 350 degrees F. (100 degrees F short of their flash point) and store a sufficient quantity to keep the oven of uniform temperature throughout a 24-hour period. Use gas or wood heat to back up this system.

Energy: Your home is probably supplied with energy in the form of electricity and natural gas. Rural homes may use wood energy and propane. These energy "sources" are converted into only a few useful forms: heat, light, mechanical motion, and sound (stereo and radio).

Heat: Heat is a cherished form of energy and the biggest load in the home. Space heating. Water heating. Cooking. Dishwashing. Clotheswashing. Both refrigerators and air conditioners are heat pumps.

Good designs of solar collectors exist to handle these heating tasks. While designing a home to use solar energy is optimal, many homes can be retrofitted to use it effectively. Thermal mass—water, concrete and rock—will store solar energy for nighttime and storms. Save wood and other fuels for really bad weather. The perceived need for air conditioning and massive heaters is a coverup for poor design, sloppy construction, and cheap materials. Good insulation is a must—floor, walls, and ceiling—to avoid heat loss in winter and heat gain in summer.

A good understanding of how heat moves (radiated, conducted, and convected) and what happens to radiated heat (transmitted, absorbed, and reflected) helps collect, contain, store, use, and release it.

Lighting: Lighting is essential for moving about at night, or in dark places. Still, night is for sleep, even in emergencies. Rest is important in survival. And sleeping saves light!

This design of solar water heater exposes the tanks directly to the sun in an insulated box.

Incandescents, fluorescents, LEDs, and oil lamps all have value in lighting.

1. Incandescents, like standard household 120V bulbs and spotlights, gobble energy. Reserve their use to short durations. 12V automotive (turn signal type incandescent) bulbs are inexpensive, work directly on 12VDC, and are low-wattage. Still, use them sparingly.

2. Fluorescents, particularly those that are high-frequency (20KHz or above) are efficient and long lived.

3. LEDs are light-emitting diodes that operate at extremely low power. LEDs may be grouped together to increase voltage and light intensity. They're expensive but have a service life hundreds of times longer than incandescents.

4. Oil lamps will burn natural oils that may be pressed from many types of plants.

Motors: Motors convert electricity into mechanical motion. Motors power appliances in the home and tools in the shop. Pumps, fans, hair dryers, coffee grinders, juicers, turntables, tape decks, CD players, vacuum cleaners, computers, answering machines, and electric can openers use AC or DC motors.

High-wattage motors are difficult to power with low-voltage DC directly. Use an inverter or generator, as needed. Low-voltage DC motors may be substituted for AC ones under 2 HP. Or seek their 12V DC counterparts. Of course, manual tools don't need electricity to work.

Electronics: Electronic devices may be divided into two categories: high voltage and low voltage. The bigger and heavier the electronics, the more likely the need for 120V, 60-cycle AC. This includes the family stereo system, computers and peripherals, printers, television, and microwave ovens. Inverters and generators will be needed to power these units.

Light-duty electronics work around low-voltage DC, often below 12V. This includes remote phones, answering machines, portable radios, calculators, and portable CD and tape players. Look for a black module that plugs into the wall receptacle. The other end plugs into a DC input jack. DC input jacks may also be found on battery-powered units.

With a suitable DC-DC converter (or a dropping resistor), these electronic gizmos can be directly powered from a 12V car battery. (With a small modification, the jack can be re-wired to also recharge NiCads while they're in the radio.) Note the voltage printed near the jack to find the unit's voltage. Or count the number of cells (batteries) the unit contains and multiply by 1.5V to calculate the voltage. Or read the rating on the black module that plugs into the wall. This will help select the dropping resistor or converter setting.

Most electronic devices are polarity sensitive. By law, manufacturers are required to show the polarity of DC inputs, usually with a symbol. Wire the jacks and plugs accordingly.

Small 12V B&W TV sets may also prove handy, providing local coverage of a crisis. (Sorry, 12V color TVs gobble energy. Avoid using them.) These and other 12V devices often use a cigarette lighter plug (like the one that plugs into the car dash). If your vehicle doesn't have one, buy a lighter receptacle from an RV or renewables dealer. It can be clamped to the car battery posts or hardwired into the vehicle.

Communication: Details of what is happening beyond your own influence during a crisis is useful and, perhaps, crucial. In a blackout, the AM-FM radio in a car or truck may be the only communication at your disposal. At low volume, a radio will work for many days on just the car battery. You may need to position the vehicle (and antenna) away from buildings to get good reception. The news may not be reassuring if you're expecting help, but it will help you make better guesses or decisions about what you can and can't do.

Battery-powered, multi-band radios or boomboxes that use dry cells are equally good. With rechargeable cells (i.e., with NiCads) installed, there is no end to their useful service life. The cells can be recharged from renewable energy sources or even the 12V battery in a car. Note the actual voltage, use a converter or dropping resistor, and observe polarity. At low volume (or with earphones), these radios use only a tiny amount of energy in operation.

Transceivers, ham radio sets, walkie talkies, and CB (Citizen Band) radios are all useful, particularly for communities. Understand the power requirements to ensure that you can meet them. As well, recognize that sophisticated radio gear doesn't mean more effective communication. The semiconductor junctions in transistors and chips are extremely vulnerable to EMP (electromagnetic pulses) generated at high altitudes by both nuclear weapons and meteor strikes. The more complex something is, the more there is that can go wrong with it.

Transportation: Transportation may be adversely affected by crisis. Roads blocked with debris or other vehicles, bridges out, power lines down—these are common themes in a disaster. Owning a 4WD vehicle helps but it will need fuel, oil, tires, and parts to operate.

Vehicles converted to electric propulsion have an advantage over gas engines. There are only a few sources for gasoline. An electric vehicle (EV) is "fueled" by electricity from utility power, a standby generator, and renewable energy systems (solar, wind, or hydro). An EV has an additional advantage over vehicles with engines: it is silent in operation.

It may be easier to get around with motorcycles (noisy unless electric) and bicycles (mountain-type). Closer to home, carts, wagons,

This electric motorcycle is recharged daily from two solar modules.

wheelbarrows, and garden carts will help with everyday work or emergencies. Again, with self-reliance, there is simply less need for transportation. Δ

Chapter 16
Emergency power for $950

By Jeffrey Yago, P.E., CEM

For less than the price of a desktop computer you can have the piece of mind that your lights and small appliances can operate for months without the utility grid.

It is relatively easy to provide emergency power for most appliances and lighting fixtures with a gasoline generator, but what if the power outage lasts weeks or months instead of days? You may feel prepared owning that 4 kW gasoline generator that you purchased last year to keep your refrigerator, television, and lights operating after storm-downed power lines, but what do you do when you run out of gasoline? What if the gas stations do not have electricity to pump the gasoline and your car's gas tank is also empty?

Most metropolitan areas in the United States rarely experience a power outage that lasts over a few hours. A power outage lasting one or two days during a winter snowstorm or spring hurricane is not uncommon for more rural areas, but very rarely will any part of the United States be without electricity for more than two weeks.

Even when a major hurricane takes down power lines across an entire state, temporary emergency assistance from relief agencies, linemen from unaffected states, rented commercial generators, and other make-do efforts can bring back basic services until all the lines are repaired.

But what if the downed power lines or failed power grid affects a very large part of our country at the same time? What if the damage is so widespread that most homes and businesses will be without power for months, not days? If this widespread grid failure was caused by a terrorist attack or sabotage, we may have more to worry about than beer getting hot in the refrigerator. Under these conditions, remaining in any large city would be almost impossible, but for those living in more rural areas, many will stay home and try to make do. Even a little electric power can bring a lot of needed comfort for these people.

As a basis for this scenario, let us assume you live on several acres of land in a rural area, and you probably already own a wood stove, flashlight, have a well-stocked pantry, and use a well and septic tank. Let's also assume that even if you own a generator, its gasoline supply is limited and after several days you too will be in the dark if a working gas station is hundreds of miles away. You have just used the last of your candles and flashlight batteries, and are cooking on your wood stove or propane barbeque grille. That all-in-one backup battery power cart you bought at the discount warehouse store was cute, but it only operated your home computer or color television a few hours on the first day of the outage, and now its small battery is also dead. There isn't a functioning utility grid to recharge your battery-operated appliances, and you now have lost all contact with the outside world.

So now what? What can you do to be prepared for this type of long-term situation without spending your life savings to build that underground bunker with the 5,000-gallon fuel tank or buying a $50,000 solar power system?

Small pre-packaged single light kit including gel cell battery, charge controller, solar module, and light

Our first step is to identify the absolute minimum electrically powered devices you need to maintain a very basic level of lifestyle during a long-term power outage. Keep in mind that many luxury appliances like color televisions, home computers, refrigerators, electric water heaters, and drip coffee makers will be useless. Even if you could keep them operating, the refrigerator will run out of things to keep cold, the local television stations may be off the air, the downed phone lines will end your Internet surfing (unless you have a satellite connection), and it may be many months before you will have air conditioning and a hot bath again.

Let's start with the basics

Television has a very short range transmission and in rural areas reception is poor beyond 30 to 50 miles from the transmitting tower. Satellite receivers may allow watching distant television channels if they are still operating and you still have emergency power, but a very good all-band radio can receive stations from around the entire world using very little battery consumption. You will want a radio with long range AM band and shortwave reception capability and uses the larger rechargeable C or D cell batteries. Make sure it includes a plug and adapter allowing it to be powered directly from a car's 12-volt cigarette lighter. The CC radio from the C. Crane Company is an excellent radio for emergencies and costs $159.00. It also receives all emer-

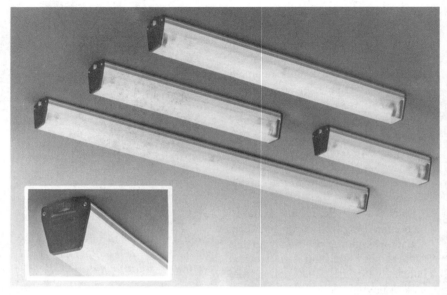

*Popular 12-volt DC high efficiency fluorescent fixtures
with end-mounted on/off switch*

gency alert frequencies and has an optional solar panel to recharge the battery.

Now that you have a reliable window to the outside world, your next concern is lighting up the darkness. For this we turn to the RV and boating industry. If you have not walked into a boating or RV supply store in the past five-years you are in for a surprise. They have any household appliance and light fixture you can imagine, and they all operate from a 12-volt DC battery. I will address in a moment how you will provide this long term 12-volt DC power, so at this point purchase those items you can't live without and that will operate on 12-volt DC electricity.

Most low cost light fixtures use standard incandescent bulbs that soon burn out and consume too much electricity when used with a small battery backup system. Select lighting fixtures designed for either compact flourescent lamps or the smaller T-8 style 2-foot fluorescent tubes. These provide excellent room lighting, the lamps last several years, and they use very little electricity. If you have electrical skills, buy the 12-volt DC surface-mounted wall sconces and ceiling fixtures. Install these in rooms, corridors, and stairwells where your family spends the majority of their time at night. You can mount them beside your existing 120-volt AC fixtures to achieve the same light distribution.

For a more temporary installation, wire each fixture with very long flexible cables of suitable size. Keep the unmounted fixtures and attached rolled up cables stored until needed during a power outage. Be sure you label each light fixture by room location so it will have the correct length of cable back to the battery location.

Do not try to put these 12-volt DC fixtures in every room since you can use a flashlight in any lesser used areas, or just don't use these spaces after dark. Since you will be powering these DC fixtures from a centrally located battery, your battery wiring must be kept separate from all existing 120-volt AC house wiring. If you purchase DC fixtures that include their own on/off switch, you will not need to wire separate room wall switches, which makes installation much easier. Also keep in mind that at 12-volts, it takes 10 times the number of amps to supply the same watt-

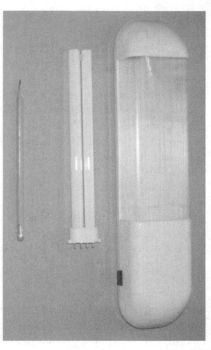

12-volt DC side-wall mounted compact fluorescent fixture with switch

age light fixture as a 120-volt circuit, so you will need larger wire sizes than normally used for AC circuits.

Follow manufacturer's installation recommendations for all wiring and wire sizing. Operating kitchen appliances like microwave ovens and refrigerators would make life easier and these larger appliances can be powered from a DC to AC inverter, but this will significantly increase your backup power system's costs and battery bank size. An inverter large enough to power a refrigerator, medium size microwave oven, or well pump can cost over $3,000 and that still does not include the hundreds of pounds of batteries it requires to operate. If you are interested in installing a whole house off-grid backup power system, refer to the larger solar power systems described in previous issues.

Battery power supply

Since we are limiting your emergency electric needs to only those lights and appliances typically installed in a recreational boat or camper trailer, you do not need to buy a room full of batteries, expensive inverters, sub-panels, and generator transfer switches. If you keep your system needs down to only six or eight high efficiency 12-volt DC fluorescent light fixtures and a quality portable radio or small black and white television, then you will only need a few moderately priced components to build your own long-term backup power system.

List of materials:

2 quality gel cell 6-volt batteries-$250
2 solar modules at 50 to 75 watts each-$600
12-volt solar charge controller-$75
2 safety disconnects and fuses-$25

Total: $950

Do not use car batteries as these will not provide the long-term reliability you need.

Remember that this bare bones solar power system is not intended to reduce your electric bills or to replace your existing lights and appliances that you use every day. This will be lighting that only operates during emergencies.

Your best choice for batteries is the 6-volt gel cell golf cart T-105 size battery. Each battery should have a 180-amp hour storage capacity and will weigh about 70 pounds. Their thick lead plates and sealed gel electrolyte will provide very reliable deep discharge capability and require no maintenance or refilling. It can be located almost anywhere; however, ambient temperatures above 90 degrees or below 40 degrees will substantially reduce their storage capacity. Since this is a 6-volt battery, you will need multiples of two in order to provide 12-volt power.

A good rule of thumb is to figure approximately 1 kWh of usable stored electricity in a battery this size. If you keep your electrical loads low, two 6-volt batteries should give you several days of emergency operation before recharging is required. You will not want to operate so many DC lights or appliances that you totally discharge the batteries each night. This will significantly shorten battery life and require a much larger solar array to keep them charged.

For a rough estimate of system performance, assume an average of six hours per day of direct sunlight (9 am to 3 pm), using two 75-watt solar modules, and allow 20% efficiency losses in the battery charging process. This system will have a maximum daily energy collection of 720 watt-hours (75 watt x 2 x 6 hours x 80%). This would power four 25-watt compact fluorescent fixtures for seven hours per night (4 x 25 x 7) plus a radio. It should be obvious that you must keep your electrical loads to a minimum.

The more solar modules you have and the larger they are, the more appliances you can power, but since this will be the most expensive item in this system design you will want to keep your load needs small and within budget. For quality solar modules you will normally pay at least $4 to $6 per watt, but with smart shopping you should be able to find a pair of 75-watt modules for under $600.

Shop for the larger 50 to 100-watt modules as these have a lower cost per watt and you will have fewer panels to interconnect. For this size system, a good rule of thumb is one module per golf cart battery. You can mount these on a frame made from 2" x 2" aluminum angle and $^5/16$" stainless steel bolts purchased from any home supply store. Remember, solar modules will be like kites in a strong wind, and even though they are reasonably lightweight, your structural concerns are wind uplift. A well built mounting structure is worthless if the entire assembly blows away.

Solar photovoltaic modules can be permanently mounted on your roof or garage with the help of a few friends.

Store it away

Since this will be a last defense emergency power system, you could make it portable and store the solar modules in your garage until needed. However, you do not want to allow the gel cell batteries to be discharged for any length of time or they will permanently be unable to hold a full charge later. A high quality trickle charger can be purchased to keep these batteries charged if your solar array will be kept in storage. However, you must use a charger that shuts off when the batteries are fully charged if you plan to keep it permanently plugged in. Also note that any charger used to charge gel cell batteries must be adjustable since gel cell batteries have a different charge voltage than liquid filled batteries.

Whether your solar array will be mounted on a garage roof, van roof, or tall pole, it must face as close to south as possible and tilted up 30 to 60 degrees depending on your latitude.

Charge controller

When shopping for your own solar modules, you will also need to purchase a charge controller. This device controls the battery charging process and a high quality controller will squeeze more charging capacity from any given

Solar modules can also be portable or stored until needed. The 100 watt module shown next to RV measures 59" x 23-1/2".

solar array. Two 75-watt 12-volt modules will require at least a 6-amp charge controller; four modules will require a 12-amp controller. Expect to pay at least $75 for a quality 12-amp unit, and be sure you select a unit with the correct charge voltage output for gel cell batteries.

To round out your system you will need fuses and safety disconnects as shown in the wiring diagram. The Square D QO brand of circuit breakers can be substituted for the fuses shown in the diagram. These are the only AC switchgear you will find in a home improvement center that is also UL rated for use with low voltage DC circuits.

Most AC fuses or circuit breakers are not rated for DC voltages and can be extremely unsafe if used. Purchase only DC-rated fuses and fuse holders. The automotive type 12-volt DC fuses and fuse blocks you will find in the RV and boating supply stores will protect your DC system components; however, they are not UL approved for permanent wiring installation in a residence.

If you are not familiar with these electrical safety issues and the National Electric Code, obtain the assistance of a licensed electrician to help with your final electrical connections.

Portability

You may want to have your 12-volt DC lighting and appliance wiring terminate at a common point in a garage or utility room and be able to quickly disconnect the batteries, charge controller, and solar array. This would allow you to relocate your system to an RV or van if you are forced to relocate during a major crises.

The wiring diagram provides a basic guide for connecting the individual components. Be sure to note that the solar modules are nominal 12-volts

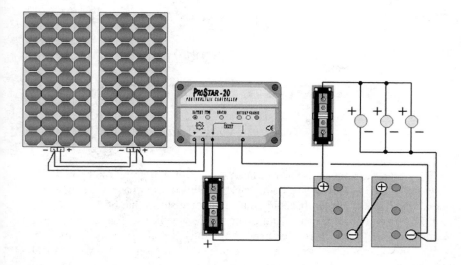

*Wiring diagram for a 12-volt DC solar battery charger
and emergency power supply*

(they will be labeled 16 to 17-volt) so they must be wired in parallel, not
series like the 6-volt batteries or you will end up with 24-volts.

Material sources:
Dunimis Technology Inc., Solar power kit shown, 1-804-784-0063, www.
dunimis.com
Port Supply, 12-volt marine appliances, 1-800-621-6885, www.portsupply.
com
Lehman's, Non-electric appliances,
1-888-438-5346, www.lehmans.com
S. King Company, 12-volt RV appliances, 1-888-892-2547, www.skingco.
com
RV Parts Outlet, 12- volt RV appliances, 1-866-333-0999, www.rvpartsout-
let.com
C. Crane Company, Battery powered radios, 1-800-522-8863, www.ccrane.
com Δ

Chapter 17
How do you live without electricity?

By Anita Evangelista

It's going to happen. Sooner or later, the power will go off, and you won't know when (or if) it will come back on. This doesn't have to be the work of evil-doers, either. It could be a sudden ice storm that brings down the power lines. It could result from other severe weather such as a tornado or hurricane, or from a disruption caused by faulty power company equipment, or even something as simple as a tree branch falling on your own personal segment of the grid. The effect is the same: everything electrical in your home stops working.

For most modern Americans, the loss of power means the complete loss of normalcy. Their lifestyle is so dependent upon the grid's constancy that they do not know how to function without it. How do you cook a meal if your gas stove has an electric ignition? How do your children find their way to the bathroom at night if the light switches don't work? How do you keep warm if your wood heat is moved through ducts by an electric fan? What do you do with a freezer full of expensive meat? How do you find out what is happening in your area with the TV and radio silent? What will you drink if your water comes from a system dependent on electrical pumps?

These are questions that both the Red Cross and Federal Emergency Management Agency are asking people to seriously consider. Both of these agencies have suggested that preparations for three days without power are prudent commonsense actions that all Americans should now undertake.

We'll look at these issues in the broad context of living without access to the grid, whether you've chosen to separate from it or whether the choice is made for you by outside forces. What you can do now to mitigate your difficulties if the power goes off in the future, and what you can do then to help keep your situation under control, will be the focus of this article.

Remember, too, that an important principle in all preparations is that you maintain as much "normalcy" in your lifestyle as possible. For example, if television is part of your relaxation and unwinding process, don't assume you can easily do without it. The closer you can keep your daily routines to "the norm" for your family, the more easily you can deal with power outages.

There are five primary areas that are easily disrupted if the power goes off. Each of these is critical to daily survival, as well, so when making preparations for emergencies keep these in mind. In order of importance, they are: **light, water, cooking, heating/cooling,** and **communication.**

Light

While living on our Ozark farm without the grid, we spent some time rising with the sun and going to bed when the sun set. This would probably have been a pretty healthy way to live, if everyone else in the world did the same thing. Our children's bathroom needs didn't stop when the sun went down, our neighbors figured that nighttime visits weren't out of the ordinary, and those midnight raids on the pantry for crackers and peanut butter turned into fumble-fests. Sometimes the barking of our livestock guardian dogs meant strange predators were too close for comfort, somewhere in the countryside darkness. Light is the most important item on our Big Five list because without light we are not able to efficiently carry on the other activities of daily living.

The most simple and familiar form of emergency lighting is a **flashlight.** Do you have one that you could find in the dark, right now? If so, congratulations. You are among a very small percentage of Americans. Better yet if you have one for each member of your family, with fresh batteries, plus three extra sets of batteries for each flashlight. That should be your minimum "safe" number. Store your flashlight where you can quickly reach it in the dark night—under the mattress of your bed, for example. Each child old enough to walk should also have his or her own flashlight, and be taught how to use it.

Flashlights range in price from the 79 cent cheapie to the fancy multifunction $80 special. Consider a small 2-AA battery flashlight with a halogen bulb. These cost about $4-5 each, give an excellent clear white light, and are easily portable in a pocket or purse. Additionally, when we discuss communications later in the article, the most common battery used in these devices is also the AA, so your life will be simplified if you stick primarily to one type of battery and don't have to buy various odd sizes for different needs.

Batteries wear out rapidly if your flashlights are used continuously: figure two changes per week of regular use. Alkaline batteries last longer, give a more powerful light, but cost more than regular batteries. Most rechargeable batteries are suitable for flashlights, but should be recharged when the light begins to dim a little. Don't let them get completely drained. This means you would need several sets of rechargables for each flashlight (some would be recharging while you use the others).

*Cooking bread outdoors
in a Dutch Oven*

Recharging can be done by means of a charger plugged into your car's cigarette lighter outlet. These DC-powered rechargers can be found at auto supply stores and at Radio Shack for about $30 or less. Solar rechargers work slower but produce the same results for about $30.

Candles are available, slightly used, at garage sales and thrift stores (5 cents to 10 cents each or less), and some outlet stores like Big Lots have new candles for 25 cents. We have a cardboard box weighing 35 pounds that is filled with various sizes and shapes of candles. This would be about a year's supply for my family. We've acquired them gradually, every time we found them inexpensively. They never go bad! Candles are easy to use and familiar. Most of us can adjust to using candles easily. The light is soft and wavering. You'll need at least three candles if you hope to read by the light. If you have small children or indoor pets, care must be taken where you place them. Metal candle holders that hang on walls are probably the safest. Remember to place a heat proof plate underneath the holder to catch drippings. Save your wax drippings, too, to make more candles later.

Oil (kerosene) lamps produce a steadier light than candles. Department store oil lamps cost about $10 each and come in attractive styles. Lamp oil is about $3 per liter. A typical lamp will burn one to two cups of oil per night, so you would use about two liters each week per lamp. The light from these lamps is not quite adequate to read by unless it is placed very close, and the light does waver a little. A single lamp can provide enough light in a room so that you don't bump into furniture, but two or three may be needed to provide good functional light. As with candles, if you have children, these lamps need to be placed securely and out of reach. The smell of burning oil (kerosene) can get heavy in a closed room so keep ventilation open. Keep an extra set of wicks ($2) and chimneys ($3) in case of breakage.

The Cadillac of oil lamps is the **Aladdin Lamp**. These run from $60 up to several hundred each. The light given off is as good as a 60-watt bulb, clear, and unwavering. You can read or do needlepoint by the light of one lamp. These burn the same oil or kerosene as typical lamps, but because they burn hotter, there is much less odor. Position these lamps so that they cannot accidentally be overturned, and so that the intense heat coming from the chimney won't ignite something. Purchase an additional "mantle" (the light-giving portion of the lamp - $3), and chimney ($15), as backups.

Solar powered lamps ($80-$120) are typically small fluorescents, and can be run off of battery systems. It may take more than one day of bright sunlight to recharge these lamps, so you may need several—one to use, while others are recharging. The light is white and clear, good for area-lighting, and rather difficult to read by. Have extra fluorescent bulbs on hand, too.

Don't forget to store matches!

Water

If you live in a town or city, the loss of power to homes and businesses probably will not immediately affect your water pressure, but it could affect the purification process or allow reverse seepage of contaminants into the lines. If, instead, your water comes from an electrically-powered home water pump, your water stops flowing the moment the power does. Either way, with the loss of power comes the loss of water (or, at least, clean water). Water that is free of bacteria and contaminants is so crucial to our survival that it should be a special concern in your preparations.

The easiest way to guarantee quality water is to store it right now. The important question is: how much? Both Red Cross and FEMA suggest a minimum of one gallon per day per person. This is an absolute minimum, and covers only your real drinking and cooking needs; bathing is out of the question.

The typical American currently uses around 70 gallons a day, taking a nice long hot shower, flushing the toilet several times, washing a load of laundry, letting the water run while brushing teeth, and for cooking and drinking. In a short-term emergency situation, only drinking and cooking water is crucial, but if that short-term incident drags out to weeks or months, daily consumption would rise to include bathing and clothes washing. And this presumes that the family has prepared a sanitary "outhouse," so flushing isn't needed. In that case, 5-10 gallons per day per person would be a more reasonable amount, with a weekly communal bath becoming the routine.

One to three-gallon jugs, direct from the supermarket, run about 60 cents to $2; these store easily under cabinets and counters. A few tucked into the freezer will help keep things cold if the power goes off. You can also store water inexpensively in large, covered plastic trash cans; they hold 36 to 55 gallons each. Refresh the water every two weeks, so it will be ready in case the power goes off. Kiddie swimming pools—a 12-foot wide, 36-inch deep pool holds 2500 gallons and costs about $250—also make excellent above-ground holding tanks. Buy a pool cover, as well, to keep bugs out.

Farm supply stores often sell "water tanks" made of heavy grade plastic. These can be partially buried underground to keep water cooler and less susceptible to mold and bacteria. These run about $1 per gallon of holding

A "shepherd" or "camp" stove offered by Cabela's catalog. It has a detachable shelf on the right, detachable five-gallon hot water tank on the left, and an oven sitting above the stove body. The whole thing breaks down and is portable. It cooks very nicely, too. Costs about $500 for all components, excluding stove pipes, and it can be bought piecemeal. The light in the upper left-hand photo is a lit oil lamp, placed to give light when using the stove.

capacity, so a 350-gallon tank new will cost $350. Plan to filter and purify the water before use.

Collecting water can be done by hand with 5-gallon plastic buckets if you live near a river or stream (it *must* be filtered and purified before use). You can also divert rainwater off your roof, through the rain gutters and downspouts into plastic trashcans. If you live in the Midwest, Northwest, or East Coast, rainfall is adequate to make this your primary backup water source. West Coast, high desert, and mountain areas, though, won't have sufficient rainfall to make this a reliable source.

A drilled well with an electric pump can be retrofitted with a plastic hand-pump for about $400 - $600. These systems sit side-by-side with your electric pump down the same well-shaft, and can be put to use any time the power is off. Typical delivery is about 2 gallons per minute, and pumping strength varies from 11 to 20 pounds—a good but not exhausting workout.

Water can be purified inexpensively. Fifteen drops of bleach (plain unscented) per gallon of water costs less than 1 penny, and ¼ cup of hydrogen peroxide (3%) per gallon will also destroy bacteria. Twenty minutes of a hard, rolling boil will, too. Bleach is effective against both cholera and typhoid and has kept American water supplies safe for decades. The chlorine taste can be easily removed with a charcoal filter system (such as Brita Pitcher or Pur brands for home use, about $30).

British Berkefeld water filters, along with various other brands, are more expensive ($150-$250), but can filter and purify water indefinitely. Both eliminate bacteria, contaminants, and off-flavors. We've used a "Big Berkey" for four or five years, and it is a very reliable gravity-fed system. When shopping for filters, if they only offer "better taste" they won't protect you from bacterial contaminants.

Noah Water System's travel companion will work great in case of a power outage, or your water supply becomes undrinkable. The Trekker is a portable water purificationn unit. With the Trekker you can get water from any river, lake, or pond. It's small enough to carry like a briefcase.

Cooking

A person can survive indefinitely opening cold cans of beans for meals, but it wouldn't be a very satisfying existence. In times of crisis, a hot meal goes a long way toward soothing the day's troubles. The simplest way to heat a meal is the Boy Scout method: a couple of bricks or rocks set around a small outdoor fire, with the bean can propped over the flames. It's low cost, and it works. However, the cook doesn't have much control over the outcome.

Outdoor cooking of all kinds, including **grilling** and **barbecuing**, all work during emergency situations, provided you have the charcoal or wood (and matches!) needed to get the heat going. These are familiar methods, too, so family members don't have to make a huge leap to accept these foods. It's difficult to cook much more than meats and a few firm vegetables over open heat like this, though. Also, never use these devices in a confined space, as they emit carbon monoxide.

"Campfire" cooking can lend itself to some baking, if you also have a cast iron Dutch Oven—a large, heavy, cast iron covered pot. Place a well-kneaded pound of bread dough into a heavily-greased or oiled Dutch Oven and put the cover in position. Make a hole or pot-sized well in the ash near the fire, and line this with glowing coals. Put about an inch of ash over the coals, and place the Dutch Oven into this. Now, pile about an inch of hot ash around the oven and cover with glowing coals, then another layer of ash to keep the heat in. Uncover and check your bread in about 35 minutes, it should be done.

Propane and **butane camp stoves** are so much like ordinary home stoves that there is no difference in the cooking results. Portable RV 2-burner propane stoves are often available used—mine cost $5 at a garage sale—and can even do pressure canning because the heat is consistent and reliable. A typical 18-gallon propane cylinder, the kind used for barbeques, costs around $30 new, and a propane fillup is about $7. This will last for nearly a month of daily use. You'll also need a feeder hose and pressure regulator for the stove, which can be prepared by your propane dealer for $20 or so.

Butane stoves are also portable and run off of a cylinder of the same kind of butane that is used in cigarette lighters. These stoves are $80-90 new, and cylinders are $5 and last for 8 hours of cooking.

attach to sides
4 REFLECTORS

DUCT TAPE HINGES
TO HOLD
GLASS IN
PLACE

SHEET
OF GLASS

BLACK
INTERIOR

3 nested
cardboard
boxes

A solar oven design made with cardboard boxes, aluminum foil, and a piece of window glass. Interior of the box is flat black paint.

General camp stoves (around $65 at department stores) operate on "stove fuel" (basically, propane in a small 1-pound cylinder - $3). A cylinder lasts for around 8 hours of cooking. You can also find camp stoves that will cook off of unleaded gasoline, and there are some that are "multi-fuel," using either kerosene or gasoline—handy in case of a shortage of one fuel or the other. Use outdoors or on a covered porch to prevent carbon monoxide buildup in your home.

Solar cooking is another option, if you have plenty of unobstructed sunlight and someone who is willing to adjust the cooker to face the sun every half hour or so. A **solar oven** need be no more fancy than a set of nested cardboard boxes painted flat black on the inside with tempura colors, a sheet of window glass, and some aluminum foil glued to cardboard panels. Total cost for this, if you can scrounge leftover glass and cardboard, is about $1.

Place your food in a covered lightweight pan inside the box, prop it so the entire interior is exposed to the sunlight (about a 45-degree angle), cover with the sheet of glass (and tape the glass so it won't slide), then prop the aluminum foil panels so that they reflect more sunlight down into the box. Move the box every 30 minutes so it maintains an even temperature. It will get hot fast, easily up to 325 degrees, and hold the heat as long as it faces the sun. Remember to use potholders when removing your foods! Our first solar oven had a black plastic trash bag as a heat-absorbing inner surface; it worked superbly until the plastic actually melted.

Keeping foods cool if the power goes out can be as simple as looking for shade, even under a tree. Some Ozarkers have partially buried old broken freezers in the shade of backyard trees, storing grains and winter vegetables inside. During the winter, your parked car will stay at the same temperature as the outside air—below freezing on those cold nights—so you can store frozen goods there safely. During the daylight hours, the car interior will heat up, though, if it's in the sun. Park it in the shade of the house, or cover the windows and roof with a blanket to keep the interior cool.

Kerosene refrigerator/freezers are alternative appliances that will continue to function with the power off because they are "powered" by kerosene.

Their cooling and freezing capacity is exactly the same as a regular refrigerator, and they come in the same colors. Typically, they are a little smaller than conventional 'fridges and cost up to $1500, but they'll last for decades with care.

Portable battery-powered refrigerators that keep your foods 40-degrees cooler than outside temperatures are available at most department store sporting-goods sections ($90). These run off of both DC and AC power, so they can be plugged into your car battery through the cigarette lighter outlet or into a solar power system.

What about that freezer full of expensive meat if the power goes off? First step is to cover the freezer with blankets to help retain the cold. Then, find dry ice (if everyone else in your town hasn't already bought out the supply). Blanket coverings will keep a full freezer frozen for two days, and the addition of dry ice will prolong that to three or four days.

If power stays off, it's time to eat and time to can the meat remaining. Canning low-acid foods like meat calls for a pressure canner ($90), canning jars ($6 for 12), a source of consistent heat (like a propane RV stove), and some skill. In considering your time requirements, it took me two days of steady canning to put a 230-pound pig into jars. Each quart jar holds 3 pounds of meat.

Heating and cooling

It's a funny thing that even though we know winter is coming, we put off cutting our wood until after the first really cold night has chilled the house below comfort levels. But with the instability in the world today, it is sensible, and reasonable, to prepare well in advance of season changes. Putting in supplies a year ahead of time is a traditional farm practice, and it gives a cushion of safety against uncertain conditions.

Woodstove heating is more common, and comfortable to use, than it was two decades ago. New wood heaters run from $100 to several thousands, depending on materials, craftsmanship, and beauty. Better stoves hold heat longer and may have interior baffles that let you use less wood to produce more heat. Even so, the most basic metal-drum-turned-stove also works to heat a room or a house.

Heating a 3-bedroom home that is moderately insulated will use about 8-12 cords of wood throughout the winter. The size of a cord (sometimes called a "rick" or a "rank") is not standardized from region to region, but typically will be about 8' x 8' x 2', roughly a pickup truck bed loaded even with the top of the sides. Prices will vary between $65 per cord to $150, depending on the region and type of wood. Hardwoods, such as oak and walnut, and fruitwoods like apple and pear, burn better and longer than softwoods like poplar. Don't use resinous woods, such as the pines, cedars, and spruces for the main heating—only as firestarters—because they burn too hot and fast and generate creosote. Better home insulation and better quality hardwoods will decrease the amount of wood you need to use.

If you plan to secure and cut your own firewood, be willing to acquire a good-quality chainsaw—any that cost below $200 will only give you grief. Keep an extra chain on hand. Use safety precautions, too: wear ear and eye protectors, heavy gloves, and don't chainsaw alone. Cutting your own wood will decrease your heating costs significantly, but increase your labor. It typically takes us a full week of constant work to put up a winter's worth of wood.

Woodstoves require heat-proof surfaces surrounding them, an insulated chimney pipe (about $90 per 3-foot section), and some building skills in order to install. Installation costs can equal or surpass the cost of the stove itself. Chimneys need to be thoroughly cleaned of the black crusty buildup, creosote, at least twice each year (and more often if you use the stove continuously).

Propane heaters that don't need venting to outdoors are a relatively new product. A plain one ($200) can be mounted on the wall in the home's main room, or more fancy models that look like built-in fireplaces complete with fake logs ($450) are available. You will need a propane tank, regulator, and appropriate copper lines, but these will all be installed by your propane company for a small charge. Propane has varied widely in cost from year to year, but typically runs around $0.95 to $1.30 per gallon.

Kerosene heaters ($120) are freestanding units that burn kerosene in a way that is something like a lamp—it uses a wick system and flames to provide heat. These are best used in areas that can be easily ventilated, because of the potential for buildup of carbon monoxide. Kerosene has a strong odor, as well. Kerosene costs about $1 per gallon or less (in quantity).

Solar heat can be "grabbed" anytime the light from the sun hits your house. Even in the dead of winter, the south-facing walls will feel noticeably warmer than the shaded north-facing ones. You can "store" the sun's heat in any surface. Ceramic floor tiles, for instance, are excellent at retaining heat. So will a flat-black painted covered plastic trash can filled with water. If these surfaces are exposed to sunlight, say, indoors next to a south-facing window, they will absorb heat during the day. At night, with the window curtains closed, the surface will release heat slowly and steadily into the house.

One of the most efficient ways to heat is something else we have forgotten in the past 50 years—close off rooms that are not being used. If doors aren't available, you can hang curtains in doorways (or even tack up a blanket, in a pinch), and keep your heat restricted to the room you are actually in. In an emergency situation, you can curtain up a room and set up a tent-like "den" for the family to snuggle in under blankets. Body heat alone will keep the den's interior comfortable.

Cooling a residence during a hot summer requires just as much thought and advance planning as winter heating does. Battery and solar-powered fans help keep air moving, windows can be shaded by fast-growing vines and pole beans, and—planning way ahead—fast-growing trees like poplars can be planted on the house's south side to shade the yard.

In areas where wind blows routinely in the summer, you can soak a sheet, ring it out, and hang it in front of a breezy window. The air passing through the window is cooled as it moves against the wet sheet, and helps to cool the house. Remember that heat rises, so make it easy for too-hot air to escape from the attic and upper floors by opening windows and vents.

Communications

In a time of distress, keeping in contact with family and knowing about local and national situations is important to maintaining both continuity and confidence. In general, telephone systems are on a different system than the electrical power grid, but they can be disrupted if there are earth movements or as the result of terrorist activities.

During the Loma Prieta earthquake in 1989, we kept informed about the damages by watching a 4-inch black and white TV set (bought used for $25) that was plugged into our car battery through the cigarette lighter. At night, we heard reports from the BBC via a 4-AA battery powered shortwave radio ($70 from Radio Shack). I consider these two devices—shortwave and TV—the required minimum communication/ information devices during a crisis, especially if the phone system is down.

Satellite internet hookups, using a battery-powered laptop, could be an excellent communication tool, both for accessing news and for staying in touch with friends and colleagues by email.

Citizens Band (CB) radios are excellent tools, as well. These portable devices can be carried with you into the field and used to stay in contact with neighbors and family when you are away from the house. Basic models run $60—you'll need at least two—and ones with greater ranges and features are more costly. They'll run on 6 to 8 (or more) AA batteries.

"Family Radios" are FM-band devices that have a short range, about ¼ mile ($60 for a pair). These are handy for keeping family in contact during outings, when traveling in a caravan, or when one member needs to go out to the barn during a storm. They run on 2 AA batteries.

Keeping things normal

Even though circumstances may change in the world, we can choose how we wish to react. We can live in a state of helpless anxiety—or control what we can. We can control our responses, in part, by maintaining as much normalcy in our lives as possible.

If your family relaxes in the evenings with a video, plan to continue doing that. Acquire a battery-powered TV/VCR combination, and make sure you have enough power sources to keep that going for at least two weeks. (If things get dicey, you can wean off the system in two weeks.) A cassette player or CD player with external speakers can provide relaxation and entertainment, and they run off of AA batteries as well.

Children have difficulty adjusting to sudden changes in their environment, so if you expect them to play board games if the power goes out, they should be comfortable with board games now. Keep routines consistent, arising at the usual time in the morning and going to bed as you have in the past. Prepare familiar meals with foods everyone enjoys. Have "fun foods" and goodies on hand. Remember to reach out to your neighbors and older folks who live nearby, and provide extras to help them, as well.

Use the knowledge you've gained, and your experience with non-electric living, to make your neighborhood a more secure and adaptable place.

Resources

Aladdin Lamps: Lehman's carries an excellent selection, plus many non-electric items.
Lehman's, P.O. Box 41, 4779 Kidron Rd., Kidron, OH 44636
www.lehmans.com, 330-857-1330
British Berkefeld water filters:
Noah Water Systems, Inc., 46373 Galway Dr., Novi, MI 48374
www.noahwater.com, 877-356-6624
New Millennium Concepts, LTD., P.O. Box 201411, Arlington, TX 76006
www.bigberkey.com, 888-803-4438
Hand pumps: A websearch can find many manufacturers and sellers. Two are:
Kansas Wind Power, 13569 214th Rd., Holton, KS 66436
www.kansaswindpower.net
785-364-4407
Ready Made Resources, 239 Cagle Rd., Tellico Plains, TN 37385
www.readymaderesources.com
800-627-3809

(Anita Evangelista is the author of *Living Without Electricity and Liking It*, available from *Backwoods Home Magazine*, 1-800-835-2418.) Δ

Chapter 18
Medical kits for emergencies

By Jackie Clay

Tbere may be a time, as close as tomorrow, when your loved ones need medication or medical treatment and there is no drug store open or doctor available. This may be as simple a situation as a head cold coming on during a weekend night, or more drastic, such as nothing available after a civil disturbance, terrorist attack, or natural disaster.

Family medical kits

Here at home, we've always had a medical kit. Several, in fact. One is quite large, made up of a poly box, originally designed as a field box for trap and skeet shooters. This "drug store on wheels" is a well-packed medical utility box that will handle nearly everything from a cold to severe lacerations. This one we carry when traveling in remote locations.

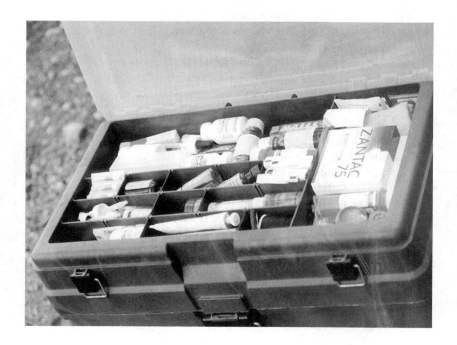

But while it is loaded with most medical needs, far surpassing a first-aid "kit," it is heavy, weighing over 30 pounds, and it is not something we carry for short trips.

An intermediate kit is lighter and fits into a flat, moderate-sized fishing tackle box. While this does not contain such a wide variety of medical supplies and medications, it is a very well thought out first-aid—and then some—medical kit. This is light enough to pack in our canoe (if we don't foresee many lengthy portages, when every ounce counts), with camp supplies on a horse packing trip, or small enough to take up little room in our truck.

Besides this kit, we also carry a small first aid kit under the seat of the truck and Suburban, containing bandages, antibiotic ointment, burn medication, sterile gauze, tweezers, aspirin, sterile eye wash, and cold tablets for ourselves and our eight-year-old son, David. In the glove box is a smaller snap-open plastic box with Bob's oral diabetes medication, my blood pressure pills, and a few aspirin. This has come in handy many times when someone forgot to take prescribed daily medication or a headache suddenly popped up. As the glove box does get hot during the summer, this small stash of meds is rotated routinely to make sure the strength does not fade.

Learning to use your kit

No matter how comprehensive your medical kit is it can be useless or even harmful if you do not know how to use it safely. You don't have to have extensive medical treatment to handle most emergencies that occur in real life. Most of ours consist of splinters, minor cuts and scrapes, sprains, and an occasional head cold or the flu. While these are scarcely life-threatening, they are uncomfortable and the afflicted party sure appreciates quick, competent aid.

Our family is lucky; I have spent a lifetime as a veterinary field technician riding on calls and acting as an assistant on everything from broken legs to pneumonia. Bob is a Certified Nurses Assistant (CNA) with additional military medical training in Vietnam.

But you'd be surprised at how much free medical training is out there for you to pick up. Many communities provide first-aid classes, including invaluable cardiopulmonary resuscitation (CPR) training.

During these classes, ask questions to boot up the amount of knowledge you receive. Attend volunteer firemen's training sessions, as available (again, ask around). Ask your veterinarian if you could accompany him/her on calls one or more days a week free in exchange for the knowledge you gain. Yep, I know, they're animals, not people, but basically, a mammal is a mammal, especially when it comes to shock, wounds, and common illnesses such as pneumonia.

Pick up a good first-aid manual (which should be in your large medical kit at all times) and a book or two from a preparedness company which details medical treatment when no doctor or dentist is available. Then *read* these manuals carefully. I know they're not great reading, but they can save someone's life. Share the reading with your spouse or older children, and even practice at home. It can be interesting, learning to suture gaping wounds on a piece of that chicken you're having for dinner. After it's butchered and ready to cook, of course. I'm not that morbid.

Real life medical treatment basics

While some survival first aid manuals assume your family's injuries will need treatment for nuclear blast and gaping wounds, in reality most will be of a much more mundane level no matter where you are, from arctic tundra to urban sprawl. They will consist of minor cuts, scrapes, slivers, blisters, the flu, colds, a fish hook in the skin, etc. We have lived for years in very remote locations and, although the worst injury any of us sustained was Bob's green stick fracture of his leg in a snowmobile accident, the most painful was my severely sprained ankle, suffered when I missed a step going downstairs in our farmhouse in "civilization."

Let's look at some real-life possibilities and what to do about them, assuming that there is no doctor or hospital available. Remember that if trained medical help is available, one should always consider this course first as many conditions can be made worse by incorrect diagnosis and treatment.

Hypothermia

Believe it or not, hypothermia (the condition where the body temperature is lowered below normal) kills more people in survival/stress situations than does gunfire, wild animal attacks, poisonous reptiles and spiders, wounds, or drowning.

Hypothermia has many causes, from shock following an accident to remaining outside in cold weather without adequate clothing or shelter to getting dunked in icy water—even for short periods of time. It is definitely something to watch for in any survival situation.

Identifying hypothermia can be a problem with the uninitiated, as it comes on slowly and the person still can walk and talk. But by paying careful attention, one can usually notice body shaking, paleness, and a tendency toward poor judgment and/or speech that doesn't make sense.

Taking the victim's temperature, you will quickly see that it is subnormal.

SUGGESTIONS FOR YOUR MEDICAL KIT (LARGE)

ITEMS	USES
thermometer	detecting fever
aspirin/Tylenol	fever/pain
zinc lozenges	head off colds/flu
cough/throat lozenges	comfort with colds
antifungal medication	fungus infections of the skin
antibiotic ointment	heal cuts/abrasions
eye medication	infections/irritations
oral expectorant	clear lungs, reduce coughing
burn medication, such as Burn Free	reduce severity and pain from burns
oral electrolytes	treats dehydration
rolls of 2" sterile gauze	covers wounds, control bleeding
several packs 2" sterile pads	covers wounds, gauze controls bleedng, holds medication in place
rolls of elastic leg wrap	supports sprains, holds meds in place controls bleeding, protects legs
rolls of sterile cotton	cleaning area, controls bleeding, etc.
alcohol, soap, Betadine	cleaning, disinfection, wound healing
oral antidiarrheals	treating moderate diarrhea
any family daily meds	maintaining health
oral antibiotics/sulfas	treating systemic or local infection
injectable antibiotics/sulfas	treating systemic or local infection
injectable ephinephrine	shock, as in drug allergy
injectable antihistamine	allergies; bee sting
surgical instruments, such as forceps, needle holder, scalpel w/blades, scissors, etc.	facilitate minor surgery
assorted sizes suture material; absorbable	allows suturing of gaping wounds
stethoscope	monitoring vital signs
sterile needles and syringes	giving injections
sterile IV kit (if experienced)	makes IV injections possible for severe dehydration
IV electrolytes	severe dehydration, shock
first-aid manual	instructions

Of course your family's personal medical kits (small, medium, and large) will probably contain different items, depending on your foreseeable needs, medical experience, and preferences. And you will probably think of many more items that would be provident to carry, especially in your large kit. There are no hard and fast rules, only suggestions. The main thing is to be prepared—and confident.

Hypothermia must be treated vigorously and immediately. Warmth is the key. As the body has lost its ability to warm itself, simply putting a blanket around the person is not enough. Build a warm fire. If the victim is wet, get them into warm dry clothes quickly. Warm a blanket or sleeping bag, then wrap it around them while they sit or lie in front of the fire. If they are not too bad, a drink of warm coffee or tea often helps. But do not give anything to eat or drink to a victim that is dazed or unconscious.

If nothing else is available, have one or more persons crawl into a sleeping bag or blankets to provide bodily warmth to the victim. Then keep the person warm and dry until they are fully recovered. You don't have to be a mountaineer to suffer hypothermia. I have had several encounters: falling through thin ice while crossing a beaver dam, getting stuck out in an unexpected blizzard in June, and getting drenched in the rain while making a mile and a half canoe portage in Minnesota's Boundary Waters. Hypothermia can be just plain uncomfortably miserable, but it can also kill.

Wounds

Most wounds that folks suffer in a survival situation are relatively minor, and though they may be uncomfortable and even bleeding, they are not usually life-threatening. The thing is not to panic. A little blood looks like a lot, especially when it is on yourself or a loved one.

If the wound is combined with possible other injuries, such as following a tumble down a rocky slope, you have to first assess the possible damage. Could there be a broken bone? A concussion? Internal injuries?

Don't panic. However, if you suspect such complications, do not move the injured party unless absolutely necessary, and then do it with great care.

Talk to the victim. He can usually tell you a lot about where he hurts and how much pain he is in. If the only injury seems to be the wound, reassure the victim and begin treatment.

Check the wound. Is it visibly dirty? Is the blood simply flowing from the wound or is it spurting? In survival situations, more people die from infected wounds than bleeding to death.

If the wound is relatively minor and the bleeding is minimal, you'll want to gently clean it before any attempt is made to bandage it. Nothing causes infection more than bandaging an unclean wound, even if it contains no visible dirt. Remember that deadly staph organisms are commonly found on human skin.

A good way to clean most wounds is to gently bathe the area with mild soap and water. Mop away from the wound, as one would sweep a floor, instead of scrubbing back and forth. The latter only moves bacteria around rather than removing it from the area. Rinse or soak the area well, removing any debris carefully with sterile tweezers.

When the area is clean, pat it dry with sterile gauze or air-dry it, then apply Betadine or antibiotic salve. We use Betadine for deeper wounds, and antibiotic salve for lesser injuries. Minor wounds seldom require bandaging, healing quicker by air exposure. Deeper wounds and ones in areas where they will be constantly irritated by clothing or work should be bandaged. A simple adhesive strip usually does the trick.

If the wound is bleeding quite a bit, simply applying pressure to the area with a sterile gauze pad will usually stop it within a few minutes. Where tourniquets were once advised, it has been found that more damage was done by the tourniquet than the bleeding would have caused in most instances. The application of firm pressure directly to the wound is very effective. After the severe bleeding has been stopped, gently clean the wound, but do not destroy the clot that has formed or bleeding will probably resume.

Should you be dealing with a more severe wound, covering it with a Betadine soaked (but not wet) sterile gauze, then a plain sterile gauze square, then adhesive tape is usually sufficient. If the edges of the wound gape or there is a flap of skin hanging down, either gently match the edges with butterfly adhesive strips or suture them, if you have the experience. Remember that most wounds will heal fine without suturing, especially with a little help from gentle butterfly adhesive strips. Sutures that are too tightly drawn will cause pain and scarring.

Never bandage a wound tightly with gauze bandage or anything else. This will restrict circulation and can cause pain and severe problems and even gangrene.

In the following days, keep the wound clean and dry. Change the dressing as needed, usually twice a day, leaving the dressing off and the area open to fresh air and sunlight as much as possible. This will greatly reduce the healing time and reduce chances of infection. Bacteria love damp, dark, warm areas, including a wound which is bandaged.

Watch for ugly redness or a fever in the patient, which would indicate infection in the wound. In this case, keep the area soaked in Betadine and give the patient antibiotics for 10 days, even if they seem better within a day or two. Immersing the infected wound in a hot Epsom salts solution also helps reduce pain and swelling along with cleansing the area.

Simple pain and swelling from the injury can be alleviated by plain aspirin, taken orally. Do not give aspirin immediately following an injury if there is a possibility of internal injuries, as aspirin may enhance hemorrhage. Do not give aspirin to young children. Use Ibuprofen instead.

Colds and flu

These common conditions are bad enough when things are fine, but are downright miserable in a survival situation. And remember that stress helps these overcome your body.

At the first sign of a cold or the flu, do those things your grandmother told you: keep warm and dry, rest, and drink plenty of fluids. Then add vitamin C and zinc lozenges, and most folks can overcome that mean cold or flu in a few days. If you need to alleviate symptoms, such as fever, runny nose, or coughing, take a cold/flu medication that covers your symptoms. By now, you probably know what works best for you and your children. The key is to have the medication on hand.

If the cold or flu lasts for longer than 10 days or seems to get worse, it may have turned into bronchitis or pneumonia, and antibiotics are necessary. Remember that home treatment is only for when no doctor or hospital is available.

Sprains

Believe it or not, sprains are one of the most common injuries in a survival situation. And often one of the most painful. The sprain can arise from walking over debris, logs, rocks, and even urban curbs. It can come from a fall or even an ankle turning over. (Your family will experience less sprains if they wear good, sturdy footwear, not flats or sandals. Ankle support is very important.)

When a sprain is new, immerse the affected part in cold water or apply ice packs to reduce pain and inflammation. I've found that when I take two plain aspirin immediately following such an injury that it greatly reduces both pain and inflammation later on.

If possible, rest the sprain, keeping it immobile and elevated for as long as reasonably possible. I continue taking the aspirin to keep down the inflammation. If you must move about, gently wrap the area with an elastic bandage to support it. Do not wrap area tightly or you will restrict circulation and make the pain much worse. Use a cane or crutches if the sprain is in a foot, ankle, or knee to reduce the amount of weight put on the injury. If the sprain is in the hand, wrist, elbow, or shoulder, keeping the arm in a sling will greatly reduce the pain and help it heal.

After a day, begin using hot Epsom salts soaks or packs to reduce the swelling and pain. And remember, the more you use a sprained joint, the longer it will take to heal and it may not ever heal completely if you persist ently use it before it heals. Rest is the key.

Slivers and spines

Getting a sliver or sticker of some kind is awfully common, especially in a survival situation, when one may be building a wood fire or foraging for food. Most of the time you can simply get hold of it and pull it out and be no worse for wear. But sometimes it is in too deep and painful and seemingly impossible to remove.

For relatively minor, but painful slivers, I use a sterile hypodermic needle, choosing the gauge (diameter/size) to fit the sliver size. Most smaller slivers are removed very easily with a 20-gauge needle. Now I use a hypodermic needle for several reasons, as opposed to using a sewing needle. First, and most important, they are hollow. This allows one to slip them into the sliver track with little pain, as less bulk is pressing on that tender skin. They are also sharp, which lets me carefully pick away the skin layer above the sliver which has no feeling because there are no nerves, until the sliver is exposed and can be either snagged with the needle and drawn out or picked up with a pair of sterile tweezers and removed.

With larger slivers, I use an 18-gauge needle, which does the same thing but is a bit stronger. When the sliver is very painful, using a local anesthetic, such as oral medication or antibiotic ointment containing an anesthetic on the area about 10 minutes before the procedure, helps a lot.

The main thing is to keep the sliver aligned with its track, and not to pry it upright in removal, which is extremely painful.

Once the sliver is out, a little alcohol or Betadine will disinfect the area and let it heal quickly.

I've discovered a great treatment for small stickers and cactus thorns which break off when you try to remove them from tender skin. Should you or a family member fall into a cactus or other plant with fine stickers, simply coat the area with *Shoe-Goo* or *Sportsman's-Goo*, which is a clear silicone-type product. Just a thin coat is fine. In about fifteen minutes it will be dry, and you can just peel it off, complete with all of the painful stickers.

Of course, there are many other possible injuries and illnesses. With a little advance preparation and study, you'll be surprised at what you can glide smoothly through. There is seldom any benefit to panic; a positive mental outlook can save lives. Δ

Chapter 19
What to do
when there's no doctor!

By Gary F. Arnet, D.D.S.

We are used to being able to see a doctor at any time for any reason, no matter how small. Will this always be the case? Not necessarily.

There are many scenarios in which access to medical care may be restricted. You could be on your own for a few days to a few weeks. All it takes is a major natural disaster, such as a blizzard, earthquake, or flood, a sustained power outage, or a terrorist attack to disrupt routine care. Doctor's offices and walk-in clinics will close. In a disaster with mass casualties, doctors will all be at hospitals dealing with the seriously injured.

New threats, such as biological or nuclear attacks, could cause hundreds of thousands of casualties. Unlikely? We all hope so. If one occurred, however, there may be regional or national quarantines and doctors from around the country will be sent to the affected area, causing shortages locally.

During any sustained natural or man-made disaster you may be doing things that you normally would not. Cutting or lifting firewood, cooking over an open fire, using a gasoline generator, working by flashlight, lifting sandbags, and any number of other activities may expose you to the chance of injuries or burns that you would normally not face. Improper food storage, sanitation problems, and contaminated water during a disaster can expose you to illness that you would not normally have to worry about.

Are you prepared for the many situations that could limit your availability to medical care? Many individuals and families are not. During one earthquake in southern California, people lined up outside hospitals for Band-Aids, while overworked staff struggled to deal with the seriously injured. Now is the time to prepare. You need to be able to take care of your own medical needs when no doctor is available.

The information presented here is intended to help you plan and prepare for the possibility that you might need to manage your own routine medical care and minor injuries if medical care is not available. It is not a substitute for seeking proper medical care when it is available.

In life-threatening situations, always seek medical care whether there is a disaster or not. Call 9-1-1 or your local emergency number for serious prob-

*Be prepared—You can't assume that help will arrive
in a crisis. Know first aid and have a family first aid kit
and medicines available before disaster strikes.*

lems such as a person who is unconscious, has trouble breathing, has chest
pain or pressure, is bleeding severely, is vomiting blood, has a seizure, severe
headache, or slurred speech, has injuries to the head, neck, or back, has possible broken bones, or appears to have been poisoned.

Preparing for the worst

Well before a disaster strikes, you need to prepare by having the knowledge
and supplies available to take care of yourself. Educate yourself in first aid
and medical care by taking a class in first aid and CPR, available through the
American Red Cross and other community organizations. Obtain first aid
books that you can refer to, if necessary. Many first aid and home care books
are available at your local bookstore or on the Internet. Several that cover a
wide spectrum of injuries and illnesses include *Community First Aid and
Safety* by the American Red Cross, the *Boy Scout Handbook* by the Boy
Scouts of America, *Wilderness 911* by Eric Weiss, M.D., and the *Mayo Clinic
Family Health Book.*

Next, have a good first aid kit and a stock of medicines that you might
need. You should have a first aid kit in every car and a larger family one at
home. You can buy a ready-made kit or make one up yourself. I prefer to
make my own so that I am sure it has what I need for every situation. It may

First aid supplies

Disposable gloves	Splint materials
Sterile gauze pads	Rolled elastic bandage (Ace
Rolled gauze bandages	wrap)
Tincture of benzoin	Triangular bandage
Steri-Strip wound closure strips	Adhesive tape
Butterfly bandages	Ice packs
Nonstick dressings (Telfa)	Eye wash
Spenco 2nd Skin	Dental first aid kit
Assorted sizes of Band-Aids	Tweezers
Polysporin antibiotic ointment	Bandage scissors

be more costly, but you can be confident that you have enough of the right materials.

Several variables will influence what your kit will contain, including your medical expertise, the distance to and availability of medical care, the number of people in your family, any preexisting medical conditions of family members, and your geographic location. For example, you would want a *Sawyer Extractor* for snakebites if you lived in Arizona, but not if you lived in Alaska.

To make your own first aid kit, use a list from one of your books and supplement it as needed. When I do this, I make a list of problems I might need to treat and then list the materials for each. For example, you will want materials to treat bleeding and lacerations, burns, sprains and fractures, and medicines for fever, pain, vomiting, diarrhea, coughing, and rashes. Include over-the-counter medications for any other problems you may have including heartburn medication, *Preparation H*, or *Milk of Magnesia*. Also, make sure you have an ample supply of any prescription medications that you take, along with a written copy of the prescription, which would be handy if your doctor is unavailable to authorize a refill. Depending on your situation and the remoteness of your location, you may want to ask your doctor about the advisability of having some prescription antibiotics and pain medicines in your family medicine kit.

Keep your first aid kit and medicines in a container or pack that you can easily grab in an evacuation and make sure everyone in the family knows its location.

Once you have your family medical supplies together, consider what health and sanitation problems you could be faced with in a disaster or survival situation. Where are you going to get water once you have used up any that you have stored? Will it be potable or could it be contaminated, needing to

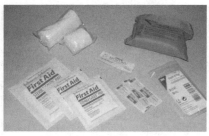

Your first aid kit should include materials to treat lacerations and bleeding. Some of the materials you will want include sterile gauze pads, pressure dressings, rolled gauze bandages, wound closure strips, antibiotic ointment, and Band-Aids.

be purified. What about food? How will you keep it from spoiling?

Sanitation is even more important in a disaster than other times. Diseases can be spread easily so be sure to have soap to wash hands and appropriate facilities to deal with human waste.

Finally, the healthier you are when a disaster or survival situation strikes, the greater the chance that you will survive. Exercise regularly, eat well, have preventative medical and dental care, and be happy.

When disaster strikes

Now that you are prepared, what do you do if a disaster occurs? First, stay calm and make sure to account for everyone. If in an unsafe area, move to safety. Treat any injuries and comfort those around you.

Once you are safe and injuries are treated, stop and think. How bad is your situation? What risks do you face? Is there a continued threat from the disaster? Can you expect outside help? How long will you likely need to depend on yourself? What shelter, food, water, medical, and other resources do you have available? Develop a well thought out plan of action.

Include preventative and safety measures for your food, water, sanitation, health, and safety. Accidents and injuries can occur during disasters as individuals are performing activities that they are not used to doing. You do not need to complicate your already difficult situation with injuries. Try to stay as healthy as possible, avoiding illness or injuries.

The remainder of this article will give you some ideas of common medical problems that you might be faced with. Again, it is recommended you take a course in first aid and not depend solely on this article.

Managing common injuries

Lacerations: Cuts (lacerations) are one of the most common injuries and can be caused by knives, broken glass, scissors, or falls. Deep cuts can damage blood vessels and nerves.

The first step in treating a cut is to stop the bleeding. While wearing a disposable latex or nitrile glove, place several sterile gauze pads over the cut and apply pressure directly over the wound for at least five minutes. Most bleeding can be stopped this way. Sometimes pressure may need to be held for up

Medications

Analgesics (pain medicines)	Poisoning
Ibuprofen	Syrup of Ipecac
Aspirin	Rash and itching
Tylenol	Benadryl tablets
Fever	Hydrocortisone cream
Tylenol	Cough medicine
Antidiarrheal	Earache drops
Imodium or Lomotil	Eye drops
Antinausea	Other over-the-counter medi-
Pepto-Bismol	cines you use
Mylanta	Prescription medications

to 30 minutes. Nasal sprays that contain blood vessel constrictors, such as *NeoSynephrine* or *Afrin*, can help stop minor bleeding. Moisten a sterile gauze pad with the spray and pack it into the wound for five minutes before removing.

After the bleeding has stopped, clean the wound to remove bacteria, dirt, blood clot, and damaged tissue. Use a 10 to 15-ml syringe filled with water to rinse the wound. This works like a high-pressure squirt gun to clean the wound of debris. Inspect the wound to make sure all particles of dirt or dried blood are gone, as they will be a source of infection.

Some wounds need to be stitched (sutured) by a doctor to help the healing process, improve the appearance of scars, and reduce the chance of infection. A general rule of thumb is to stitch any wound over an inch long or one where the edges of the skin do not fall together. Any wounds that show bone or muscle, are large or deep, involve joints, hands, or feet, or that could leave conspicuous scars, such as those on the face, should be seen by a doctor.

If wounds do not need to be stitched or if medical care is not available, they can be closed with wound closure tape strips, such as *Steri-Strips*, or butterfly bandages. Apply a thin layer of tincture of benzoin to the skin on each side of the wound and let it dry for 30 seconds. Apply the tape to the skin on one side of the cut, gently pull the wound closed so the skin edges just touch, and attach the tape to the skin on the other side. The tape should extend about one inch on each side of the wound. Apply more strips of tape about ¼ inch apart until the entire wound is closed.

After closing the wound, place a non-adherent dressing, such as *Telfa* or *Adaptic*, over the wound to keep it clean, followed by an absorbent gauze, and, finally, an elastic bandage or rolled gauze bandage to keep the dressings in place. Check the wound daily for infection, which will present as increased pain, redness, swelling, pus, or greenish drainage from the wound. If infec-

For sprains and fractures, splinting materials should be part of your first aid kit. Shown here are a SAM splint, wire splint, foam-board splint, finger splints, triangular bandage, elastic bandages, and adhesive tape.

tion develops, seek medical care since antibiotics may be necessary.

Strains, sprains, and fractures: Injuries to the bones, muscles, and joints are common. Sprains are stretching or tearing of ligaments that attach bones together and strains are tearing or stretching of muscles or their tendons that attach them to bones. The ankle and knee are the joints most often sprained. Muscle strains from overexertion or lifting are common, with back strains being particularly disabling.

Pain or tenderness at the site, swelling, bruising, and pain on movement of the injured area are signs of a strain or sprain. These are also present with a fractured bone and it may be difficult to distinguish between fractures and strains or sprains.

Standard treatment for any sprain or athletic injury is summarized by the acronym RICE—rest, ice, compression, and elevation. Take the stress off the injured area by resting to prevent further damage to the ligaments or muscles. Apply ice early to reduce the swelling and pain. It should be used for up to 20 minutes 3 to 4 times per day. Swelling will return once the ice is removed unless a compression wrap is used. Place padding, such as gauze or socks, over a sprained joint and wrap with an elastic bandage. It should be comfortably tight and loosened if there is increased pain, numbness, or tingling. Elevate the injured area to reduce swelling. Continue the RICE treatment for the first 72 hours. After that, tape or splint the injured area to stabilize it and prevent further injury.

Non-steroidal anti-inflammatory medications, such as ibuprofen *(Motrin)* 600 mg. three times a day with food, can be taken to reduce both inflammation and pain.

Bone fractures are characterized by pain, swelling, bruising, deformity, the inability to put weight on or use the injured part normally, or the grating sound of bones rubbing against each other. The injured person may have heard a snapping or popping sound at the time of the injury.

Sometimes it can be difficult to tell the difference between a fracture and sprain without an x-ray. All known or suspected fractures require medical evaluation. Unstable or displaced fractures should be stabilized with a splint by emergency medical personnel or, if not available, by first aid methods before transport to a doctor hospital.

Back injuries: Muscle strains from overexertion or lifting heavy objects are the most common cause of acute back pain. Pain can be mild or so severe that the injured person is unable to sit or stand. Generally, the pain is worsened by bending, moving, or touching the area and made better by lying flat with the knees bent or supported by a pillow.

Bed rest is the initial treatment. Have the injured person lie on their back with a pillow under the knees, or on their side with a pillow between their legs for 1 to 2 days, while taking anti-inflammatory medications such as ibuprofen 600 mg three times a day with meals. Ice packs will reduce swelling and decrease pain.

After two days, resume gentle activity as longer bed rest can slow recovery. Most people with back strains recover on their own in 2 to 4 weeks.

Ruptured (herniated) disks are ruptures of the cartilage discs in between the vertebrae of the back. Heavy lifting can cause discs to rupture and put pressure on the spinal nerves causing pain which can radiate down the buttock and leg (sciatica). The pain is worse with sitting, bending forward, coughing, and lifting the leg. Numbness or tingling of the leg may occur. Treatment is initially the same as a back strain, however the injured person should seek medical care.

Severe back pain that is not made worse with movement or change of position can be a sign of a serious abdominal problem, including a kidney stone or kidney infection. Seek medical care.

Burns: Burns can be caused by heat, flames, chemicals, or by electricity. The severity of the burn depends on the temperature of the heat source, the length of time of exposure, the size of the burn, and the location on the body. First-degree burns, such as minor sunburns, injure the first layer of skin and cause redness and pain. Second-degree burns injure deeper layers of skin, causing blisters. Third-degree burns destroy the skin and burn into deeper tissue layers or muscle and are very serious. They can look charred, black, or brown and may be painless if nerve endings have been burned. When burns damage the integrity of the skin, the body loses fluid and is susceptible to infection.

The first thing to do to care for burns is to stop the burning. Put out flames on clothing and cool the burned area with large amounts of cool water for several minutes. Cover the burned area with dry, sterile dressings to help prevent infection. Don't apply any type of ointment or burn cream as it seals in heat and does little to reduce pain. Blisters should be left unbroken to prevent infection.

Critical burns require immediate medical care. An ambulance should be called for burns that are large, involve breathing difficulty, are on the head, neck, feet, or genitals, cover more than one part of the body, or result from chemicals, explosions, or electricity. Stop the burning, cover the burned area to prevent infection, and keep the victim from becoming chilled while you wait for the ambulance.

Managing common illnesses

Bad Water: Drink water that you have stored and know is safe. If that is not available, you can collect rainwater, which is safe to drink without purifying. If you use water from other sources, you must purify it before drinking.

Water taken from natural sources such as rivers, streams, and lakes may be contaminated with protozoan parasites, such as Giardia and Cryptosporidium, or bacteria, such as E. coli and Salmonella. Wells that have been in flood waters may also become contaminated with these organisms. City water supplies occasionally become contaminated and there is a potential threat of terrorists attacking our water supplies.

Boiling water is an effective way to kill Giardia and other waterborne diseases. Water above 185°F (85°C) will kill all microorganisms within a few minutes. Therefore, in the time it takes water to boil at 212°F (100°C) all potential disease-producing organisms will be killed. While an excellent method of purifying water, the problem with boiling water for drinking is that it takes a long time and considerable fuel, especially if you are with a large group.

Iodine and chlorine products have long been used to chemically treat contaminated water both in the wilderness and in municipal water supply systems. Iodine products, such as *Polar Pure* and *Potable Aqua* work well against Giardia, the most common contaminant, but are not effective against Cryptosporidium. Chlorine based products, such as halazone tablets and liquid chlorine (unscented chlorine bleach) may be used to purify water for people with iodine allergies or restrictions, although they are less effective than iodine products in treating water infected with Giardia. Follow manufacturer recommendations for any of these products.

A convenient way to purify water is with a commercial backpacking-type water filter that is designed to catch disease-producing microorganisms. Water is pumped through a microscopic screen that filters out microorganisms of a certain size. It would be worth having one with your emergency preparedness supplies.

Drinking bacteria or parasites in contaminated water will often produce a syndrome of diarrhea, gas, and abdominal cramping, in the case of Giardia beginning about 7 to 10 days after exposure. Nausea, loss of appetite, tiredness, vomiting, and weight loss may also occur.

Seek medical care if you have such symptoms for over 24 hours. Antibiotics, such as Flagyl 250mg three times per day for seven days used for Giardia infections, can cure the problem.

Diarrhea: Diarrhea is frequent (more than three a day) loose stools that can be caused from viral illnesses, bacteria from bad water or food, parasites from bad water, food allergies, inflammatory bowel disease, and anxiety. Abdominal cramps, nausea, vomiting, fever, and fatigue may also be present. No treatment may be necessary if it lasts only 1 to 2 days. Diarrhea may be serious if it lasts longer or if there are more than 10 bowel movements a day. In severe diarrhea, up to 25 quarts of water can be lost in a day, rapidly leading to dehydration.

For diarrhea lasting more than three days or when accompanied by blood or mucous in the stool, fever greater than 101°F, severe abdominal pain or distension, or dehydration, the victim needs medical care for intravenous fluids and treatment of the underlying cause.

If these are not present, treat diarrhea by rehydrating the victim with water and electrolytes to replace lost salts, potassium, and bicarbonate. Oral rehydration salts containing the proper electrolytes are available commercially. Anti-diarrheal medications, such as *Imodium,* can reduce cramping and fluid loss. *Imodium* has fewer potential side effects than *Lomotil. Pepto-Bismol* and *Kaopectate* can also be used, but are less effective.

Dehydration: Dehydration is water loss greater than the amount the body needs to maintain its balance. It occurs when lost water is not adequately replaced and it decreases the ability of doing even the simplest of activities. Dehydration will also increase the chance of severe shock if an individual is injured.

Normally, the body needs 2 to 3 quarts of water a day to maintain normal balance. Sweating from heat, exercise, or work increases the amount of water loss dramatically. In conditions of heavy activity, 5 to 6 quarts (1½ gallons) or more can be needed per day.

By the time an individual is thirsty, they are already dehydrated. A 5% loss of body water, only 2.5 quarts for a 150-pound person, will cause thirst, irritability, nausea, and weakness. A 10% loss, 5 quarts for the same person, will result in headache, dizziness, inability to walk, and tingling sensations of the arms and legs. A swollen tongue, dim vision, numb sensations on the skin, and painful urination can occur with a 15% loss of water and any greater can cause death.

It is easy to forget to drink or to have inadequate water available during a crisis situation. Dehydration is largely preventable, so plan your daily water needs.

Treatment for dehydration is to replace the lost fluids. Replace fluids by drinking water, juice, lemonade, soup, decaffeinated coffee, *Gatorade*, or similar sports drinks.

Vomiting: Many things can cause vomiting, including food poisoning, stomach flu, viral illness, motion sickness, anxiety, pregnancy, and irritants to the stomach such as medications. Drink small amounts of clear liquid such as soup, tea, *7-Up*, or diluted *Gatorade*. Be careful not to drink too much too soon, which will distend the stomach and cause more vomiting. Once vomiting has stopped, bland food such as toast or crackers may be started, progressing to a normal diet as tolerated.

Medical care should be sought for vomiting that is associated with head or abdominal injury, fatigue or confusion, severe abdominal pain or distention, fever over 101°F, fresh or dried blood in the vomit, or if it lasts over 24 hours. The source of the vomiting needs to be determined and prescription anti-emetic (anti-vomiting) drugs are available.

Take care of yourself

Our ancestors had to depend on themselves to treat most of their medical problems. Despite our excellent access to health care, we also may be faced with such situations. Be prepared by staying healthy and fit, learning first aid and CPR, having family medical books available, and by having a well-stocked first aid kit and medicines available. Take the time now to prepare. Your life may depend on it. Δ

Chapter 20
No dentist? Oh, no!

By Gary F. Arnet D.D.S.

Enjoying lunch while looking out over the gorgeous view from your backcountry home, you bite down hard on a nut, hear a loud crack, and immediately feel excruciating pain from a broken tooth. Rare? No, it occurs all the time.

Dental emergencies can occur at home or in the wilderness without warning and can incapacitate a person in an instant. "No problem, I'll get right over to the dentist," you think. Hopefully, that is possible, but not always. You may live some distance from a dentist, it may be a night or weekend when it is hard to find one, or there may not be any available.

One of the first things that stop during a disaster is dental care. Major natural disasters, such as earthquakes, fires, or floods, and human disasters, such as terrorism or riots, close dental offices in a second. Electrical shortages, as seen in California recently, or any disruption of the regional power grids and there is no help since dentists can't operate without electricity. Hospitals rarely have any dental services, so you could be on your own for hours or days.

Since dental first aid is rarely taught in first aid classes, information presented here is intended to help you in an emergency situation when no professional dental help is available. It is not intended to be a substitute for proper dental care.

Prevention

Living in a rural area, avid hunter, fisherman, and dentist Dr. Kenneth Lund has much experience with dental emergencies. "Nothing can ruin a good hunting trip like a toothache," Dr. Lund says. "Anyone going on an extended trip, say over a week, should make sure they are current with their dental check-ups." This is good advice for everyone, whether traveling or staying at home.

A routine visit to the dentist can prevent many painful dental problems. Professional cleanings help prevent gum infections. Fillings that are starting to fail can be fixed before breaking at an inconvenient time. A small cavity in a tooth that causes no pain can be easily repaired before it does.

Proper care of teeth is important. Brush and floss teeth regularly to avoid cavities and gum infections. This is especially important during a time of

A toothache is the last thing you need when no dentist is available. Basic knowledge of dental first aid and a few things added to your first aid kit will help you until you can find professional help.

crisis, such as a disaster or evacuation. While brushing is the last thing on your mind, gingivitis or gum infections are more frequent during times of emotional and physical stress, especially when coupled with poor oral hygiene.

A toothbrush with toothpaste is always the best way to clean your teeth. If one is not available or you find yourself in an emergency survival situation, clean your teeth in other ways. A wash cloth or towel can be used to remove the soft, sticky, bacteria-laden plaque that develops on the surface of the teeth. The end of a thin green twig from a non-poisonous tree or bush can be used. Chew it until it is soft and fibery and use this end as a brush to clean the teeth and gums. Even your finger will work if nothing else is available.

Dental first aid kit

The first time I needed to treat a broken tooth while backpacking, I opened my first aid kit and there was nothing that would help. I'll bet yours is the same. A few small, lightweight items available at a drug store or market can be added to your first aid kit to treat dental emergencies. I recommend the following:

Dental floss
Soft dental or orthodontic wax
Cotton pellets
Tempanol or Cavit temporary filling material
Oil of cloves (eugenol)
Small dental tweezers

When working in the mouth, remember to always wear protective gloves from your first aid kit to prevent the spread of infectious diseases.

Toothache

A toothache is caused by the inflammation of the nerve inside a tooth, called the dental pulp. Decay from a cavity that extends into the pulp can

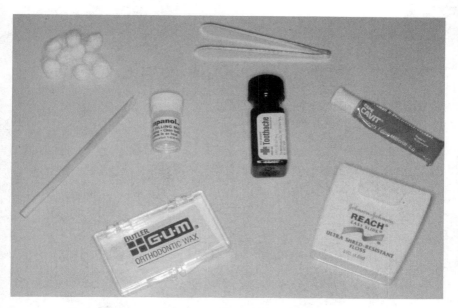

*Dental items to add to your first aid kit: Cavit or Tempanol
temporary filling material, eugenol or benzocaine-based toothache medicine,
cotton pellets, small tweezers, small tool for placing filling material,
soft dental wax, and dental floss.*

cause a toothache, as can a fracture of the tooth. If infection occurs in the tooth, it can cause excruciating pain and can spread through the root of the tooth into the jaw causing an abscess.

Symptoms of a toothache include pain in a certain tooth or over several teeth. At first, the pain may be mild, intermittent, and made worse with hot or cold foods or drink, cold air, and the pressure of biting. As it progresses, the pain may become constant, excruciating, and incapacitating.

Sometimes, an abscessed tooth will slowly drain infection into a large cavity. After a meal, when food is packed into the cavity, the drainage may be blocked and the pressure will increase in the tooth causing the toothache to become worse until the food is cleaned out.

Treatment of a toothache consists of locating the painful tooth and checking for any obvious cavity or fracture. Clean out any food with a toothbrush, toothpick, or similar tool. Then soak a small cotton pellet or, if not available, a small piece of cloth, in a topical anesthetic, such as a eugenol or benzocaine solution. This should then be placed in the cavity. A small pair of dental tweezers, like the type provided in commercial toothache kits, tick removing tweezers, or a small instrument like a toothpick is helpful in placing the cot-

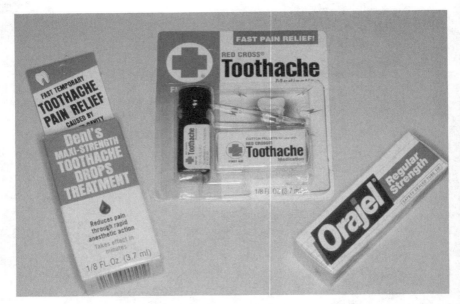

Over-the-counter toothache medicines will help ease the pain from a toothache or broken tooth. Many are available, including those containing eugenol (oil of cloves), such as Red Cross Toothache Medicine, benzocaine, such as Orajel, and those containing both, such as Dent's Toothache Drops.

ton as it is often hard to get your fingers into the mouth. This topical anesthetic should give quick relief.

The type of topical anesthetic used is important. Dentists use pure eugenol for emergency treatment of toothaches since it is long-lasting, but this can be difficult to find. Oil of cloves is the same thing and is available without prescription at pharmacies and some health food stores. Be careful, however, as pure oil of cloves can cause chemical burns to the mouth and tongue if it gets off the tooth.

Commercial toothache medications that are available include *Red Cross Toothache Medicine* containing 85% eugenol, *Dent's Toothache Drops* containing benzocaine and eugenol, and *Orajel* containing benzocaine. Some products include the small dental tweezers and cotton pellets that you will need.

Once the medicated cotton is in place, cover it with a temporary filling material, such as *Tempanol* or *Cavit* to prevent it from falling out. These are all soft, putty-like materials that can be molded into the cavity. If they are not available, soft dental wax or softened wax from a candle can be used. If a candle is used, melt some wax and let it cool until it is pliable before placing in the mouth.

A pain medication, such as 800mg *Motrin* every 8 hours, or prescription pain medicines, such as *Vicodin*, 1-2 every four to six hours, can be used if available. Do not place aspirin on the gum next to a painful tooth. Not only doesn't it help, it causes a large, painful burn to the gum tissue.

Seek help from a dentist immediately. If it takes some time to find one, it may be necessary to replace the cotton pellet with another freshly soaked in topical anesthetic.

Gingivitis

Gingivitis is an inflammation of the gums (gingiva) most commonly due to inadequate tooth brushing. Gums become red, swollen, and may bleed while brushing the teeth. It is largely preventable by good oral hygiene and regular dental check-ups. When gingivitis causes pain and bleeding in the field, improve oral hygiene by brushing three times per day, followed by warm salt-water rinses. Over-the-counter anti-bacterial mouthwashes may also help.

Dental abscess

An infected tooth or gum infection (gingival infection) can cause a dental abscess, also known as a pus pocket. Food lodged between the teeth can also do so if not removed with dental floss.

Abscesses are normally located next to the offending tooth and cause pain and swelling. They can spread beyond the tooth to the face, floor of the mouth, or neck and it may be difficult to open the mouth or swallow. On rare occasions, dental abscesses can become life-threatening by getting so large that they block breathing or by causing fever or generalized infection throughout the body. Deal with any abscess immediately.

Antibiotics are required to treat abscesses. Go to a dentist immediately. If one is not available or if there is severe swelling go to a physician or hospital emergency room. When dental or medical help is not available and the situation is an emergency, oral antibiotics, such as penicillin 500 mg every six hours, can be given, after making sure the person is not allergic to the medication.

Warm salt-water rinses of the mouth every four hours may help the abscess to spontaneously drain, giving some relief of the pain. Do not place hot packs to the outside of the face unless directed to by your dentist or physician, as heat can spread the infection outward. Pain medications may be used as described above.

In the rare situation where no professional help is expected to be available for some time and no antibiotics are available, an abscess that is localized next to a tooth can be drained to remove the pus. A sterile scalpel, needle, or a fishhook (with the barb removed and disinfected by heating with a match) may be used to puncture the abscess. It will be painful to do, but there should be immediate relief from the abscess.

Broken filling or lost crown

Biting down on candy, nuts, ice cubes, and other hard or sticky foods are common ways to break a tooth or filling. If the tooth is not painful, be careful not to break it further during eating and see a dentist as soon as possible.

A temporary filling can be placed to prevent the tooth from becoming sensitive to hot or cold and to avoid food from packing into the hole left by the filling. Place a small amount of a temporary filling material, such as *Tempanol* or *Cavit*, into the hole in the tooth using a dental instrument or a flat tool such as the blade of a knife, popsicle stick, or similar tools. Have the person bite down on the temporary material to form it to their bite and then have them open their mouth and remove any excess material. These materials will harden some and remain in place. Soft wax also can be used in the same manner as filling a cavity described above.

Crowns (caps) can be pulled off teeth by sticky foods, such as caramel and salt-water taffy. If the tooth is not sensitive to hot or cold, save the crown and see a dentist as soon as convenient.

If the tooth is so sensitive that it prevents the person from eating, it may be necessary to replace it temporarily. Do this only if really necessary, as this is only a temporary solution and there is a risk that the crown could come off and be swallowed. Clean out any dry cement or material from the inside of the crown with a dental instrument or knife. Place a thin layer of temporary filling material, denture adhesive, or even a thick mixture of water and flour inside the crown. Making sure the crown is aligned properly on the tooth, have the person gently bite down to seat the crown all the way and see a dentist as soon as possible.

Injuries to teeth

A fall or blow to the mouth can injure teeth, most commonly the upper front teeth. Teeth may be in a normal position, but loose when touched, may be partially out of the socket or pushed back, or may be completely knocked out. Unless it is completely knocked out, the first thing you should do is see a dentist.

When one is not available within a reasonable time, a tooth that is out of place may be repositioned with steady, gentle pressure to bring it back into proper position. If it is very loose, gently biting on a piece of gauze can help hold it in place. A dentist should be seen as soon as possible, as the tooth may need to be splinted to hold it in place until healing occurs.

When a tooth is completely knocked out (avulsed), what you do in the first 30 minutes determines whether the tooth can be saved. The ligaments that hold a tooth into the jaw are torn along with the nerve and blood vessels when it is knocked out of its socket and it is essentially a "dead tooth." When re-implanted into the tooth socket within 30 minutes the body will usually accept it and the ligaments will reattach. While it will require a root canal to remove the dead nerve and blood vessels, it will be a functioning tooth.

Over 30 minutes before it is re-implanted and the body treats it like foreign material and slowly dissolves the root over a period of weeks to months. Often the tooth needs to be extracted.

To treat an avulsed tooth, find the tooth on the ground or in the person's mouth. If the socket is bleeding, have the person bite down on gauze pads placed over the top of the socket. A moistened non-herbal tea bag may also be used.

Check the tooth to make sure it is whole and not broken. Handling the tooth only by the crown, the part that normally shows in the mouth, clean off any dirt or debris by gently rinsing the tooth with sterile saline, disinfected water, or milk. It is important that you do not touch the thin, whitish colored layer of soft tissue covering the root. This is the important layer of periodontal ligament that will allow the tooth to reattach. Replace the tooth into the tooth socket and with gentle, steady pressure push it into place. Have the person bite down lightly on a piece of gauze to hold it in place and see a dentist immediately to have the tooth stabilized.

If a tooth cannot be immediately re-implanted, it should be wrapped in gauze and soaked in a container of sterile saline solution, milk, or the injured person's saliva while they are immediately taken to a dentist. Some recommend keeping the tooth moist by placing it in the victim's mouth. This does work, but the tooth can also accidentally be swallowed.

Dental emergencies are more common than most people realize. While you most often will be able to obtain help from a dentist, there are times when you may be on your own. Prevention, knowledge, and a few important items in a dental first aid kit can save you and your family during these times. Δ

Chapter 21
Caring for wounds in the field

By Bill Glade, M.D.

The beautiful remote Canadian lake has provided a bountiful supply of fresh fish. You are cleaning the catch when a moment's inattention allows the knife to slip and create a deep slash into your leg. The bleeding is stopped with pressure; but now what do you do? Where is that kit with the medical instruments? When did you last check them for sterility? Where is that book on emergency medicine and exactly how do you make those sutures?

There is a common misconception that wounds need to be closed in order to heal. Texts on wilderness medicine will include sections on suturing techniques and equipment. They list recommended instruments, suture materials, and methods of making stitches. Unfortunately they don't mention that suturing is an acquired skill and not easy to do, especially on yourself. Also, anyone who is planning to suture every laceration or wound that occurs in a remote location had also better learn the signs of several interesting wild creatures such as *clostridium tetani* (tetanus), *clostridium perfringens* (gas gangrene), *staphylococcus, streptococcus,* and *pseudomonas.*

Surgeons divide wounds into four categories: **clean, clean-contaminated, contaminated,** and **dirty/infected.** The differences between each class are determined by the amount of bacterial contamination expected in the wound.

The first two categories are for patients in a hospital. A clean wound occurs when prepared (cleansed) skin is opened in a controlled fashion and no internal organs are entered. Hernia repair is a good example. Clean-contaminated wounds also happen in operating rooms, as when an internal organ is operated upon under controlled circumstances, often with antibiotic coverage. A good example is an appendectomy.

Contaminated wounds include open fresh traumatic injuries or surgery with bacterial contamination from an internal organ. Slashing your hand with the same knife you have been using to clean fish or game would be a good example of the former.

Dirty and infected wounds contain dead tissue, pus, foreign material (e.g. wood, grass, etc.), gross contamination (e.g. dirt, manure) or are contaminated wounds that have received no treatment in the first hours after injury.

The classification system is useful because it predicts the chance of an injured area becoming infected. Infection rates by classification are:

- clean: 1.5-3.9%
- clean contaminated: 3.0-4.0%
- contaminated: 8.5%
- dirty wounds: 28-40%

Obviously, the dirtier your wound the greater likelihood of a subsequent infection. This is especially true if you suture up the wound and trap the contamination inside. Bacteria in a warm, closed space feed on bloody injured tissue and are able to multiply rapidly. Using chemical bulldozers they are able to spread into the surrounding healthy tissues causing an infected wound that is red and drains pus. If drainage doesn't occur they can spread through tissue planes causing fasciitis, the so-called flesh eating disease, or spread throughout your entire body causing fatal infection.

With proper cleansing and antibiotics a contaminated wound can frequently be closed without infection but even surgeons in a hospital will usually leave a dirty wound open initially. This allows the fluid and bacteria to drain from the wound and antibiotics to kill the invading bacteria. After the wound has been repeatedly cleansed and treated with antibiotics, closure can be accomplished with little chance of infection.

Within six hours

The following are suggestions for treatment of a wound which occurs when you are some distance from medical care. They are based on one easy question:

Can you get to qualified medical care within six hours?

If the answer is yes I would recommend:

a) Stop the bleeding with pressure on the wound.
b) Once bleeding has stopped, gently clean out any gross debris, such as wood particles and rocks, but don't do it so vigorously that it restarts the bleeding. Also remember that this area may be very painful so don't torture yourself or your injured companion. If you carry local anesthetics in your medical supply kit now is the time to use them. You can inject with a needle but it can also be effectively used by dripping some into the wound. When it numbs the site a little, wet a gauze with the rest and place it in the wound. After a few minutes the wound will be less painful and easier to clean.
c) Place a sterile gauze or clean piece of cloth into the opening and wrap the site with gauze or an ace wrap. If it is near a joint, try to immobilize the joint to prevent further bleeding and pain.
d) Transport expeditiously to a hospital. Don't take any antibiotics unless it is going to be a long trip. The hospital personnel will likely sample the wound for bacteria and prescribe appropriate antibiotics. If

you have a long transport and carry antibiotics, cephalexin or cipro-floxacin would be good choices.

e) If there hasn't been a lot of blood loss and the person isn't nauseated, give them some pain medication for the trip.

Over six hours

If you cannot get to medical care in six hours or are in a really isolated area:

a) Stop the bleeding by pressure on the wound.

b) Once bleeding has stopped, gently clean out any gross debris, such as wood particles and rock, but don't do it so vigorously that it restarts the bleeding. In this circumstance try harder to physically remove the materials. If you have access to a lot of water, irrigate the area thor-oughly. The water won't be sterile but shouldn't be grossly dirty or contaminated. Again, do not clean so vigorously that you restart any bleeding, and make use of any local anesthetics as directed above.

c) Place sterile gauze or clean cloth into the wound as deep as you can without causing undue pain. Cover the site with more gauze pads, and wrap the site with gauze or an ace wrap. If it is near a joint, try to immobilize the joint to prevent further bleeding and pain.

d) This wound will seep a lot of fluid and the dressing may need to be changed frequently in the first 48 hours. Make an effort to cleanse the site with water and then replace the gauze pack. Removing the pack will help to remove a lot of the debris that you couldn't easily get out initially. After several days the wound will not be nearly as painful and the dressing change will be easier to do.

e) If you have antibiotics go ahead and take them in this circumstance. Topical antibiotic ointments such as *Bacitracin, Triple Antibiotic,* or *Bactroban* could also be helpful. I would place some on the gauze that is placed into the wound.

If there has been extensive blood loss, an open fracture exists, or there are other serious associated injuries (head, chest, abdomen) begin expeditious transport to medical assistance or use any available communication to sum-mon help to the scene.

If this is simply a contaminated laceration and you have adequate dressing supplies, you may continue to treat the wound in an open fashion. It will heal on its own in two to four weeks. It may leave a wider scar than desired, but you can later find a plastic surgeon who will revise it.

I recently watched a movie called *The Professional* in which our hit man/hero bravely dealt with a gunshot wound in his chest. In true Rambo fashion, lacking anesthesia, he sutured up the bleeding edges and continued his fight. He was later killed by the bad (worse) guys saving a surgical team the need to try and save him from his infected wound. A bullet containing oil and gunpowder passing through cloth and dirty skin creates a grossly contaminated wound. Closing the skin over trapped blood, dead tissue, and foreign material creates a buffet table for bacteria. Don't make the same mistake. Pack it open, avoid the infection, and let it heal cleanly. Δ

Chapter 22
Smallpox vaccine

By Dave Duffy

A t the start of 2003 the United States began the vaccination against smallpox of half a million health care workers so America can respond to a possible terrorist smallpox attack. It is only the beginning of a plan to vaccinate millions of Americans, beginning with health care workers and the military. The fear is that terrorists, and possibly Iraq, have acquired the deadly and disfiguring smallpox virus and intend to use it against us.

Many people may think no sane human being would consider using a disease like smallpox as a weapon. After all, even the diabolical Nazis of World War II possessed nerve agents and biological weapons but refrained from using them, even as they were bombed into obliteration during the last months of the war. But think again. According to many muslim terrorists, it is God's will that America the Infidel be destroyed.

It is not an unheard of rationale. In at least one documented case during the conquest of the Americas, a British colonel deliberately distributed smallpox infected blankets to Indians, which led to an epidemic among them. And during the Spanish conquest of the Aztecs, which coincided with another smallpox epidemic among the Indians, a Spanish priest wrote in his diary: "Thank you heavenly Father for sending this plague to destroy our enemies." There is even some evidence that the British tried to spread smallpox among the Colonists, and during America's own Civil War, there is an undocumented report of a Confederate supplying unsuspecting Union soldiers with smallpox infected blankets.

Man, historically, has always justified his most reprehensible actions, and muslim crusaders will have no problem justifying a smallpox attack against us.

What is smallpox?

Smallpox is a highly contagious disease caused by the variola virus, which is an orthopox virus in the same family as monkeypox, mousepox, camelpox, rabbitpox, and cowpox. Cowpox is used to make smallpox vaccine, called vaccinia.

Smallpox no longer exists as a naturally occurring disease, having been wiped out by the World Health Organization's (WHO) worldwide smallpox eradication program in the 1960s and 70s. But for thousands of years, since it first appeared about 12,000 years ago in settlements in northeast Africa, small-pox had been one of the most feared of plagues, killing hundreds of millions of people, decimating whole civilizations, and not even sparing kings. The mummy of the great Egyptian pharaoh Ramses V, who died in 1156 BC, bears the distinc-tive smallpox scarring on his face, and the Roman Emperor Marcus Aurelius was killed by smallpox in a plague that

Man with smallpox. Smallpox has been eliminated thanks to vaccines.

killed millions in the Roman Empire about 180 AD. In the last decades of the 18th century smallpox killed 400,000 Europeans a year, including four reign-ing monarchs, and in the 20th century the disease killed an estimated 300-500 million people. By comparison, wars in the 20th century, which was history's bloodiest century for warfare, killed 111 million people.

Historically smallpox has killed 30% of its victims, although that number has been higher in very susceptible populations. The New World populations of Indians had never experienced smallpox so were very susceptible. Between 1580 and 1620 smallpox reduced the Aztec population of Mexico from about 20 million to less than 2 million, after Spanish conquistadors had inadvertently introduced it there, and smallpox is the main suspect in reduc-ing the overall North American Indian population from about 100 million at the time of Columbus's arrival to about 10 million a mere 50 years later.

How is it spread?

Smallpox is normally spread through direct contact with an infected per-son, and transmission of the virus occurs when a person inhales a virus-containing airborne droplet of an infected person's saliva. But it can also spread from contact with an infected person's fluids, clothing, and bedding. It is not spread by animals or insects.

The virus is very stable and will survive for months in an infected person's clothing and bedding, even dried in the dust in his sick room, in the form of viral material from the smallpox pustules or from the pustules' crusted scabs. These are much less infectious than the airborne droplets, but infected cloth-ing and bed linens have historically been a source of smallpox outbreaks in Europe.

Smallpox victims are infectious with the onset of rash, which occurs 2-4 days after the onset of fever, which occurs 10-14 days after initial exposure to the disease. Victims are most infectious during the initial week (after

Smallpox lesions at day 17 of rash on a 5-year-old convalescing

development of rash) when they develop lesions in the mucous membranes of the mouth, tongue, larynx, pharynx, and upper part of the esophagus. The victim sheds part of the lesions in airborne water droplets during this period. As the lesions develop on the skin, the person remains infectious to a declining degree until the lesions turn to scabs and the scabs fall off.

Types of smallpox

There are three types of smallpox, **ordinary**, **flat, and hemorrhagic**, that can occur in unvaccinated persons, plus a fourth type, **modified**, that can occur in previously vaccinated people.

1) Ordinary smallpox (Variola major): This is by far the most common type. Once exposed to **ordinary** smallpox, it takes from 7-17 days for symptoms to appear. (The average incubation time is 12-14 days.) Then symptoms are flu-like, progressing from a high fever, cough, and fatigue to headache, backache, and other body aches with occasional vomiting and disorientation. After two to four days of these symptoms, the fever peaks and begins to decline, ushering in a rash that develops into hard painful lesions. The lesions appear first on the mucous membranes and pharynx, then on the face, forearms, and hands. Within a day or two, the trunk and lower limbs, including the palms of the hands and soles of the feet, also become involved with the rash. The rash lasts for about two weeks and becomes most pronounced on the face, forearms, and lower legs. At the end of 14 days the lesions, which by now have developed into hard raised painful sores called pustules, begin to dry up and crust over. By about day 19 the scabs begin falling off, with the scabs on the palms and soles falling off last. The resulting scars, which are most pronounced on the face, are the result of the destruction of the underlying sebaceous glands.

Thirty percent of victims will die, usually from toxemia leading to respiratory or heart failure. Death, if it occurs, is usually in the second week. Some victims will also become blind, generally as a result of opportunistic bacterial infections.

Ordinary smallpox can sometimes be confused with chickenpox. With chickenpox, however, the rash is more uniformly distributed on the body, with no rash on the palms or soles.

2) Flat type smallpox: This is very rare and is believed associated with a deficient immune system. It occurs more frequently in children and is characterized by intense toxemia. The lesions remain soft and velvety, and never

216

> ## The ring method of stopping a smallpox outbreak
>
> At present the Centers for Disease Control's (CDC) plan to contain a smallpox attack includes widespread *voluntary* vaccination but, if necessary, *forced* quarantine of infected individuals and *mandatory* tracing and vaccination of anyone who may have come in contact with them.
>
> They will employ the "ring" method to control an epidemic, namely vaccinate everyone who has had contact with an infected person, then vaccinate the ring of people who have had contact with the first set of contacts. It's the method used so successfully in the 1960s and '70s to finally eradicate smallpox.
>
> Keep in mind that for up to four days after exposure to smallpox, vaccination will either keep a person from catching the disease or lessen its severity.

progress to the pustular stage. Although the majority of cases are fatal, survivors typically are not scarred.

3) Hemorrhagic smallpox: This is also rare and associated with people with a compromised immune system. It occurs more frequently in adults. The virus multiplies in the spleen and bone marrow and leads to the inability of the blood to clot, resulting in spontaneous bleeding from spots on the skin and from the mucous membranes. The illness includes a shortened incubation period followed by severe high fever, headache, and stomach pain. These victims are highly infectious, and death occurs in the fifth or sixth day after incubation, before lesions typical of **ordinary smallpox** have a chance to develop.

4) Modified type smallpox: This type usually appears in previously vaccinated people. The incubation period, followed by headache and body pains, are similar to **ordinary smallpox**. The rash, however, develops without the presence of fever, and lesions are fewer, more superficial, and progress more quickly, with crusting accomplished within 10 days. These victims are infectious, but not nearly as infectious as victims with **ordinary smallpox**.

History of smallpox vaccine

The decision by President Bush to resume smallpox vaccination marks the first time in U.S. history that a nationwide public health preventive measure has been put into operation to defend against attack with disease.

The vaccine for smallpox is called vaccinia. It is a live virus derived from cowpox, a relative of smallpox but much milder.

The earliest form of smallpox inoculation was developed in China and India about 1000 B.C. Called variolation, it consisted of taking the pus from the pox of an infected person and inoculating a healthy person with it. A mild form of the virus developed and granted the person lifelong immunity. The practice spread to Europe and the New World in the 1700s.

In Britain in the mid 1700s, cowpox was a disease that primarily affected milkmaids, and it was noticed that they became resistant to smallpox after they recovered. In 1774, a British farmer from Dorset inoculated his family with material taken from the udders of a cow with cowpox, thereby granting his family immunity from smallpox. And in 1796 a British surgeon extracted fluid from the pustule of a cowpox victim and injected it into a healthy child, conferring smallpox protection on him. By 1800 smallpox vaccination campaigns using cowpox began throughout Europe.

Modern science has now learned that cowpox is a virus that primarily infects rodents and only occasionally infects cows. It exists primarily in Europe.

The World Health Organization's (WHO) worldwide smallpox vaccination program, designed to eradicate the disease, began in 1967 and ended in 1980 when smallpox was officially declared eradicated, making it the only human disease ever eradicated. The last reported case of smallpox was in Somalia in 1971, and in the United States the last reported case was in 1949. Vaccinations for U.S. civilians stopped in 1972, and U.S. military smallpox vaccinations stopped in 1990. Vaccine production discontinued in the U.S. in 1982.

When eradicated, the world community agreed to keep two samples of the disease in laboratory repositories in the United States at the CDC in Atlanta, and in the Soviet Union at the Russian State Research Center of Virology and Biotechnology in Koltsovo, Novosibirsk, which is in central Siberia.

Vaccination has begun again under a renewed threat of the return of the disease. It is feared that hostile states such as Iraq and North Korea, and possibly terrorists like Al Qaida, now have the smallpox virus and may use it against us. The threat has become more credible since the terrorist attacks in New York on Sept. 11, 2001 and the subsequent anthrax attack by an unknown person or persons shortly thereafter.

Types of vaccines and availability

There is currently enough smallpox vaccine to vaccinate all 288.6 million residents of the U.S. This includes about 75 million doses of the 1970s era Dryvax vaccine and about 300 million doses of the 1950s era Wetvax vaccine. The old vaccine has been stored cold and has been tested every two or three years to test its potency. Some of the vaccine has been diluted up to five times to make it go further, but tests indicate it is still potent.

The U.S. has ordered 209 million more doses of a more modern smallpox vaccine from Acambis Inc., a Cambridge, Massachusetts based company, and it should be ready for use in early 2004. It hasn't been fully tested but initial tests indicate it will be safe and effective. The FDA has not yet licensed enough of any of the vaccine for general public use, but it will be made available to the public without licensing in the event of a smallpox epidemic emergency. There is no definitive way to test the potency and safety of the new vaccine in the absence of an outbreak of smallpox.

Protection

Successful vaccination produces total immunity to smallpox. Once vaccinated, it takes approximately 7-10 days to achieve protection. However, if you are vaccinated within 3-4 days of initial exposure to smallpox, you may receive total protection from the disease, or at least protection against severe illness. The vaccine is then good for about 5-10 years (no one knows for sure). If you are later revaccinated it is believed immunity from smallpox lasts even longer, although how long no one knows. There is no danger in being vaccinated multiple times. Dr. D.A. Henderson, the director for the Center for Civilian Bio-Defense Studies at Johns Hopkins University, who in 1966 was the WHO director overseeing the global eradication of smallpox, says he has been vaccinated between 25 and 100 times. The live vaccinia virus vaccine, he says, must grow in your skin to produce immunity to smallpox. If you are already sufficiently immune, the vaccine simply does not grow in the skin.

The severity of lesions from smallpox can vary greatly, either naturally or because vaccination years before has given a person partial, but not complete, protection. With nearly complete protection from vaccine, few lesions will appear, but even if a person was vaccinated many years before, lesions may be far less and more superficial than for a person who was never vaccinated. In this case a person could get a mild case of smallpox, with an accompanying mild rash. He will not die and may not even get very sick, but he may be contagious, capable of passing along fullblown smallpox to another person.

Vaccinia Immune Globulin

A major difficulty in treating adverse reactions to the vaccine is that in past years bad reactions were treated with vaccinia immune globulin (VIG), which is serum derived from people who recovered from infection with the vaccine virus. Due to the absence of smallpox vaccinations for 30 plus years, the supply of VIG is now about 700 doses, which is enough for anticipated adverse reactions if only 6 million people get vaccinated. Additional doses of VIG are being produced.

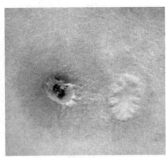

Close-up of the skin reaction at a smallpox vaccination site

Adverse reactions to vaccine

Smallpox vaccine has a higher adverse reaction rate than any of the modern vaccines generally given. Based on the statistics of the 1960s and 70s smallpox eradication program, as many as 50% of people being vaccinated will have some sort of reaction from the vaccine, ranging from a sore, swollen arm and swollen glands to flu-like symptoms. In a study of adult primary vaccinees, it was determined that 36% became sufficiently ill to miss school, work, or a recreational activity, or to have trouble sleeping. In another study 17% had fever of at least 100 degrees Fahrenheit within two weeks of vaccination, 7% had a fever of 100 degrees or more, and 1.4% had a fever of 102 degrees or more.

One or two of every million people who get the vaccine for the first time will die from it, 15 to 50 will have life threatening reactions including eczema vaccinatum, progressive vaccinia (vaccinia necrosum), and post vaccinal encephalitis, and approximately 1,000 will have serious reactions including a toxic or allergic reaction at the vaccine site and spread of the vaccinia virus to other parts of the body. If all 130 million Americans never vaccinated got vaccinated, about 250 would die and 2,000 would have life-threatening reactions. This does not include people with AIDS, who could be very severely affected.

The data showed that the death rate and adverse reaction rate for those being revaccinated was cut by two-thirds, but still if all 158 million Americans who were previously vaccinated were to get revaccinated, it is expected that 40 would die and 800 would have life threatening reactions. Again, this does not take into account people with AIDS or other immune system problems.

Compare these adverse reaction rates with a more modern vaccine such as the measles/mumps/rubella vaccine, which has experienced 11 adverse reactions and no deaths among the 30 million people vaccinated in the last 12 years. The newer smallpox vaccine, the 209 million doses still under final testing, is expected to have fewer adverse reactions than the older smallpox vaccine.

The death rate and adverse reaction rate may be much higher today because the U.S. population, or any modern population, is highly susceptible to smallpox because it has been so long (1949) since the disease has been present in the U.S. and because it has been so long (1972) since vaccinations were discontinued. Health officials expect the death and adverse reaction rate to be much lower among that older 58% of our population that has been vaccinated in the past, even though for most of them it has been the distant past, and they expect the adverse reactions in the younger 42% of the population never vaccinated at all to be significantly higher.

The most frequent complications of smallpox vaccination

From previous data, adverse reactions from vaccination occurred most often in people receiving their first dose of the vaccine, and among children under the age of 5. Following are the most frequent complications.

Inadvertent inoculation at other sites. This accounted for half of all complications of vaccination. Occurring in 1 of every 2,000 primary inoculations, it generally resulted from the hand touching the vaccination site, then touching another part of the body, thereby transferring the vaccination. The most frequent inadvertent inoculations occurred on the mouth, eyelid, rectum, genitals, nose, and face. It generally resolves itself.

Generalized vaccinia. This occurred in 1 of every 5,000 primary vaccinations, and it is the result of blood-borne dissemination of vaccinia virus. It generally resolves itself unless there is an underlying condition involving an immune deficiency. Vaccinia Immune Globulin (VIG) (See Sidebar) can be used to successfully treat cases involving the eye.

Eczema vaccinatum. This occurred in 1 out of every 26,000 primary vaccinations, and it occurred in people who had current or healed eczema or other chronic skin problems. It typically covers the area affected by the skin condition, and it is usually mild and resolves itself. But on occasion it can be severe or fatal. VIG is used to successfully treat serious cases.

Progressive vaccinia (vaccinia necrosum). This is rare, severe, and often fatal, and it is caused by the vaccine site's failure to heal. It occurs in people with underlying immune disorders and can occur after primary vaccination or revaccination. VIG is used to treat it, but with varying success.

Post-vaccination encephalitis. Also rare, this occurred in 1 out of 300,000 cases of primary vaccinations, with most occurring in children under the age of one year. It is characterized by fever, headache, vomiting, and sometimes convulsions, paralysis, or coma. Symptoms manifest themselves 8-15 days after vaccination. About 15-25% of cases died and another 25% had permanent neurological damage. VIG is not effective.

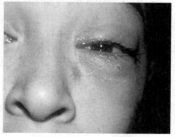

Secondary infection of the cornea in a 12-year-old male

221

Sufficient voluntary vaccination means high U.S. "herd immunity"

A survey of Americans in late 2002 indicated that more than half of Americans would be willing to get vaccinated. But the survey was taken before there was widespread understanding of the risks involved.

At present the vaccine is being made available only to the military and the 10 million or so emergency health care "first responders" such as police, firefighters, ambulance crews, EMTs, hospital emergency care workers, etc. When the vaccine is made available to the public, it will be on a voluntary basis. People will simply have to weigh the risk of having an adverse reaction against the risk that we will be attacked with smallpox. The idea of making it widely available on a volunteer basis is to build up "herd immunity." Since a certain number of people will opt for the vaccine, the nation's "herd immunity" will increase. Then if we are attacked with smallpox, the increased herd immunity will lessen the severity of any resulting epidemic.

In the event of a smallpox epidemic, the Centers for Disease Control and Prevention (CDC) recommends everyone get vaccinated, even if you have AIDS. The risk of getting smallpox far outweighs the risk of having an adverse reaction from the vaccine. The vaccine can be taken for up to four days after exposure to smallpox and still be effective in either preventing the disease or greatly lessening its effects.

Although the CDC says smallpox vaccination will be on a voluntary basis, it is anticipated that in the event of an attack and subsequent smallpox epidemic, smallpox vaccinations will likely become mandatory in affected areas. Quarantines and isolation will definitely be mandatory. Based on historical experience, there is no other way to contain an epidemic.

You won't be able to sue

If you are one of the unlucky ones who does get an adverse reaction to the vaccine, you won't be able to sue anyone. The *Homeland Security Act* has a provision protecting vaccine makers and healthcare providers from such suits. People injured may sue in federal court, but they will have to prove negligence, which will be just about impossible because the vaccine is advertised as coming with risks. The liability protection for vaccine makers was deemed necessary in light of the fact the U.S. needed a new vaccine fast and no company was willing to make one unless they got liability protection.

Genetically-altered smallpox

All of the above may become moot if we are attacked with a genetically-altered form of of the smallpox virus. No one knows if such a virus exists, but Soviet defector Dr. Ken Alibek, the former chief scientist and first depu-

People who should not get vaccinated

Eczema, dermatitis. People who have had or now have atopic dermatitis or eczema should not get the vaccine unless they are exposed to smallpox. As many as 40 million Americans, or up to 15% of the population, have had or currently have eczema, which puts them at higher risk for a potentially fatal skin infection called eczema vaccinatum. The risk is particularly great for children, who have experienced a threefold increase in eczema since smallpox vaccination ended three decades ago. In a study from the 1970s, 123 people out of one million vaccinated people got eczema vaccinatum, most of them children. In another study in Europe, 6 percent of people infected with eczema vaccinatum died from it. Running the numbers, if the 40 million Americans suspected of having had or currently having eczema were to get the vaccine, the death toll among them would be 295.

AIDS, other immune deficiency disorders. People who have a suppressed immune system, such as people who have had transplants or who have cancer, leukemia, lymphoma, or people with HIV and AIDS, are high risk groups. AIDS was not a known disease when vaccinations were given 30 years ago, so the severity of reaction for people with AIDS is not clear. Side effects can include brain swelling and extensive toxicity. Of particular concern to health authorities are the 100,000 to 350,000 Americans who have AIDS but who don't know it. Also, if you are taking immune suppressive medications such as corticosteroids, or if you are undergoing radiation, you should not be vaccinated.

(continued on next page)

ty director of Biopreparat, the former Soviet Union's secret offensive bioweapons program, says the Soviet Union was working on such a virus when he left their program in 1992. Dr Alibek is now a U.S. citizen and chief scientist at a private company in the U.S. that specializes in researching and developing medical defenses against biological weapons.

Also, both *NBC News* and the *New York Times* have reported that another former Russian virologist, the late Dr. Nelja Maltseva, may have given the genetically-altered strain of smallpox to Iraq.

Researchers have tested their ability to alter a related orthopox virus. They inserted the gene interleukin-4 into the mousepox virus, then exposed mice previously vaccinated against mousepox to the genetically altered virus. As

(continued from previous page)

Pregnant women, children. Pregnant women should not be vaccinated, nor should they be vaccinated if they plan to get pregnant within one month of vaccination. Infants should also not get the vaccine.

The current recommendation that infants not be vaccinated is in sharp contrast to the smallpox vaccination programs of the 1960s and 70s, when most of the vaccinations were given to children under the age of 1. Now, children under the age of one year are considered at increased risk for vaccine-caused brain infection. Children have been omitted from all of the current studies involving smallpox vaccines. Because children are more prone to touching the vaccination site, then touching other parts of their bodies such as their eyes, or even touching other children, the vaccination site should be covered with a special extra sticky bandage.

Also, if you have any of the following conditions you should not get the vaccine until you have completely healed: burns, shingles, impetigo, herpes, severe acne or psoriasis, and chickenpox.

Since the vaccinia vaccine is a live virus and can accidentally spread to others causing inadvertent vaccination, those people living with any of the above at-risk people should not be vaccinated. A vaccinated person is infectious until the vaccination site scabs over. A vaccinated person could spread the vaccinia virus by touching the vaccination site, then touching another person. In the 60s and 70s it was common for this to happen among young siblings.

In all, about 50 million Americans should not get the vaccine, either because they have one of the conditions mentioned above or because they live with someone who does.

they feared, many of the mice died. They are not sure if a genetically altered smallpox virus would defeat the smallpox vaccine, but it is definitely a fear.

The Iraq connection

Before they were thrown out in 1998, U.N. inspectors had discovered that Iraq had experimented with camelpox, another relative of smallpox, and one fear is that camelpox, which ordinarily does not harm humans, might be modified and used as a biological weapon. The smallpox vaccine, however, protects against all orthopox viruses, including camelpox. During their inspections in Iraq, U.N. inspectors found a freeze-drier labeled smallpox. Also, after the first Gulf War, 69 Iraqi prisoners of war were blood tested and

---

How vaccine is given

The vaccine is given by dipping a bifurcated (two-pronged) needle into the vaccine, then puncturing the skin of the upper arm 15 times in a few seconds. The puncturing of the skin is not deep. If the vaccination is successful, within three to four days a red, itchy bump will form, then develop into a large blister that fills with pus and drains. In two weeks the blister dries up and a scab forms. The scab falls off in the third week and leaves a small scar. To prevent the vaccinia virus in the vaccine from spreading to other people or other parts of your body, the vaccine site should be covered with a bandage. Children especially should be watched so they do not touch the site, then inadvertently touch, say, their eye.

---

were found to have built up immunity to smallpox, indicating prior vaccination against the disease. The obvious question is why?

Genetically engineered vaccines and anti-viral agents

U.S. scientists meanwhile are working on a genetically engineered vaccine that will be more effective with fewer side effects than old vaccines. They are also working on anti-viral agents that could, for the first time in history, effectively treat a person already infected with smallpox. No one knows if these efforts will be successful any time soon, but early laboratory studies suggest the drug cidofovir may be effective. Tests with animals are ongoing and being monitored by the CDC and NIH. There are 3500 doses of cidofovir on hand at present, which is enough to handle anticipated reactions if 15 million people are vaccinated. It will be administered under an investigational new drug protocol. Otherwise, there is no treatment beyond intravenous fluids and medicines to control pain and secondary infections.

Resources

For up to date information on the vaccine situation, you can call the CDC hotline: English: 888-246-2675; Spanish: 888-246-2857 or send them an email: cdcresponse@ashastd.org. On the internet you can find lots of information on smallpox and the smallpox vaccine, as well as on other biological and chemical threats, at the following sites: CDC.gov, WedMD.org, Cato.org, pbs.org, hopkins-biodefense.org, mipt.org, fas.org. Δ

Chapter 23
Emergency gear for your vehicle

By Jackie Clay

J ust as everyone knows it's sensible to carry an inflated spare tire, a jack, and lug wrench for your vehicle so it won't get stuck, carrying emergency gear for you and your family's safety and comfort makes just as much sense.

A good flashlight with fresh batteries is a must in every vehicle. We carry ours under the driver's seat and check it frequently to be sure the batteries are in good shape. Nothing is more miserable than having some sort of trouble in the night and being in the dark.

Carry as much emergency gear in your vehicle as you can conveniently. If you have the room, carry a gear box, such as we have under the shell of our pickup. It's large enough for a sleeping bag for each member of the family, a change of warm socks, a warm jacket, a small bow saw, a small propane stove and cartridge, candles, a few butane lighters, a pan, and other gear.

Most vehicles will provide room for nearly this much emergency gear in a trunk or other little used cargo space.

Every vehicle should have at least one warm blanket in it. Even during the summer. At night, or during a rain, it can get cold without the heater to run periodically.

A few warm clothes, tucked in a dust-proof bag in the trunk, can be a life-saver, especially in wet or winter weather. Be sure to have something for all members of the family.

Heat, in the form of a candle or propane stove or lantern, is a good idea. Be careful when using a candle, as they can easily be knocked over inside a vehicle, causing a flash fire of toxic fumes. But even a smallish candle can provide enough heat to keep a family from freezing to death inside a vehicle that is disabled. It will also provide light to attract the attention of rescuers and help prevent the vehicle from being struck by passing traffic or a snow-plow.

When using any form of heat, whether it be from starting the vehicle from time to time to keep warm or a candle, be sure to crack open a downwind window, preventing carbon monoxide poisoning. This odorless toxic gas has killed hundreds of stranded motorists, silently, without warning.

A means to make a fire is a must. The fire can draw attention to you if you need help, it can cook food and can keep you warm. Fire starters can range from butane lighters to windproof matches to a flint, magnesium, and steel kit. This last is the best.

Always carry vital motor and radiator fluids, as well as a gallon jug of water in the trunk. These include anti-freeze, brake fluid, transmission fluid and, most important, motor oil. For the lack of a quart of oil, you could blow the engine. And it could be a long walk to "civilization," especially knowing you face a $1500 engine job.

Stick a good shovel in the trunk. If you don't have room for a full sized shovel, cut the handle off one to fit, leaving as much of the handle as you can, or use a folding Army shovel. The new Army issue folds down to 12 inches. A shovel could save your butt if you get stuck in snow or mud.

Likewise, always carry a set of jumper cables. You can usually find someone willing to give your dead battery a jump, but he doesn't always have his own cables.

A basic tool box is essential. Simple tools, such as a couple of screwdrivers, an adjustable wrench, a pair of channel lock pliers, wire cutters, a battery terminal cleaner, hammer, electrician's tape, and duct tape can save the day. Even if you don't know much about auto mechanics, a knowledgeable passer-by may be willing to help, if he has the tools.

In this vein, be sure you have a box of assorted fuses tucked away in the glove box. Something as simple as a blown fuse may disable a vehicle. (One tip here, if you are lacking a correct sized fuse, rob a like sized fuse from something non-essential, such as the radio, replacing it when you get to a service station.)

Have drinking water with you at all times. This can be that gallon of water in the trunk, but if it is, change it from time to time, keeping it fresh. People have died from lack of water, and not always in southwestern deserts.

A fire extinguisher is a good addition to a vehicle's emergency gear. I've had a van I was driving catch fire without warning. Luckily a fire extinguisher was handy. All that burned up was the wiring under the hood. Check the fire extinguisher at least twice a year, to make sure it is charged.

Carrying a good, moderate sized first-aid kit is essential. Many of our little emergencies happen periodically. The kids skin a knee, your husband gets a steel sliver in his hand, you burn your arm checking the radiator. Nothing earth-shattering, but, at the time, emergencies nevertheless.

ON YOUR PERSON

On your person you should carry some or all of the following:

• means to make a fire, whether it's a butane lighter, wind-proof matches, or better yet, one of those pocket-sized magnesium and flint and steel tools such as you find sold at the Preparedness Expos.

• pocket knife or *Leatherman* type tool with can opener, pliers, screwdrivers, saw, tweezers, etc.

• vital medical prescriptions

• emergency money

Also wear proper footwear, not sandals. If you wear a fanny pack you can carry more, such as a tiny fishing kit, consisting of hooks, line, and sinker placed in a film canister. Also some granola bars, a garbage bag (raincoat), and a tiny flashlight. Some people even carry a gun in their fanny pack.

Find a sturdy, flat plastic box that will fit under the seat and fill it with commonsense first-aid gear: assorted adhesive strips (cuts, scrapes, blisters, etc.), eye drops, a needle and tweezers to remove slivers, antibiotic ointment, Betadine or iodine, a roll of two-inch gauze and gauze squares (sterile), burn ointment, aspirin, Tylenol, and anti-diarrheal tablets. Tailor your kit to your family's lifestyle. Make it comprehensive, but not bulky.

A little "survival" food, tucked in a bag or box in the trunk or under the seat, is a great idea. We certainly won't starve without a few meals, but I, for one, would rather have a little something to munch on than to go without. This is especially true during times of duress. This survival food can be high energy bars; small cracker and cheese or peanut butter packages; pop-top foods such as chili, stew, wieners, MREs (military meals ready to eat), dehydrated fruit slices, etc. The main thing is to choose foods that are not affected by heat/cold, will not go stale quickly, and will provide energy and satisfaction.

Now don't laugh, but toilet paper should be in every vehicle. Yep, you can do without it, but wiping on sticks and rocks is one aspect of my Native American heritage that I don't want to return to. Besides, toilet paper can be used to start a campfire, wipe the oil stick when checking the oil, stop minor bleeding, clean up messy kids, and blow your nose.

A transistor radio, especially one of those little ones that is both solar-powered and rechargeable with a built-in crank, would be handy to keep track of weather and/or riots. And don't forget snow chains for winter.

I'm sure, with these hints, you can think of things you'd like to include in your family's personal vehicle emergency kit. No two families are the same in their needs, but the point is to be ready for the unexpected, then relax and enjoy life. Δ

Chapter 24
Preparedness for travelers

By Brad Rohdenburg

W hen the subject of preparedness comes up, do you think of having a stock of supplies in your kitchen pantry in case of a storm? Maybe a backpack in your office or the trunk of your car with the things you'd need until you could return home?

If you travel for business or pleasure, the concept is likely to apply to an unfamiliar city thousands of miles from home. Being ready for the unexpected while traveling will give you options you wouldn't otherwise have. Sometimes what might have been overwhelming becomes merely an inconvenience, or even an adventure.

General preparedness

Clothing is your first layer of shelter. Pack for what's expected, of course, but anticipate more. A trip might start in Miami and end in Fairbanks. Dress appropriately, not only for your destination, but for possible diversions along the way, unnatural weather extremes, heating or air conditioning problems, and extended stays.

Synthetics are warm and they dry quickly, but will do skin damage if they melt. (I'm a little paranoid about this as I've seen it happen.) Natural fibers are a better choice if fire is a hazard—and it is in your car, mowing your lawn, starting a barbecue, or going to a nightclub.

Cotton is comfortable, but loses its insulating value if it gets wet, and it dries slowly. Wool provides some warmth even when wet, but gets heavy and some types are itchy. Silk combines the best attributes of both, and is my favorite first layer. It can be washed in a sink by hand at the end of a day, and will dry overnight—both you and your travel companions will appreciate that if your one-day trip becomes a five-day trip.

Impractical shoes are the biggest clothing mistake I see travelers making. I love the look of a woman in heels, for example, but the leggy girl of your dreams will wear on you pretty quickly when her feet start to hurt. Bring along something comfortable just in case there's walking to be done.

Airline preparedness

Airline travelers have the highest standard of resourcefulness to meet in order to be prepared. Not everything you'd like to have when things get difficult will fit in checked luggage, let alone in carry-on bags. The Transportation Security Administra-tion (TSA), a government agency that helps terrorists by disarming the 282 million of us who *don't* want to go on a suicide ride (but that's another article), won't allow so much as a Swiss Army knife onboard. Before a recent international flight, even nail clippers and a book of matches were confiscated from me. An elderly woman behind me had her sewing needles taken. (Of course, if a weapon were ever needed by either a terrorist or a law-abiding citizen, one can always be improvised. So far, at least, a can of soup in a sock isn't illegal.)

Personally, I'm armed wherever it's legal for me to be so. Armed or not, don't attract attention to yourself by acting like easy prey. Behave confidently but inconspicuously. In third-world countries, don't be a loud, rich American wearing expensive jewelry. Keep your wallet in a button-down pocket, and some of your money in a money belt or an ankle pouch. Make a copy of things like your passport information and keep it in a separate place. Ask your hotel's concierge about neighborhoods to avoid, and have them choose a taxi for you. Ask for a room above the ground floor. Most problems can be avoided simply by being alert, but consider taking a self defense course.

When I fly somewhere, I feel naked without at least a pocket knife. It's permissible to take one in your checked baggage. If you have only carry-on luggage, an inexpensive one may be purchased at your destination. Use it while you're there, then make someone's day by giving it away when you leave. In any case, I take a small course-grit diamond sharpening stone. It's weight and bulk are negligible. If necessary, even a scrounged piece of metal or plastic could be sharpened.

Keep a bottle of water in your carry-on, and top it off it when opportunities arise. The collapsible kind takes up less space and won't slosh annoyingly if you squeeze the air out. I bring a water filter or iodine crystals, too. You might not always be able to get water out of a tap. Pack some lightweight, nutritious, compact food. You're still free to patronize restaurants if that's your choice, but you won't be forced to rely on them.

Ear plugs and an eye mask will help you get some sleep on a crowded bus or plane. Other essentials for my "carry-on survival kit" are a toothbrush and floss, sunscreen, sunglasses, one of those candles-in-a-can, disposable lighter, a small first-aid kit (if you take medication, bring extra), a tiny LED flashlight or headlamp, and above all else: a good book. Something like, oh, say, a *Backwoods Home Anthology*.

Automobile preparedness

Have a fire extinguisher and a first aid kit. Know where they are and how to use them.

A duffel in my car also contains a sleeping bag, insulated ground pad, saw, jumper cables, tow strap, first aid kit, flashlight, a pot for cooking or melting snow, an ice scraper, and a couple of MREs (the militarly meals, ready-to-eat). I have used all of those things. I replace the MREs every year. (Want to make friends with the neighborhood kids? Give them your old MRE's. They'll be fascinated by them.)

Throw in whatever's appropriate for changing seasons, forecasts, or local conditions. In winter I add a hat, mittens, boots, shovel, and snowshoes. A candle or two will keep a stalled car reasonably warm. Be careful with fire, of course, so the solution doesn't become worse than the problem. A cell phone can summon help and reassure family. Keep your car's gas tank as full as is practical—it costs the same as leaving it empty, and again that phrase: It gives you more options.

A bicycle in the trunk, with an air pump and a spare inner tube, is my favorite automotive insurance. Walking a few miles with anything to carry is a time-consuming ordeal. On a bike, twice as far with twice the load is a pleasant outing.

Hotels

When you check into a hotel, make it a habit to look at the fire escape route posted on the inside of your room's door. Then open your door and look at the route the way you will look at it at 3 a.m. when you've been suddenly roused from a sound sleep. Count the number of doors and corners to get to it in case darkness or smoke prevent you from being able to see. (Do the same thing, while we're at it, when you board a plane, ship, or train: familiarize yourself with the way out. Count the rows of seats to it so you could get there in the dark, and look at how the doors or hatches operate.)

Don't use elevators during a fire because a power failure may immobilize them. Smoke tends to hug the ceiling. If it becomes a problem, stay close to the floor. (So why are the fire exit signs at the tops of the doors?)

If a fire alarm sounds while you're in your room, feel the door. If it isn't hot and you don't see smoke or flames through the peephole, evacuate. Remember to take your room key in case you must retreat to your room again. If you can't open the door, fill the bathtub with water and seal openings that smoke may come through with soaked towels. Breaking windows might create a draft that brings smoke in, so it's a last resort. Sit tight if you're more than a couple of stories above the ground. Most fires are confined to a few rooms or floors. We have a natural fear of fire, but smoke and panic are usually the greater threats. Δ

Chapter 25
Tools and hardware for the backwoods home

By James Ballou

A certain degree of self reliance is obtainable by those who have the knowledge and skills, resourcefulness, courage, common sense, and tools to perform most of the tasks necessary to their own survival and way of life. Living any distance outside populated areas requires a greater level of do-it-yourself capability than within metropolitan areas, where citizens tend to live under a system of interdependence.

One of the reasons why I like tools is because I associate them with individual freedom. The proper tools can help people produce much of what they need, make necessary repairs to their equipment themselves, and maintain their own homes, farms, yards, gear, and machines. The more people are able to do themselves, the less they have to rely on others. Greater independence means greater freedom.

Obviously, having a vast array of tools and hardware alone does not make a person highly capable. Knowing how to use the tools is every bit as important as the tools are themselves. But having a healthy assortment of good tools can sure make life a lot easier, and anyone with the desire and determination can learn how to use them.

When you think about it, just about everything we do, whether it's brushing our teeth, cooking and eating, driving to work, mowing the lawn, tilling the garden, typing a letter on a typewriter or computer, or even talking to friends on the telephone, involves using some device you could think of as the tool for that particular task. Modern folks are heirs to thousands of years of technological advancement in the sophistication of the tools we use. And we use many of them without much thought, often taking them for granted. But without any of them where would we be?

Making a list of the necessary tools you should keep at the homestead can be quite a task. A mostly self-sufficient country home can be expected to require equipment to serve a variety of different functions that are not generally concerns to most people who live in cities. The need for good tools in the country will always be great.

For the sake of order, you could categorize tools into groups according to their main application. At least it's a place to start, but you might want to reserve several pages for your list. It seems that every time I attempt to make a top-ten priority list of tools, I end up actually making a list of categories. For example, a wilderness backpacker will carry an assortment of tools needed on the trail and around camp, a mechanic will need an assortment of automotive tools, a carpenter will need building tools, and so on. Just listing the categories can get exhaustive, because within each category you might find subcategories. The carpenter category may include tools for rough framing, finish carpentry and cabinet making, tile setting, roofing, etc., each subcategory requiring its own specialty tools. Metal working might include machinist and lathe tools as well as tools for welding, blacksmithing, tinsmithing, and so on. And of course there are a lot of crossover tools as well. A simple

An anvil and forge can be especially handy for making and repairing other tools.

pair of pliers might be just as useful to a mechanic as to an electrician, or to a gunsmith. There are so many different kinds of tools which could be considered essential to the backwoods home that it's sometimes hard to know where to begin and where to end. But there are certain basic tools that perhaps every household should have, and covering those will be the main focus of this article.

There are some basic hand tools no home should be without.

At the top of the list we might include those tools with which we could most easily produce other tools. It used to be common to see old anvils and coal forges around farm houses and in barns. They were used for a lot of different purposes besides making horseshoes. On the anvil, a variety of knives, axes, chisels, punches, brackets, hinges, and every imaginable type of farm implement could be shaped or repaired. Basic blacksmithing tools can be extremely useful in a rural environment. Although often overlooked in this day and age, I would place the forge, anvil, hammer, tongs, and other hot metal working tools at the top of the list for the backwoods home.

Gun maintenance tools

Second on our list we might include the multi-function tools popular now. These would include the plier-type combination tools from Leatherman, Gerber, SOG, and Buck, as well as the Swiss Army Knives from Wenger or Victorinox. Although somewhat limited by size, these tools combine a list of capabilities into a single device, making them quite versatile and useful for small jobs. With the Leatherman SuperTool, you can slice, carve, scrape, saw, remove bottle caps, dig, file, crimp, and grip, among other things. It's a wonderful product in my opinion, and certainly something I would choose over a number of bulkier single-function tools whenever forced to prioritize.

Before leaving the topic of multi-function tools, I should also mention the basic fence pliers that have been around for many years in one style or another. Most of these have a hammerhead opposite a pointed horn for pulling large staples, and the tool can be used as pliers, hammer, staple puller, and wire cutter. It's a four-in-one combination tool, and it is hard to imagine a farm without one or more of these around.

Most people would probably put some type of knife at the top of the list. This makes sense because knives have hundreds of different uses. A knife would be at the top of my list whenever the tools to produce a knife aren't

Burning wood in the home can involve an assortment of wood gathering, log splitting, and chimney cleaning tools.

practical, such as wherever space and weight limitations dictate. But I would agree with those who believe that a knife is a basic item that belongs in every category.

Drills and drill bits should be high on the list. Drilling holes in things is one of the most important tasks common to several categories. I use my own drill press as much as I use any tool in my shop.

Another commonly overlooked category of tools with really a fundamental purpose is the thread-cutting taps

Everything here was purchased at garage sales for around $100. That wouldn't buy much at new prices. You can make money go a long way if you buy used.

and dies category. You won't find these in every toolbox, or even in the majority of American homes, but wise do-it-your-selfers keep a few of the common taps and dies in their shops. With them a person can make their own screws, nuts, and bolts. It can be inconvenient having to run into town every time you need some tiny machine screw with a special thread size because you can't find one in your screw bin. Some are hard to find anyway, possibly not even available at the local hardware store. It is extremely handy to be able to cut your own as needed.

We can continue adding the usual hand tools—hammers, saws, pliers, screwdrivers, clamps, vises, wrenches, files, rasps, squares, tape measures, levels, pry bars, etc.—and assemble a comprehensive list of basic items until we're confident that we could tackle most jobs around the ranch. And of course, there's no telling where all this will take you.

It's probably a good idea to focus on basic hand tools first and add power tools last. For one thing, power tools require more care and understanding to safely operate. They tend to wear out faster than simpler hand tools, and they cost more. And out in the country you may not always have electricity available. You can always accomplish a great deal with basic hand tools, just as your great grandparents did years ago.

Quality tools can be expensive, but the good news is that amazing bargains are to be found almost everywhere. Thrift stores, pawn shops, flea markets, and garage sales often sell good used tools unbelievably cheap. Sometimes they need cleaning, or they may even need to be repaired or sharpened in some cases, but most of the things I've found could be restored to service with little or no additional investment. It's always a good idea to look for quality. American made or European tools are usually worthwhile, but I tend to avoid products from China or Taiwan. The more tools you collect, the better you'll be able to fix and restore the broken ones.

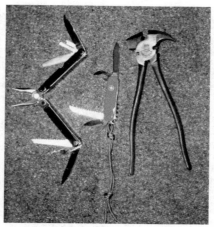

Multi-function tools are valued for their excellent versatility.

There's nothing quite like a good tool shop for dealing with so many of the chores around the house. If you don't already have a shop set up at your country home, now is a good time to get started. If you are set up already, I hope I've got you thinking about how to make it even better. Δ

Chapter 26
Sensible gun choices
after September 11th

By Massad Ayoob

Many Americans responded to the terror of September 11 by arming themselves. Autoloading rifles and short barreled shotguns moved briskly, dealers tell me, and I saw gunshops where the handgun display cases had been all but emptied by the sudden demand.

The terrorist threat against America continues. The model of what to expect has been in front of us for years. We've seen it in Israel.

Again and again, when terrorists have opened fire in that land, armed citizens have drawn their guns and put a quick stop to it. It happened most recently a month or so after the attacks on the World Trade Center and the Pentagon. A terrorist opened fire in a bus, killing two and wounding several more. An Israeli citizen drew his semiautomatic pistol and emptied it into the murderer, dropping him. A soldier and guard arrived on the scene with M-16s and shot the downed gunman again just to make sure. The local chief of police credited the armed citizen with saving many lives.

Lt. Col. David Grossman, the eminent authority on terrorism and mass murders, has suggested that off duty police and private citizens licensed to carry guns be sure to pack them when going to religious services. Grossman's research indicates that a particular sore point in the Palestinian consciousness is the massacre some years ago in Hebron in which a crazed Israeli militia-man with a government issue M-16 automatic rifle opened fire in a mosque, killing many Muslims and wounding many more. Grossman anticipates a response in kind, targeting houses of worship in the USA. Jewish synagogues would be particularly at risk. He also warns that sporting events, particularly in large arenas, are likely targets. Ditto large shopping malls, which many in "have-not" countries see as a symbol of American wealth and materialism.

I know one rabbi who is carrying a compact Colt Officers .45 auto. He has a customized Remington 11-87 12-gauge semiautomatic shotgun with extended magazine, kept securely but accessibly in a discreet location on the premises. In another synagogue in another part of the country, members of the congregation have quietly gotten together to work out a plan of action should such an incident take place. Armed members are strategically seeded throughout the synagogue during services. All carry handguns, discreetly concealed. The weapons range from .380 autos and snub-nose .38 revolvers to .357 Magnums and service-size 9mm, .40, and .45 automatics.

Rifles...

My sources believe Bin Laden and his puppets already have small, crude nuclear devices that they intend to use in our country. Such post-atomic devastation could leave survivors amidst a level of anarchy and chaos that has been predicted by survivalists since the early days of the Cold War. Facing starving criminals rather than enemy soldiers, a defender would find good use for the versatility of a semiautomatic military rifle. Caliber .223 makes much sense for the urban dweller. However, those assaulting a backwoods home would likely have come by vehicle, and the steel-penetrating ability of the .308 Winchester cartridge (7.62mm NATO) would make it a better choice.

A number of good auto-rifles in this caliber are readily available. I serve a rural community, and on "Y2K night" when it was predicted that a massive power shutdown could trigger a wave of bank robberies, I sat stakeout on two adjacent banks armed with a match grade, telescopic sighted Springfield Armory M1A. Loaded with a 20-round magazine of .308 and backed up by more, this would have been an ideal tool for the task. Fortunately, nothing happened.

Shotguns...

For close-range home defense, the shotgun loaded with buckshot is hard to beat. A short barrel pump gun with extended magazine, delivering seven- to eight-shot shell capacity, is also quite affordable. Loaded with rifled slugs and equipped with good sights, the shotgun can reach out to a hundred yards or more, but still isn't quite as versatile in this application as a rifle.

Handguns...

September 11 found my wife and elder daughter trapped in Las Vegas with no planes flying. Fortunately, my wife holds a Federal Firearms License, which allows her to purchase handguns anywhere in the country. I faxed her a copy, and a visit to a local gunshop equipped her and my daughter. Two attractive women traveling alone by ground are an inviting target for all sorts of indigenous predators. The technology she chose was simple: the Smith & Wesson .38 Special revolver, hammerless and Airweight. Such a gun can be fired through a coat pocket without snagging, is easy to conceal and constantly at hand. For a while, even rental cars were not to be had. If they'd had to hitch-hike, a small .38 apiece would get them home safely.

On my first post-attack trip I was almost 3,000 miles from home, and the Taliban was threatening that "the rain of airplanes" would continue. Another shutdown of mass transportation would leave me hitch-hiking a long way with what I could carry by hand. The 9mm cartridge—adequately powerful in the 115-grain high velocity Pro-Load Tactical ammunition I chose—made sense. I could carry more of it if it was impossible to resupply. During that trip I carried a Glock 17, loaded with 20 rounds thanks to a pre-ban magazine with +2 extender. On the hip were two spare magazines, each with 17 rounds. In an Alessi ankle holster was my backup gun, the baby Glock 26 fully loaded with 11 rounds of the same ammunition. It would feed the longer magazines of the bigger 9mm in an emergency. Carrying two lightweight guns with polymer frames, and 65 rounds of ammo on my person, was no problem at all.

A later trip included a swing through California, where a technical reading of that state's new law indicated that it might be illegal for me to bring in a high capacity magazine not registered there. I simply went with an eight-shot 1911 .45 pistol, and a five-shot .38 Airweight revolver for backup.

In the end, when you face the sort of crisis that requires a defensive firearm, the question isn't so much, "Did you have the ideal gun?" The question is more, "Did you have a gun at all?" Δ

Chapter 27
Rifles, shotguns, and handguns for survival

By Massad Ayoob

You bought it for a worst case scenario. If that doesn't come to pass, you'll still own it. I'm talking about rifles, shotguns, and handguns that'll get you through bad times and good. Consider this approach: Prepare yourself with things you can use if society doesn't break down.

Experienced rural people have known for a very long time that having a generator just makes good sense. I'd be surprised if there's a hospital in the land that isn't outfitted with generators in case the power goes out for some reason. If you have room to store it, isn't it just practical to buy staple foods, toilet paper, sanitary napkins, et al in bulk and stockpile them, saving money compared to the usual urban "wait 'til we run out and then buy as needed" paradigm?

So it is with the guns. Let's look at some rifles that would be awfully good to have on hand if society breaks down and would be good to have on hand anyway.

.308 rifles

Springfield M1A. As currently produced, this is a splendidly-made example of the M-14 rifle, a design that goes back roughly half a century and is essentially an improved WW II M-1 Garand. With up to 20-round magazines still readily and legally available, it fires the 7.62mm NATO/.308 Winchester cartridge. Ammo is abundant. The rifle is utterly reliable.

The M-14 was constructed for a projected battlefield in which it was thought that the hedgerow fighting and house to house combat of the European Theater would be the small arms battle plan of the future. This is remarkably close to defending a home against armed invaders on foot or in cars and trucks in a "post-Armageddon" scenario.

No Armageddon? No problem! A five-round magazine makes this accurate, reliable autoloader an excellent hunting rifle in rugged country. More than a decade ago, in Namibia, I used a sniper grade M1A Springfield to shoot a springbok at 350 yards. The local rules said "no semiautomatics," so I used the gun without a magazine as a single shot with just the one round in the

*This 7.62 NATO HK91 has served the
author for 20 years without malfunction.*

chamber. Ben Mozrall, then head of the New Hampshire State Police SWAT team, shot a 1.5-inch group with this same rifle at 200 yards. In a weak moment, I sold it with its exquisite Leupold scope to John Groom. Later I came to my senses and bought a stainless Match Grade Springfield Armory M1A to replace it. Target shooters, be advised that this is the rifle that kicks butt in national class High Power competition. The prices are excellent these days. An added feel-good bonus: no American gun manufacturer has been more vocal about individual citizens' Second Amendment rights than Springfield Armory.

Other fine .308 "battle rifles" include the European **FN SLR** and **HK91**. In the score of years I've owned it, I can proudly say my Heckler and Koch HK91 has never malfunctioned.

.223 rifles

With ammo readily available, the 5.56mm NATO/.223 Remington round will get you through the darkest of human conflict nights. It's the choice of not only the entire US military, but most of the cops. If I was going into battle, I'd want the superb ergonomics (speed reloading, ambidextrous use around cover in any configuration, fine balance) of the **AR-15**. For my own needs, the short, handy, super accurate **Steyr AUG** is a personal favorite, but I bought mine back when the price was reasonable. For a "best buy" today that's still user-friendly, you can't beat the **Ruger Mini-14**, which, in stainless steel, is the mainstay of this magazine's publisher, Dave Duffy, and its senior editor, John Silveira.

An Olympic Arms match-grade ultra-lite AR-15 upper mated with a Colt lower and fitted with C-More electronic dot sight. It's great for recreational shooting and formidable for home defense. It weighs less than 6.5 lb and belongs to Ayoob's youngest daughter, Justine Lauren.

The .223 is also ideal for "back porch to garden and beyond" sniping of local animals who figured you planted your garden for them instead of you. With light, high velocity hollowpoints, such a rifle is still a devastating man-stopper for home defense, offering light recoil with high hit potential on multiple targets at close range under stress in short time frames. And .223s are always fun for recreational plinking, which is what my youngest has used hers for (**Olympic Arms AR-15** with C-More red dot electronic sight) since she was twelve.

7.62 X 39 auto rifles

This ComBloc cartridge, Kalashnikov's updating of the first (German, WW II) assault rifles, approaches the classic American .30/30 hunting round in effectiveness when used with a soft-point hunting bullet. There are essentially three popular choices. A semiautomatic version of Kalashnikov's own **AK-47** will indeed work through mud or blood or crap or flood, but it won't be terribly accurate. Good for close fighting, not great for recreational use at significant distance. Ruger's Mini-14 in this caliber is known as the **Mini-30**, and with hunting-legal five-round magazines standard (and longer magazines available "aftermarket") makes more sense as "survival situation insurance

Two of the best defensive shotguns available today. Top,
Remington 870 pump; bottom, Mossberg 9200A1 auto.
Folding stocks shown are handy but not essential.

for now, and a lightweight, light-kicking deer rifle for later." Finally, there's my own choice in this caliber, the **SKS**. This old ComBloc beast is at least twice as accurate as the AK-47, rivaling the Mini and the AR. It's as ruggedly reliable as the AK, generally has a better trigger, and 10 shots instead of a bigger magazine is its only shortcoming. They're cheaper than dirt, as gun prices go, even now. I prefer the well-made commercial Norinco guns from China, and the Russian Paratrooper versions, because they both have short stocks that work well for petite females, or for adult men in heavy cold-weather coats. The same softnose hunting ammo you'd use in a Mini-30 can make the SKS a useful "farm gun" once any perceived societal crisis has passed.

I don't care for AK rifles much. Factory magazines of 20- and 30-round capacity for the Mini-30 are limited to cops under current law. For an ordinary law-abiding citizen getting started, I'm not sure you can beat the cost effectiveness of the SKS. I won one in a match, gave it to my oldest kid, and then bought an identical SKS for my youngest. In the best of all worlds, I'll have died of old age and each of my daughters will have an SKS, ammo, and accessories secured safely in their homes for their kids, far in the future.

.22 rifles

Survivalist guru Mel Tappan said you should have it. Gun experts say you should have it to teach marksmanship to your kids and other new shooters. Fast and in-the-eye-socket accurate, the gun we're talking about is a top-quality autoloading .22 rifle. The ammo is cheap, and so light it's portable.

Mel Tappan's "survivalist's choice" pistol, a Colt .45 automatic, remains a very sound alternative, especially for those trained in its use. It's a potent manstopper even with the round-nose "GI ball" ammo shown.

A box of 50 rounds of .22 Long Rifle is the size of a small survival ration of wooden matches.

For accuracy, reliability, and cost effectiveness, you can't beat the time-proven **Ruger 10/22**. I hate to sound like a PR man for Ruger, but that's just how it is. There are more aftermarket accessories (folding stocks, match-grade barrels, extended quick-change magazines, etc) available for the 10/22 than for any other .22 rifle. A close second on my list would be the **Marlin Model 77**. Over a million of these neat little rifles have been made. They're accurate, they're reliable, and the only reason I don't rate them over the Ruger is that you can't readily get extended quick-change magazines for all of them. (Most Marlins have tubular magazines, which are comparatively slow to reload.)

I enjoyed my 10/22s and my Marlin 77 before any threat to society appeared. I'll enjoy them once it's over. An accurate .22 caliber semiautomatic rifle will still pick the squirrels off your bird-feeder, still zap the woodchuck in your backyard garden from your kitchen window, and still put a 50-grain bullet through the rapist's eye and into his brain as he breaks through the bedroom door.

Other rifles

"Other rifles" is a world to cover, and I want to keep this short. Sure, a lever action .30/30 will get you through the night, but it's slow to reload in an emergency involving high-volume shooting. Yeah, the Lee Enfield .303 Jungle Carbine was the best bolt-action battle rifle of its time and not a bad deer rifle even today. Yes, the Steyr-Mannlicer rendition of Jeff Cooper's Scout Rifle is superbly crafted. Liked mine, sold it anyway. These are bolt-action rifles. When you show me how I can get off five shots in one second with a bolt gun at "down the hall distance" like I can with a semiautomatic, enlighten me, OK? Until then, a gun that would do to protect one's innocent family against many-to-one lethal odds needs to be semiautomatic as far as I'm concerned, and for purposes of this article, the topic is worst case scenario family defense guns that can be useful later. If the emphasis seems to be on later, I apologize, but we can't ignore realistically-perceived short term needs now.

Shotguns

The shotgun is a versatile firearm. But is it the ideal defense gun for a worst case scenario...or even for the best of times?

Los Angeles cops used to call it "the tube." Westerners called it "the scattergun." A whole lot of folks have called it the single most versatile of all hand-held firearms, and within its limitations, they may be right.

The "shotgun" is so named because when you drop its hammer on the ammo it was primarily designed for, it expels a cloud of pellets known as "shot." There is birdshot, a great number of tiny pellets, suitable for killing light-bodied creatures like the fowl of the air. There is buckshot, fewer pellets but each larger and heavier, which at close range act like so many old-fashioned, non-expanding pistol bullets striking all at once. These are designed to kill deer at short ranges, and other animals in the 130 to 300 pound range, animals like...oh, Hell, you figure it out. Finally, there are shotgun slugs, which turn what was once known as a "fowling piece" into .70-plus caliber rapid firing heavy rifles in close quarters.

You use fine birdshot to shoot "upland birds." You shoot heavier, coarser birdshot for "waterfowl," ducks and geese that you'll have to shoot at longer range through heavier feathers and body mass if they are to come down from their migration routes to grace your table. Buckshot ("double-ought," as it's known historically) sends nine .33 caliber pellets from the muzzle of a 12-gauge shotgun at once. It's roughly the same as shooting something nine times in the same millisecond with a .32 caliber automatic pistol and old-fashioned ammunition. Cops use it when they anticipate close-range gunfights, and African hunters used 00 Buck when going in close on wounded lions and leopards in the thickets. Finally, the 12-gauge rifled slug—an ounce of lead almost ¾-inch in diameter, flying at 1100 to 1600 feet per second—is not only the close range "shotgun deer load of choice," but is what some professional hunters in Alaska and elsewhere resort to when they have to go into the underbrush after wounded grizzly bears. It is also the ammunition the NYPD Stakeout Squad switched to after a few shootings where even the deadly "double-ought buckshot" didn't put their armed opponents down fast enough.

Good news with shotguns

Obviously, the shotgun is versatile. So are its design options. You can get a single barrel (too slow for anything more serious than sport, but cheap). You can get a double barrel, anywhere from $200 for a second-hand Stevens 311 that will get you through the night, to six figures (yes, you read it right, over $100,000) for a super-grade shotgun custom made in Europe. Or, you can get a functional pump-action shotgun (Mossberg or Remington Express) for around $300 or less. A semiautomatic shotgun will start a bit higher than a pump.

Bad news with shotguns

When the strength is versatility, the weakness will generally be found in specialty. The history of the human experience seems to be that whatever works half-ass well for everything will be found specifically deficient in something. So it is with shotguns.

So, what we're talking about here are shotguns that might be bought by someone anticipating a worst-case scenario after a societal breakdown. One study of LAPD use of (12-gauge pump) shotguns in actual gunfights indicated a 58% hit potential. That means out of every two shots fired in anger, slightly more than one was likely to put one or more 00 buckshot pellets into the opponent. If we translate that to a multiple-opponent gunfight scenario, it tells us right up front that a one-or two- or even three-shot gun will give us a limited future against multiple opponents.

This tells us that for defensive purposes, we need a baseline of a "magazine-fed shotgun," which will hold an absolute minimum of four shotgun shells in its reservoir, and if time allows the defender to load the gun all the way up, with one more shell in the firing chamber, a minimum of five shells capacity. **Important note:** There is **no** magazine-fed shotgun made today to this writer's knowledge which incorporates a firing pin safety. This means that **any** shotgun kept for emergency defense purposes needs to be stored with its firing chamber empty, so that it cannot accidentally discharge if dropped or struck on either end.

What not to look for

Don't tell me that your shotgun is cool for every distance because it has interchangeable chokes. You won't have time to change the chokes in the moment it takes you to transition from your first opponent at your doorway to the one 40 yards away in the parking lot who is aiming his stolen rifle at you.

Don't tell me that your shotgun is emergency versatile as opposed to situationally versatile because it can shoot birdshot, and buckshot, and slugs and all the rest. The versatility requires time for you to load the right shells into the magazine! That time may present itself to a police SWAT team that has the suspect in the crosshairs of multiple gunsights. It won't be there when you have to quickly change gears between perpetrator A on the front doorstep and perpetrator B, also armed with a rifle, way out there at the barn.

Don't tell me you load your shotgun with birdshot for home defense because, "It will blow away a bad guy, but it won't shoot through the walls and hurt the kids." A whole bunch of us have put our fists through the kind of sheetrock walls that separate our bedrooms, but none of us was ever able to put our fists through the opponents we punched in the stomach, as hard as we tried. If it will go into your opponent enough to blow away his internal organs, it will go through the wall and endanger your children too. If it won't go through the sheetrock your fist can go through, don't count on it to keep a homicidal antagonist you hit dead-center with it from killing your babies.

I'm sorry if that takes away something you were counting on, but somebody had to tell you in time.

Recommended shotguns

Your defensive shotgun should be a pump action or a semiautomatic. For professionals who keep their guns clean—and know how to break them down to do that—I strongly recommend the semiautomatic. For people who tend to neglect their equipment, I would most strongly recommend the pump gun.

There are damn few semiautomatic shotguns that will cycle 100% with light loads, medium loads, full power loads, and Magnum loads, no matter what you may have read in gun magazines. I have been to "gun writer seminars" where the hosting gun companies fed us up to the gills with shrimp and booze and paid for our nice hotel rooms, and some of my colleagues wrote great things about the guns that malfunctioned when we all tested them. I wrote the truth. That's why I'm not invited to some of those seminars anymore, but my duty is to you, not to the gunmakers.

When in doubt, buy a **Remington Model 870 Express** or a **Mossberg 590** pump gun as first choice, a **Mossberg Model 500** as close second choice. If you want a 12-gauge autoloader, buy a **Remington Model 11-87** or a **Benelli Super-90** or a **Mossberg Jungle Gun**. I say this not as the gunwriter who supped at the tables of the manufacturers—actually, I am that, I'm just not speaking as such.

I speak now as the full-time firearms instructor who sees what works and what doesn't, 20 to 40 students per combat shotgun training session who hose buckets of buckshot downrange at high speed and find weak points in their guns that people who shoot light trap and skeet loads never discover.

Any of the above-recommended guns will serve you well in an emergency. In the lighter-kicking 20 gauge, spewing 20 .25 caliber buckshot pellets per pull of the trigger, I'd recommend the **Remington semiautomatic Model 1100**, especially the lightweight LT-20 model with short stock that fits smaller people better and causes no shortcomings to those with taller stature or longer arms.

Handguns

Let's look at handguns for emergencies. A single gun has to be multi-purpose:

• Accurate enough to kill an animal some distance away for food.

• Powerful enough to stop a threat coming in on you quickly.

• Holding enough ammunition to allow you to shoot fast and straight and, if necessary, reload quickly and shoot fast and straight some more.

• And, when you don't worry about "panic in the streets" any longer, a gun that will still serve you well for recreational shooting, home and personal defense, and for the chores that firearms have historically performed at rural homesteads.

Single action frontier style revolvers and single shot pistols and derringers are out. Not enough firepower.

22s have a place in a survival kit for shooting small game for subsistence, and the ammo is certainly cheap and easy to carry in volume. You have to determine what you're most likely to need to shoot. .22s are cool for squirrels. In the anti-personnel function, however, they have proven effective for only two classes of people: highly trained Israeli intelligence operatives and Mafia assassins. Both seem to have the knack of getting behind the opponent and shooting him through the base of the skull. If this doesn't seem a likely scenario for your needs, then as useful as a low-powered .22 handgun is

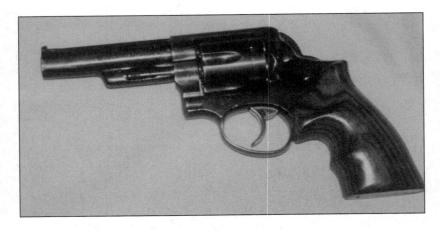

*The rugged, reliable Ruger .357 Magnum is an
excellent choice for those who prefer revolvers.*

around the rural home, you can do better for an all-around handgun whose
purposes include emergency defense.

.38 Special/.357 magnum revolvers

The .38 revolver won't take the longer, more powerful Magnum cartridge
of the same diameter, but a .357 Magnum revolver will fire shorter .38
Special cartridges. Unless there's a compellingly necessary cost saving, in
guns of the same size buy the .357 and you'll have a better chance of resupply if the future is such that ammo becomes scarce. The small ones shoot
only five rounds, a few of the new bigger models hold seven or eight, but for
the most part a .38 or .357 revolver will be a six-shooter. Have some speed-
loaders handy, of the proper size for that particular revolver, and you can
learn to quickly reload six shots at once in less than six seconds.

These guns are sturdy and reliable. If all the gunsmiths were going to disappear, I'd choose the built-to-last-forever **Ruger**. The **Colt**, **Smith &
Wesson**, and **Taurus** brands are all good choices, too.

.45 semiautomatic

Survivalist guru Mel Tappan recommended this gun, specifically the **Colt
Government Model** or one of the other 1911A1 variations, as that pistol was
known when it served the US military for most of this century. All good-
quality .45 ammo is powerful enough to trust in a fight, though the hollowpoints work a lot better and are less likely to shoot through the bad guy and
hit a good guy. Many of our readers were trained on this gun in their military

past. The gun you are most trained with is the one you'll fight best with, and when you are judged later for your actions, being trained with the gun you used is a plus. This is an advantage for the service revolver mentioned above if you were trained with one in a former life as a cop or security professional.

If you like the .45's power but don't like the necessary "cocked and locked" carry mode for the 1911 gun, you can get any of several modern double action .45 automatics. These require a long, heavy, intentional pull of the trigger to fire. **S&W**, **SIG**, and **Ruger** are all good. The **Glock** is another very reliable modern .45 automatic. In fact, it's been my experience that the .45 caliber versions are the most accurate pistols Glock makes.

9mm semiautomatic

Tappan didn't like this caliber, but that's because in his time most of the 9mm ammo available was impotent in terms of quickly stopping aggressive threats. Things are different today. You can get loads like the Triton Hi-Vel I carry in my own 9mms. A standard 115-grain hollowpoint will leave a 9mm's muzzle at 1100-something feet per second. The Illinois State Police "hot load" (so hot they won't sell it to the general public) sends the same bullet out of their **Smith & Wesson 9mm** autos at 1300 feet per second. The Triton Hi-Vel is rated at 1325 feet per second from short barrel pistols, and I recently chronographed it at more than 1450 feet per second out of the almost 5-inch barrel of one of my Berettas. This is ".357 Magnum country" in terms of potency. A pistol with 16 rounds of this 9mm, weighing the same as an eight-shot .45, is no contest for me: I'd go with the hot-loaded 9mm every time. (If you can't find Triton locally, we stock it at my place. Call toll-free (800) 624-9049 for catalog and ordering info. You'll need to mail or fax an ID card proving that you're at least 21.)

Alas, the 9mm choice presumes always being able to get the best ammo. A 9mm is very "cartridge dependent:" standard full metal jacket ("ball") ammo in that caliber is impotent for fighting determined opponents. If you may have to get ammo "wherever," go .45. If you have enough ammo stockpiled for your needs, hot 9mm has an edge.

Many readers have been trained with the Beretta M9, known in commercial circles as the **Beretta Model 92**, which the US military adopted over a decade ago. Again, the gun you're trained and proven with is the gun to have. I know one guy who taught at Fort Benning whose "preparedness kit" includes two Beretta 9mms, one for each hip, in the same kind of holsters whose use he taught to soldiers.

The Beretta is a fine 9mm fighting pistol, but the **Glock**, the **SIG**, the Smith & Wesson, the old **Browning** and many others would also deliver noble service. With 9mm, remember, the trick is having enough of the right ammo on hand.

Points to consider. You'll hear or read people saying that you should have the Beretta 9mm because you can interchange ammo and magazines with military personnel. The same argument used to come forth for having the 1911 .45. Excuse me, but I think someone has seen one too many reruns of "Night of the Living Dead." If you really think cops and soldiers are going to share their ammo with private citizens they don't know during a crisis, I would like to talk to you about buying some oceanfront property in Kansas City. The Beretta 9mm and Colt .45 are fine guns, but buy them for good reasons, not stupid ones. The same is true insofar as the thought that you should have a .38 or .357 like the cops had before, or a .40 caliber pistol like so many cops have now. The police aren't likely to share with you either.

Training

Don't just buy the handgun, train with it! The handgun is the most difficult of firearms to learn to shoot quickly and accurately. Scumbag criminals in gunfights (as opposed to murderers standing on top of their helpless victims) only hit the good guys they shoot at with 15% of their shots or less. Cops minimally trained in marksmanship will go 17% to 35% in hit potential. The cops on well-trained departments—a skill level I truly believe you can reach in home study—will go to 40% or better hit ratio per shot in real-world gunfights. The highly trained SWAT officers and graduates of private academies approach or exceed 80% hit potential with handguns in actual shootouts.

So get training and practice. Δ

Chapter 28
What's next?
What can you do?

By Massad Ayoob

On September 11, 2001, the commentators say, "Everything changed." The extent of that change is still being measured by each of us.

Every one of us will remember where we were when we first learned of the atrocities of 9/11/01. It was to our generation what Pearl Harbor had been to our parents. Amidst the horror and the rage, there was a distinct sense of loss of innocence...and of present, continuing danger.

The degree to which American lives will be changed remains uncertain. There is a strong drive to acclimatize the public to a necessary loss of liberty in the name of security. The privacy matters are a concept I will leave to John Silviera, who is better informed and more articulate on the privacy issues than I. Suffice to say that I believe Benjamin Franklin had the best handle on the matter when he said: ***"They that can give up essential liberty to obtain a little temporary safety deserve neither liberty nor safety."***

We are told by the pundits, "Everything has changed." It's the details that are not clear yet. In the days and weeks that followed, there was a run on guns and ammunition and gas masks. As we look to countries that have dealt with terrorism at home, we see something similar. During Desert Storm, we all watched on CNN as Israeli citizens donned gas masks in fear of chemical attacks by Saddam Hussein. Osama bin Laden, considered by most Americans the architect of the attack of the 11th, has been known to experiment with biotoxins as tools of terror. His minions were exploring the possibilities of crop-duster aircraft, apparently with such forays in mind. Never mind whether or not the crop-duster is a viable tool for dealing such mass death. The point is, they were looking for it.

An M-19 surplus gas mask strikes me as a sensible purchase. It also makes sense to have a few cheap gauze masks in each vehicle and in the home. They were a godsend to the rescuers in New York, who had to work in a choking haze of asbestos dust and other toxic substances.

Those I know in the intelligence services tell me that the World Trade Center and the Pentagon attacks were only the first shot of the fusillade. Enough bin Laden puppets have reportedly been sent underground in the

U.S. to deliver many more atrocities. Given the history of such suspects in the past, there are certain patterns of attack that can be anticipated.

Attacks on water, electric, and travel

The initial attacks were directed at some of the most high profile structures in major cities to "make a statement" and maximize fear with huge casualties. Poisoning reservoirs is do-able, and it's something counter-terrorism experts have warned us about for a long time. Terrorists will also be aware of what our concerns were as the nation prepared for Y2K. Attacks on power plants would fulfill those fears.

You saw what the incidents of September 11 did to air travel. Recall also that in early October a whacko slashed the throat of a Greyhound bus driver in the Nashville area, killing six when the vehicle crashed. This turned out not to be a terrorist incident, but Greyhound still froze all its bus travel for a good seven hours. It would not be difficult for terrorists to engineer events that could temporarily paralyze air, road, and rail traffic, resulting in a shortage of food and other necessary goods. All the more reason to go back to the "Y2K preparedness level": Lots of food and water on hand, generator ready, the whole bit.

Travel concerns

I am less inclined than usual at the moment to drive across large bridges. These big structures will go in a spectacular way if blown up. The cutting of the enemy's bridges is ancient wartime doctrine. We are up against people who study the ways of the ancient warriors.

Similarly, I would rather not be spending a lot of time in tunnels. Back at the time of the Olympics in Los Angeles, law enforcement was worried about terrorists hijacking a couple of fuel tanker trucks. If it's a one-mile tunnel, they travel a mile apart. As terrorist A is about to emerge from the tunnel, he pulls sideways to block all lanes of traffic, flips a toggle switch, and runs out of the tunnel and into the open air, leaving the truck behind. His partner, terrorist B, does the same at the entry to the tunnel, a mile behind him. The switches they've flipped arm time bombs that are set to go off very soon. The gasoline tankers erupt spectacularly, and every motorist trapped in that mile of tunnel is soon either burned to a crisp or suffocated.

In the early days after the Twin Towers destruction, FBI discovered that several suspects and people linked to them had acquired truck drivers' licenses, including licenses authorizing them to transport hazardous materials.

When aboard a plane

Many say that there will be no replay of the events of September 11 because of improved airline security, because the passengers will all rise up and overpower the hijackers as apparently happened on Flight 93 that terrible day, or because "they've already done that."

I can only reply, "What!?!?" The argument that "they won't do it again because they've already done it" is ludicrous. Yeah, and in 1945, Nagasaki was safe because our people had "already done that" at Hiroshima.

Improved security precautions? It'll be a while before enough sky marshals can be put in place to cover every domestic flight, if that ever happens at all.

In commercial air travel since this incident, I've only once been patted down, and then unprofessionally. Ceramic or plastic knives can still easily be smuggled through security by those who don't worry about lawbreaking.

Travelers need to follow the paradigm of the heroes of Flight 93. That aircraft crashed in Pennsylvania fields instead of into the US Capitol Building or the White House because at least four brave Americans rose up against hijackers who were armed with edged weapons. Did one or more of those courageous passengers have small knives of their own, that they were able to put to good use? We may never know. We do know that in the foreseeable future, you won't have even a nail file to protect yourself if dangerous people arise in the passenger compartment to threaten others.

I am hoping we've seen the last of the "suicide hijackings." I suspect that the bin Laden moles still in the country have been glued to CNN and are aware that American air travelers are in a mood to rise up and, bare-handed, swarm the next set of hijackers. If they choose to abandon the tactics they used on September 11, it will not be because they're afraid of sky marshals. It will be because they're afraid of people just like you.

Body armor

At this writing, there is nothing that prevents the law-abiding citizen from wearing concealed body armor, either in public or aboard a jetliner. A very sharp stabbing implement can go through a vest that would stop a .44 Magnum slug, but in the field it rarely happens. The favored weapon of the 9/11/01 terrorists was a boxcutter. This is a slashing weapon, and even with big knives, a vest made of Kevlar or Spectra should defeat a slash attack.

Travel with a gun

As long as the danger exists, it's a good idea to bring a gun and ammunition with you when traveling long distances by automobile. If we have another incident like those of the eleventh, you and I are unlikely to be the initial victims. However, air travel was shut down the last time, stranding people for days. If you have to strike out for home on land—perhaps hitch-hiking, if a run on rental cars has emptied the Hertz and Avis lots, and train or bus service have been disrupted—being unarmed and helpless just won't be any fun.

My wife was in Nevada on the 11th. There are a lot worse places to be trapped. However, thinking she might have to drive cross-country, she saw a need to be armed. I faxed her a copy of her Federal Firearms (dealer's) License, with which she bought herself a compact Smith & Wesson .38 Special at a local gunshop. Without the FFL, she would have been SOL, since Federal law prohibits a dealer from selling a handgun to a non-dealer who lives out of state. Lesson learned: she'll have her own gun in the suitcase on the next trip. At this writing, Federal Air Regulation 108.11 remains in effect, and it is legal for any law abiding citizen to fly on commercial carriers with an unloaded handgun in one hard-shell suitcase and the ammunition in another. Make sure, however, that you're going to be legal to be in possession of the gun where you land.

High risk days

Major American holidays will be high risk. Terrorists will appreciate the impact of alarming Americans on days when we traditionally celebrate peace and security: Thanksgiving, for instance, or Christmas. Large gatherings of citizens, such as stadium events, also have a high "target priority" according to what anti-terrorism experts teach us.

Carrying concealed

The first attacks focused on mass death in huge numbers. Terrorists know they can make the impact they want with lower body counts. As the Israelis have learned, bombs detonated in department stores and restaurants achieve the evil goal of terrorizing and intimidating the public. Ditto "mass shootings."

Some years ago, a group of terrorists opened fire on the citizenry on a city sidewalk in Israel. In seconds, the terrorists themselves were down; they had been riddled with the return fire of armed Israeli citizens. When he recovered from his wounds, the sole surviving terrorist seemed indignant about it: no one had warned him that his victims might shoot back.

The United States is a country which, historically, shoots back. If these incidents start happening here, I hope they at least happen in one of the increasing number of states where citizens can be licensed to carry concealed and loaded handguns in public. That can, as in the Israeli incident mentioned above, turn a massacre of the innocent into a short gunfight with as happy an ending as gunfights ever have.

Attacks in the hinterlands

What happened in New York City and Washington, DC has doubtless reinforced the decision of so many of our readers to live in rural areas. However, just because the first attacks hit metropolitan cities doesn't mean that plan is locked in stone for bin Laden and his followers. Again, look to Israel, whose enemies are largely the same as what we face now. Yes, the terrorists may strike in the heart of downtown Tel Aviv…but they are also known to strike at the remotest kibbutz.

Imagine yourself as Osama bin Laden. You want to strike terror into the heart of a people. You will reach not just to the capital, but to the heartlands and the hinterlands. People of the countryside see the cities as somehow remote from them. Terror visited upon the people of a village frightens those in the other villages. I would not be at all surprised to see small town schools or town halls on the terrorists' list of targets.

Emergency personnel

Captured materials indicate that it was part of the terrorists' plan to strike the first target, allow rescue personnel to begin their efforts, then deliver a second strike in hopes of killing rescuers. They succeeded all too well. The death toll includes over 300 firefighters, numerous emergency medical personnel, 23 New York City police officers, and perhaps 37 Port Authority cops, plus at least one Federal agent. Neither the fire service nor the police service has ever taken such a massively fatal "hit" in the history of both institutions in the United States.

The tragedy has engendered more respect for the nation's emergency service providers. People are more likely to use all their fingers when they wave at a cop lately.

If you have lived for any length of time in a rural community, you probably know volunteers on the ambulance service, volunteer firefighters, and part-time cops. You may have been invited to join one or more of these agencies. People volunteering to make up for lack of a populous tax base that can pay for a full-time, full-service department is a longstanding tradition in rural America. Be advised, those admirable people may be in more danger than before if terrorism moves to the hinterlands.

The perpetrator of what was previously our nation's worst terrorist attack, Tim McVeigh, was pulled over on a highway and captured by a lone state trooper. No cops in America work lonelier posts than the US Border Patrol, yet it was they who captured Ahmad Rasham before he could fulfill his admitted goal of detonating a large bomb at Los Angeles International Airport.

Even when terrorists strike in the cities, they often flee to the heartlands. This cancerous tumor inside the body of the United States of America has metastasized widely. More of these dangerous people are going to surface in this country. Some, perhaps more than you'd expect, will be captured somewhere off the beaten metropolitan path.

Attack on the President?

George W. Bush told us no lie. It will be a long, hard road to avenge—as I think we must—the horrors of September 11. Our nation will be misunderstood. It's happening already, worldwide, and we're seeing it in microcosm in our own country. On the day of the incident, a certain high profile newscaster implied that the President was in hiding. The President was doing his job, which included denying the enemy one of its prize targets. Not since JFK has a President been in so much personal danger. Having given the "dead or alive" order on the megalomaniac false Moslem bin Laden, the bankroller of terrorists will doubtless "shoot back." The next "big target," if the group in question wants to show its power, may not be the Sears Tower or the Empire State Building. It may be George W. Bush.

Hate crimes

Within three weeks of the atrocity, the FBI was investigating some 90 serious hate crimes against people of Middle Eastern appearance or descent. These have been committed by troglodytes so clueless they can't tell Moslems from Sikhs. Such bozos certainly will have trouble figuring out that bin Laden and company are not a problem comprised of Moslems, but a problem comprised of radical Islamists.

A false Moslem

True Moslems understand that their faith rigidly prohibits the murder of innocent children and old people, such as those sacrificed in such great number on the 11th. Only a false Moslem could claim to be ordering such murders in the name of God. Even those who think the suicide bombers were heroic martyrs will have some doubts about bin Laden when they figure out that bin Laden literally stole their souls. A Moslem who has murdered innocent children can no more go to heaven than one who has intercourse with pigs; this is clear from any reading of the Koran.

Investigations are even indicating that bin Laden and his co-conspirators sold stock short in a way to take advantage of the tragedy a short time before they caused it.

The genuine, devout Moslems will eventually figure out that the false Moslem bin Laden (a) is responsible for the deaths of countless innocent children and old people, as well as the younger and more able-bodied victims; (b) murdered his own followers by sending them on this murder/suicide mission; (c) stole those men's souls; and (d) lined his pockets while doing it.

Honest Moslems are already vehemently distancing themselves from these heinous acts by heinous people. That will accelerate if and when all Moslem clergy, particularly those in the Middle East, frankly assess the actions of bin Laden and his followers in light of their holy book.

Arming pilots

Air travel needs to be made safer. This means more and more highly trained security personnel, and it would be facilitated by arming the pilots. This is not a radical step requested by the National Rifle Association. It is a logical step presented by the Airline Pilot's Association itself. In the '30s and '40s, most pilots carried guns. It was to protet the mail they carried. History shows no record of any problems with that: no pilots shooting copilots in arguments, no passengers getting control of their guns, or anything similar. Pilots carried guns of their own aboard airlines through the '80s, when the mandate was made that ended the practice.

Yes, things will change. For now, keep your powder dry, your gun loaded and locked, your larder full, and your senses alert. Δ

Section 3
Long-term
Preparation

*It is thrifty to prepare today for the
wants of tomorrow.*

— Aesop, The Ant and the Grasshopper, c. 550 B.C.

Chapter 29
A survival garden

By Jackie Clay and Alice Yeager

Many of us have a garden and enjoy fresh vegetables during the summer and fall. Maybe we even have a few chickens for eggs and meat. But some of us want to extend our preparedness to what I call "hard-core" homesteading. This is serious homesteading, aimed at being able to provide your family with nearly all of its basic needs.

Luckily, most of us with a piece of out-of-the-way land can become nearly "store-bought-free," raising much of what we need in nearly the same way as did our ancestors.

There is a vast difference between this type of survival homesteading and stars-in-the-eyes, back-to-nature, recreational homesteading to relieve stress and provide enjoyment. The difference is not so much in how-to, but in discipline and learning.

The survival garden

It has been said that one can raise enough food for a family of four in a 50- by 50-foot space. While such an area can provide a goodly amount of food, there is no way a family could survive, year-round, off such a small patch. In reality, all that this is is a "house garden" for providing fresh produce such as greens, broccoli, cabbage, peppers, herbs, etc.

When one needs a garden to put up food, not only for the winter but possibly for a year or two, we're talking about at least an acre of intense cropping.

This includes a patch of wheat for grinding into cereal and flour, flour corn for hominy and corn meal, sweet corn for eating, canning, and dehydrating, and rows of dry beans as well as fresh beans (yellow wax, green, pole, etc.) for putting up. Here we stumble on the weak link in most folks' gardens. They say "We only use a few pounds of corn meal or dry beans a year," and they feel confident they can get by with just a few packages of such items, bought at the grocers.

But having lived in a wild corner of Montana, well above the "grocery line" (because of road accessibility), I can tell you that you will use many more pounds of these staples when you cannot eat from the store shelves.

And if there are no store shelves to choose from, we will all need to take care of our own needs at home. Remember, it takes more than one year to get a garden into full production. You can't just plow up a plot and expect to survive off of it, especially if you lack experience.

You can't grow everything, everywhere. Look at your local production capabilities. In New Mexico I could grow anything, but in the high country of Montana, nearly everything was a challenge even though I've gardened all my life. But we could survive from my Montana garden with potatoes, wheat, and beans along with a number of cold-loving crops we grew. What you need to do is put your energy into growing what will make a crop in your location.

Don't be afraid to experiment. Everywhere I've gardened I've grown crops that locals said "wouldn't grow."

To better use space, consider inter-planting as much as possible. Grow cornfield beans among the flour corn, radishes in the same row as carrots, peppers between rows of tomatoes (which act as windbreaks), pumpkins and squash next to a corn field where they can run into the corn after cultivation has stopped. (Don't do this with sweet corn or you will have a devil of a time picking the corn stumbling among rampant squash vines.) Inter-planting will do much to save garden space, a large consideration in survival gardening, especially when you must cultivate and till by hand.

Crops for a survival garden

Everyone who gardens grows some things just because they enjoy the taste. This is great, and we all do it. But in hard-core homesteading, we must consider our basic needs, as well.

We need to grow enough grain and corn for ourselves and livestock. This can be done by hand, in a relatively small plot, provided that our poultry and livestock needs are small. If you need more grain, say for cattle or horses, consider small scale farming with horses. This is a sustainable way of living as horses are easy to work, versatile, and provide manure for the fields. They also require no fuel to run. One team of moderate-sized horses can do as much work as a small tractor and cost little to maintain.

As little as an acre of ground can supply modest grain needs for a family homestead. Include a bit of rye, oats, and barley for variation. (There is a naked-seeded oat that is great for homesteaders, as at home one has a difficult task in hulling oats for oatmeal.)

Besides small grains, include your rows of flour corn for corn meal and hominy, being sure to include enough for livestock feeding.

Most folks have to double or even triple the amount of usual garden produce to allow for putting up as much each year as possible. Be sure to allow for lots of tomatoes for tomato sauces, and enough root crops, such as turnips, potatoes and carrots. (You'll eat a lot more "homegrown" when you can't run to the store for "quick" meals.)

Vegetables and herbs

The following vegetables are generally considered as good yielders and will not only produce plenty of fresh vegetables but there'll be plenty to can, freeze, or dehydrate.

Tomatoes. They're among our most versatile and best loved vegetables. An industry has been built around tomatoes. They're canned whole, diced, stewed, used in everything from chili to pizza sauce, mixed into salsa, sliced in salads, dehydrated—you name it. Tomato reigns and the recipes keep coming.

Tomatoes are not hard to grow if one follows some simple rules. Whether you buy plants or raise your own plants from seed, be aware that not every tomato variety does equally well in all parts of the country. Varieties that are recommended for hot humid areas are the best bet for our part of the United States (Zone 8, Southwestern Arkansas). Seldom do we have a summer without drought and soaring temperatures. We don't waste space with varieties recommended for cooler areas. Also, notice initials such as VNT, VFFNTA, etc., listed along with the names of varieties. These initials mean the plants are resistant to certain diseases and problem. For instance, "N" means good resistance to nematodes, those ever present, microscopic, worm-like pests that live in the soil and can cause havoc with tomato plants as well as others. (Seed catalogs always give a list of initials and their meanings.)

Some of the varieties that have done well in our area are *Arkansas Traveler, Quick Pick, Thessaloniki, Celebrity, Park's Whopper,* and *Supersteak.* One that performed especially well in 2001 was *Super Fantastic.* We also took some suckers from this one in midsummer, rooted them in water, and planted them in early August to stretch our tomato season. The new plants began bearing in late summer and continued until frost.

Don't forget the small tomatoes generally referred to as "cherry tomatoes." They are among the heaviest bearers of all and are great for making tomato juice and preserves or to eat fresh from the vine. *Sweet Million* is a favorite of ours as it bears until frost and has wonderful flavor.

Beans. Another tasty vegetable with a variety of uses. Generally, beans are either bush type or pole. Bush beans mature quicker, but pole beans will give a larger harvest over a longer period of time. Personally, I prefer to plant pole beans as the pods are easier to pick, pods are cleaner, and their trellises provide afternoon shade for shorter plants during hot weather. Pole beans are space savers.

Bush varieties that have performed well for us include *Buttergreen, Venture, Blue Lake, Romano,* and *Shamrock.* Pole beans of exceptional yield have been *Kentucky Wonder, Romano, Blue Lake,* and *Kentucky Wonder Wax* (yellow colored).

Let's not forget other beans of delicious flavor. There are lima beans (both bush and pole), soybeans, field peas (often called cowpeas), asparagus beans (pole)—the list is long. Best of all, beans are easy to grow and will give you a good return for your time and effort.

If you live in a part of the country where it is practical to grow beans recommended for drying, you can raise varieties hard to find in stores. Pods mature almost all at once and beans can easily be separated by hand from the dry pods. Be sure that beans are completely dry before storing in clean airtight jars. If there are signs of weevils or any other tiny bug, try freezing the beans for a few hours before storage. Due to summer humidity, we don't try to grow beans for drying but instead buy certain varieties we like and store them with a bay leaf or two in the jars. Bay leaves are also good to use when storing other dry foods—pasta, peas, grits, corn, rolled oats, etc.

Peppers. Every garden should have several types of peppers—another easy-to-grow vegetable. Peppers are an essential part of many recipes ranging from salads to soups and they have a taste range from sweet to yowee! Colors of mature sweet peppers range from ivory, green, yellow, orange, red, and purple to chocolate. These are particularly desirable when one wants to show off a bit with a specially prepared meal. Hot peppers have a wide color spectrum, too, but must be used with caution.

As a general rule, pepper plants will stand heat and humidity better than some other plants. If temperatures stay above 100' F. for several days the plants will slow down on production, but will make a comeback when weather cools. Some of our best blocky varieties have been *Bell Boy Hybrid, California Wonder,* and *Albino.* Cubanelle types include *Gypsy Hybrid, Aconcagua,* and *Aruba.*

One should always have some hot peppers on hand to give some zip and variety to dishes where it is appropriate to use them. Jalapeno peppers, available in both hot and mild types, are prolific bearers as well as some smaller peppers such as *Tabasco* and *NuMex Sunrise.* Not a great deal of space needs to be devoted to hot peppers, as a little goes a long way.

Suggestions for a survival garden

green beans, pole & bush
sweet corn (various maturing dates)
yellow wax beans
carrots
dry beans (several types)
tomatoes (several varieties)
potatoes
turnips
rutabagas
cabbage
broccoli
cauliflower
cucumbers
onions
greens of several types
spinach
lettuce
peas (dry & green)
pumpkins
summer squash
winter squash
muskmelon
watermelon

Seasoning plants. Those of us who love food seasoned with something besides salt and pepper are sure to grow some herbs or garlic in our gardens.

Nothing peps up a roast like bits of garlic cloves tucked in here and there. Garlic is a blessing to the kitchen and is very easy to raise as hardly any pests attack it. It flourishes in the garden and may be grown alongside fences out of the way of other crops. When the plants go dormant in the summer, bulbs may be dug and hung up in mesh bags in a cool room to be used when needed. Where winters are not severe, plants will begin their cycle of growth putting up new leaves as weather cools down in the fall and showers begin. We often use fresh garlic leaves to season food during winter and early spring.

Raising one's own herbs just adds to the fun of gardening. Not only can leaves be used fresh during the growing season, but they may be dehydrated, crumbled, and put in clean small jars for winter use. (Be sure to label and date.)

Pick out the ones you like and try your hand at raising them. There are a few that are a little finicky as to climate and soil, but most herbs will thrive under normal conditions if given some TLC. We grow plenty of sweet basil as that is one of our favorites. We also like thyme and summer savory. Seasoning plants add both to the preparation and pleasure of meals and they can be used with many dishes, and they're delightful to flavor vinegars. So, reserve a spot in the garden for some herbs.

With all survival garden vegetables, a family should buy only open pollinated varieties. This will enable folks to save seeds from year to year, which is not recommended with hybrids. Hybrid seed, while usually fertile, can not be depended upon to reproduce truly. And, contrary to popular belief, most of those old open pollinated varieties are good tasting and hardy.

Perennials for the survival garden

Along with the vegetables, a hard-core survivalist should establish a good variety of perennial edibles. These include asparagus, Jerusalem artichokes, horseradish, garlic, perennial onions, and herbs for both culinary and medicinal use. Remember to encourage native perennial edibles which do well in your area. These may include prickly pear cactus (the fruits and pads are eaten as a vegetable), wild rice, wild greens, cattails, mushrooms, etc. In a survival situation, one truly appreciates variety in the diet.

The perennials have the advantage of having to be planted only once and usually expand on their own with little human help. And, like the annuals, which must be planted each year, a family can gather and put up many jars full of winter eating. I can wild and domestic asparagus, wild mushrooms, wild greens, cactus pads (known as nopalitos in the southwest), and dry many other wild and domestic perennials.

Small fruits are nearly essential

Nearly everyone has room to plant a good selection of small fruits. These include strawberries, raspberries, blackberries, rhubarb, blueberries, and so forth. Luckily, once a patch of each has been established, one can readily take divisions or replant sprouts to greatly increase their food-producing capabilities.

As with the vegetable garden, one should grow as great a variety of small fruits as possible, and enough of each to put up significant jam, preserves, and canned and dried fruit. In hard times, a good loaf of hot whole wheat bread spread thickly with homemade strawberry jam, or a steaming blueberry pie, makes the term "survival" a joke. We call it living good.

You quickly discover that small fruits are a wonderful treat that can be easily turned into strawberry shortcake, blueberry pancakes, rhubarb tarts, blackberry cobbler, etc. In hard times, you don't eat many candy bars; instead you substitute healthier fruit snacks and desserts.

Even picky eaters greatly enjoy dried fruits and fruit leathers which are easy to make at home.

Every homestead should include a small orchard

Even the smallest homestead has room for fruit trees. With the variety of tree sizes and shapes, you can choose full-sized trees which are tremendous producers, but take room and several years to begin bearing fruit. Semi-dwarf trees, which usually require only a 10- by 10-foot spacing, produce full sized fruit in moderate amounts and only take a couple of years to bear. Dwarf and "pole" trees, which produce full sized fruit in small amounts, can be raised on a patio in a portable tub.

A hard-core homesteader can get by with two each of several varieties to provide variety and cross-pollination. I'd suggest apple, pear, pie and sweet cherry, apricot, and plum for most gardeners. Of course, if you can grow citrus in your zone, go for it. We live in zone 5 and have two Brown Turkey Figs in a protected corner of our east flower bed—protected by the house from the killer winter north winds.

Now a lot of folks say they'd need acres and acres to reach this level of self-reliance in the food department. Not so. My grandmother did it on two city lots in Detroit. Instead of normal landscaping, nearly everything she grew produced edible fruit: peach, grapes, brambles, quince, asparagus, apple, crab apple, strawberry, etc.) Having gone through the Depression as a widow with two young boys to raise, Grandma knew how to fend off hard times.

But what about meat?

Like produce and fruit, a family can grow all of their meat requirements, right at home. Now few people actually like to kill to eat, but when it comes down to eating or not eating meat, most of us can find a way around our revulsions. After all, someone had to kill that steer that went into your Big Mac. It gets ridiculous when visitors won't eat a home-butchered beef roast but will buy a tainted, chemical-laden piece of plastic-wrapped roast at the supermarket and eat it with abandon.

Folks on a very small acreage will usually have to limit their meat production to poultry, rabbits, and perhaps a little goat meat. A small flock of chickens for egg and meat production, with a couple of hutches of rabbits and the castrated male offspring of the family dairy goats will do much to help out at the dinner table. Of course, a family with these reduced production capabilities will not eat meat every day, but it will be able to enjoy regular meals with meat as a feature.

The benefit of having only a small poultry flock, a few hutches of rabbits, and very few goats is that the feed requirements and labor requirements are also minimal. In such cases, a family can easily hand-raise and harvest all feeds necessary to maintain their meat and egg supply.

Small-holders can help supplement their meat needs by hunting and fishing. But remember, if times are hard nationwide, subsistence hunting will become very difficult in most areas, as it did during homestead days and during the Depression. The game quickly disappears with overhunting. Fishing holds up much better, so it benefits a family if they hone fishing skills before they are truly needed. (Besides, it's enjoyable family "work," as well.) For lucky backwoods dwellers who live near the seacoast or a salmon stream, fishing can well be the major source of family meat.

Folks with more acreage are in better shape to truly be meat self-reliant. Using horsepower to till moderate amounts of land, a family can raise enough small grain, field corn, and forage (hay and pasture) to maintain not only the horses but a couple of dairy cows or several dairy goats. Let me stop right here and address you folks who are saying, "Goats! No way am I going to raise those stinking tin can eaters!".

Goats do not eat tin cans, nor do they run around butting people, any more than do cattle. Goats are exceptionally clean, picky eaters, refusing to take a bite of the apple you just took a bite out of, and they'll dehydrate before they will drink from a bucket containing even one berry of manure. Only bucks in rut have any odor. While in rut they will spray their neck, belly, and chin with urine as an attractant to does in heat. So do elk and deer. The normal scent glands on a buck's head, which produce scent during rut, can be removed by surgery when the buck is an adult or during disbudding, leaving a scent-free male totally capable of breeding. Does never have an objectionable odor, and with neat droppings the pen is quite clean and odor-free with even minimal daily maintainance.

We've had both dairy goats and cattle, and we know the benefits and drawbacks of each. Both produce milk which is equally good-tasting. A goat often produces multiple offspring while a cow produces one calf a year.

Cattle are easier to fence in, but goats will do great in a pasture grown over to willows and brush as they are by nature browsers like deer. And, like deer, they can hop a four-foot field fence to enter your young orchard and strip the tender trees of their bark and twigs. Cows produce beef; goats produce chevron. Both are good, but different.

Chevron comes in carcass weights from between 20 and 100 pounds of dressed weight, depending on age. They are easier to cut up and handle, but their small carcass lasts a much shorter period of time than a 600-pound Angus carcass.

Remember that worldwide there are thousands more goats used for meat and dairy production than there are cattle. There are reasons, and economy is at the top followed by the quickness of meat consumption in areas without refrigeration. A 600-pound cattle carcass is likely to spoil before it's completely consumed.

Pigs are another cog in the serious homesteader's wheel of self-reliance. Not only can a few pigs easily be raised for butchering—being fed from home-produced feed, kitchen and dairy waste (skim milk is an excellent food), along with weeds, pasture, and hog-foraged feed—but they provide excellent meat with a carcass that is quite easily handled by the family. The bonus of hogs is that they produce lard, the only homegrown cooking fat easily obtainable.

Yes, I know about high cholesterol, but let me tell you that when you are working hard everyday to put food and other necessities on the table, your cholesterol will balance easier than your finances.

Homegrown dairy products

Okay, so far you have a good vegetable plot, small fruits, small grains, and an orchard and meat/egg supply started. It's time to think about dairy products, particularly milk and cheese. After that stored dry milk is gone, your family will want something to replace it. And what is more natural than learning to run a tiny kitchen dairy and cheese plant? All dairy products are quite easy to produce at home, and as with almost everything else, it's much better when homemade.

I've made cottage cheese, cream cheese, mozzarella, colby, cheddar cheese, sour cream, cheese spreads, balls, logs and sandwich loaves, ice cream, ice milk, sherbet, and more regularly at home, both from cow and goat milk. Butter and whipped cream are easier to do from cow milk, as the cream quickly separates out, floating to the top. Goat milk is naturally homogenized and it takes more "doing" to access the cream. Both animals' milk produces good-tasting dairy products.

A good milking doe goat will produce about 3 quarts each milking, on average, where an average milk cow will produce much more—about three gallons. So your choice will depend on your facilities, labor and needs. Remember that all "extra" milk can be used to produce dairy products such as butter (which can also be used as a cooking fat) and cheese; dairy by-products can be fed to chickens and hogs. Extra milk can be used to bottle feed young calves or kid goats. On a survival homestead, there is no waste!

When planning on establishing a home kitchen dairy, be sure to stock up on such things as rennet tablets, which make forming cheese curd much easier and more reliable, cheese cultures (as you need for some "fancier" cheeses), cheese cloth and a cheese press or the materials to make one. These materials can be as simple as a #10 can or a 4-inch piece of PVC pipe and wood.

Okay, now we have your family ready with a vegetable garden, small fruits, grains, orchard, meat/eggs, and dairy production. Pretty nifty, right? You bet. For now you can also make soap from used cooking fats, which you can save in a can after each use. Soap making is easy and glitch free, requiring only strained, clean used fat and lye (which can be produced by seeping water down through wood ashes). This soap is great and can be used to wash clothes, babies, and hair.

Add a hive or two of bees, and your sugar requirements are easily met. Then too, the bees will pollinate your entire garden, grain patch and orchard, ensuring bountiful harvests. Bees are easily established and easy to work with. I've only been stung twice working with domestic bees, and probably a few dozen times by "wild" bees.

Survival homesteading is addicting. Once you get started, your mind works constantly at ways you can do more to be less reliant on the system. Now I say "can do" as few homesteaders actually practice every bit of their knowledge. I can raise and shear sheep, spinning wool into yarn to make clothes. And I can tan hides from which to fashion clothes and footwear. But I choose to use my time in other ways, which are more productive to the family at present. But the knowledge is there, should our needs change.

Survival homesteading is rewarding, financially and spiritually, as a basic instinct in human beings is to provide for their own and their family's needs. Never become overwhelmed by feeling that you must do everything at once. It is better to proceed in steady forward steps, rather than to run forward, fall and lose heart. One vital tip: start small and work your way up as your ability and knowledge increases. Your survival homestead depends on it. Δ

Chapter 30
Grow, grow, grow

By Alice Brantley Yeager

There is a sense of stability and survival if the household's food supply can be counted on under emergency conditions. Not so if the pantry has mostly empty shelves and the freezer is in about the same shape. From time to time, we hear the harbingers of doom state what can happen if produce or other food is contaminated by terrorists. We have no way of knowing what the international criminals are plotting, but now is not the time to drag our feet and become complacent. Instead, it is the time to begin preparing as much as possible to ensure that the food we preserve is as nutritious and free of contaminants as we can make it and that we put away plenty of it.

Those of us who are involved in gardening aren't too worried about the quality of produce coming from our gardens. We tend the plants from the time the seedlings appear until they mature and produce their crops. "Fresh from the garden," we take pride in saying and the excess we've put away canned, frozen, or dehydrated is a boost to our sense of well-being.

All emergencies don't necessarily result from catastrophes such as terrorist attacks. They can be produced by weather conditions—hurricanes, blizzards, tornadoes, and so on. We had one of those emergency situations in our southwest Arkansas area in 2000. It began on December 25 in the form of an ice storm, the likes of which had never before been recorded for this area. By nightfall, residents and businesses alike had lost electrical power. Folks with all-electric homes were really in a bad situation.

Fortunately, we have never put all of our eggs in one basket. We have a natural gas kitchen range and water heater and we have a real wood burning fireplace in our den. Nevertheless, due to the failure of our central heat system, our house could not be kept comfortably warm and it was downright cold in some rooms. Our electricity was off for 10 days and some folks had no power for 2 weeks or more. Our kerosene burning antique lamps from the good old days were pressed into service and we were thankful for a radio that could operate on batteries.

Trees that had endured all kinds of weather over the years were battered by the ice storm. Christmas night was like living with the sounds of a war zone. Huge limbs and tops of trees snapped with gunshot sounds and came down with enormous force burying whatever grew beneath and near them. Tree farms were almost totaled. Orchards suffered likewise. Our garden area was ringed with the remains of what had once been shade trees. If the garden had not been in an open area, it would have taken weeks to clear it of debris. As it was, we only had to remove a few limbs and prune broken branches from some fruit trees. What a mess!

Our home canned and dehydrated items came through all right in the pantry, but the contents of our freezer thawed out and had to be discarded. Ordinarily, we could have taken all of this in stride, but I was on a walker due to a strained leg muscle forcing James to fall heir to all outside chores including bringing in wood for the fireplace. After things began to return to normal, James had a bout with pneumonia. The 2000-2001 holiday season was not one of our best. To add to the area's troubles, New Year's Day was ushered in with several inches of snow. This doesn't sound like much to northerners, but the camellia and magnolia adorned South is never ready for snow and ice.

I mention this trying experience to emphasize that disasters come in many forms and that we all need to be prepared when they happen. Most of all, we need to learn from them. One lesson we learned from the ice storm involved buying a generator, one that will produce enough power to keep essential appliances operating. We may never need the generator, but, if we do, at least we won't lose a freezer full of nourishing home-grown food plus the items in our refrigerator.

Praise be that winter doesn't last forever and spring always follows. Spring may not be perfect, but it's better than trying to deal with wintry conditions. The first sprigs of new grass and even chickweed are welcome as they tell us it's time to get out our hoes, rakes, and trowels and go about the business of freshening our food supply.

A few years ago, we converted our row type garden to raised beds and we have found that we now have a tendency to coordinate plants better, thus making the most of the space under cultivation. It's easier to control watering when necessary and compost stays where we put it. Unless one is trying to harvest enough produce to sustain a large number of people, raised beds are the way to go. A surprising amount of vegetables may be gathered from raised beds and it's easy to take out depleted early plants such as lettuce or spinach and replace them with summer crops. In turn, summer crops may be replaced with a variety of greens and plants that thrive under cool fall weather.

Folks who take heed for the future always begin gardening early, and one of the first things planted in our Zone 8 is Irish potatoes. Oldtimers swear by the planting date of February 14, but it's hard to plant right on the 14th if the weather isn't cooperating. At any rate, by the time you dig your crop of potatoes, you should be able to use the space for a summer grower such as bush beans.

Potatoes come in quite a variety of choices now, some large like Red Pontiac or Kennebec and others of the mini or gourmet type. If you aren't familiar with growing potatoes, it might be well to check with your local County Extension Agent or a neighbor gardener to determine which varieties do best in your area and when to plant them. Like other plants, potatoes are subject to certain viruses, etc., and it's best to find out about diseases beforehand.

Whether you buy your potato pieces locally or from a seed company, you should get certified seed potatoes. If you buy whole potatoes, cut them into pieces containing not over three eyes. Do this a day or so before planting so that the cut surfaces will dry somewhat and be more disease resistant. To further immune them, dust the pieces with sulphur. Don't plant potatoes you have bought at the supermarket. They are not seed potatoes and your yield will be disappointing.

In our raised beds, we plant the potato eyes firmly about a foot apart on top of loose, loamy soil and cover them with about 4-5 inches of organic mulch. As the sprouts push through the mulch, more is added to keep tubers from being exposed to the sun and developing green spots. This method produces a nice clean potato and the potatoes are easy to dig.

Suggestions

1. Obtain a field guide, particularly one that gives information about wild plants growing in your area and how to forage for them. Many food plants are found on railroad dumps, in fields, and other cleared places. Some require a little more shade such as along the edge of wooded areas.

2. Buy a book on canning, freezing, and dehydrating food items. Buy one that is published by a manufacturer of canning supplies. Addresses may be found on cartons of canning supplies.

3. Unless you live in a dry climate such as New Mexico or Arizona where outside drying of fruits and vegetables is feasible, you will find an electric dehydrator very handy. It maintains a constant temperature, thus eliminating worry over humidity.

4. Anticipate what can happen to your food supply, particularly if in a freezer, when electrical power fails. Be ready with a backup system—a generator able to generate enough power to keep your essential appliances in operation.

5. Thieves seem to be on the increase. Don't place your freezer on your back porch in plain view or inside an unlocked area. Put it in your kitchen, utility room or somewhere not easily seen by prying eyes. Your freezer may be worth its weight in gold in case of a food emergency.

If you're planting in the regular way, you'll need to dig trenches about 6 inches wide and 8 inches deep in loose soil making trenches about 30 inches apart. Commercial fertilizer recommended is 5-10-10 which should be spread in the bottom of the trenches at a rate of about a pound to 25 feet. You never want potato pieces to come in direct contact with the fertilizer, so place at least 2 inches of soil over the fertilizer. Plant the potato pieces, eyes up, 12-15 inches apart and cover with about 4 inches of soil. After the first leaves emerge, start hilling up soil against the plants. As they grow, hill them with compost. Be sure that plants receive adequate water if dry spells occur.

Potatoes should be dug as soon as vines die down and the new potatoes spread out in a shady ventilated place. Any clinging dirt may be whisked off with a soft brush when dry. Potatoes will keep for several weeks stored in a cool place and even longer if refrigerated. If you haven't tasted cooked, freshly dug potatoes, you're in for a pleasant surprise. Treat your family to a good pot of potato soup. It'll go a long way toward satisfying hearty appetites. (See recipe.)

English peas grow well in early spring weather and the peas are excellent for freezing or canning. These peas may be planted when ground temperature is 45°-50°F., but if warm weather arrives early, yield will not be as heavy as vines tend to succumb to heat. You will see more English peas in northern gardens than in the South. We have had good luck with Dwarf Grey Sugar due to its heat tolerance. If we have a late spring, the pole type, Tall Telephone or Alderman, will produce well here. Both have good flavor and the Dwarf Grey is also an edible pod pea.

Peas prefer moderately rich, loose soil with pH 6.0-8.0. Plant them according to packet directions, as some varieties require a little more room than others. The vines need support—sturdy wire trellises, brush cuttings, etc. Most varieties don't grow over 3 feet high, but the Tall Telephone grows to a height of 5 feet or more thus needing a taller support.

Peas are like ears of corn in that the sooner you can cook them the better, as they start to lose flavor and quality as soon as picked. It takes a backyard garden to do justice to the English pea. Can or freeze your excess peas as soon as possible after harvesting.

Many greens including mustard, spinach, turnip greens, and Pak Choi may be canned or frozen. All of these are easy to grow and yield best when planted in early spring. They all require the same type soil and growing conditions and are certainly worth considering if you like greens. Some gardeners prefer broadcasting the seeds and others like to plant in rows. We prefer rows, as it's easier to apply an organic mulch to keep dirt from splashing onto leaves during spring rains. No one likes to deal with gritty greens.

There are numerous other early yielding crops that may be enjoyed from the garden—radishes, carrots, beets, onions, cabbage, and so on. Avail yourself of some catalogs from established seed companies, compare prices and order seeds or plants to suit your taste and space. Blessings on those companies that send their catalogs to be perused during long winter months.

Summer probably gives us more produce from the garden to preserve than any other season. That's when it seems we have an overflow of everything—corn, beans, peppers, tomatoes, squash, you name it. Summer also gives us long days with plenty of sunshine. The plants need the long, warm days to mature their crops and we need the long days to harvest and put away our excess.

Sometimes we tire of putting up each kind of vegetable individually. That's when imagination can give us some dandy ideas. For instance, how about merging tomatoes, green beans, carrots, and such into vegetable soup to tuck away in the freezer. (See recipe.) Frozen cartons of vegetable soup are very handy to have whether or not there's an emergency situation. Just put a carton in a double boiler to heat and serve with crackers or hot cornbread.

Besides your own garden, there are other places to find food plants to process. If you like strawberry preserves and you don't have space for strawberry plants in your garden, try seeking out wild strawberries. You'll find them growing in patches in fields mainly in the cooler parts of states east of the Mississippi River. We tried for several years to grow plants we had brought from Ohio and, although the plants thrived and multiplied, they were never very productive. We concluded our climate was a little too warm and humid for wild strawberries.

There are other berries, too—dewberries, blackberries, raspberries, and so on to harvest from the wild. Or, if you have space, you may want to purchase tame varieties from nurseries to plant along the edges of your garden. Wild berries have better flavor than the tame ones, but they may all be made into jellies and jams or the juice extracted, frozen, and used at a later date. Berries may be canned or frozen whole for cobblers, pies, cakes, etc.

Depending on the region in which you live, don't overlook the possibilities presented by wild plums, muscadines, persimmons, mulberries, May haws, crab apples—an endless list. There are also nut trees—hickory, pecan, beech, chinquapin, black walnut—another long list.

Growing in the wild are many vegetables—poke salad, dandelion, asparagus, wild onions, Jerusalem artichokes, mustard, wild rice, and on and on. Many of these are best enjoyed fresh, but a number may be preserved. They are a tasty source of food, full of nutrition and will certainly provide variety to meals.

Foods from the wild may be harvested yearlong beginning with early greens to nuts maturing in the fall. It's a pity that we lean heavily on what we can raise in our gardens and turn down what Nature offers us just for the taking. Pioneering people were proficient in foraging for what the land had to offer even though many of them did have gardens. We newcomers need to learn more about nature's bounty and how to use it.

During this day and uncertain time, it is foolish not to be prepared for emergencies. Even primitive people put away food to sustain them during tough winters and other trying times. We have come a long way from their methods, but we still have one thing in common with them—we still depend on food to keep us going.

We live in a land of plenty. Let's make the most of it and in so doing be prepared for the unexpected.

Some reliable seed companies:

Pinetree Garden Seeds
Box 300
New Gloucester, ME 04260

W. Atlee Burpee & Co.
Warminster, PA 18974

J. W. Jung Seed Co.
335 S. High Street
Randolph, WI 53957-0001

Totally Tomatoes
P.O. Box 1626
Augusta, GA 30903

Geo. W. Park Seed Co.
1 Parkton Avenue
Greenwood. SC 29647-0001 Δ

Chapter 31
Canning meats and vegetables at home—it's not only easy, it's safe and inexpensive

By Jackie Clay

While quite a few people still put up pickles, jams, jellies, and tomatoes, it is estimated that less than 5% of the population in the United States actively cans vegetables, meat, fish, and poultry. Why? I think it's because people fear it is difficult, dangerous, and expensive. They're afraid they will give their families food poisoning, and they think they can buy canned goods cheaper at the store.

Let's look at the arguments realistically. Difficult? I can put up 10 pounds of meat in less than 2 hours, while I work on the word processor or home school our son, and I'm no rocket scientist.

Dangerous? No, the canner won't blow up if you read common sense directions and regularly monitor the pressure, adjusting the heat as needed to keep it at the correct pressure. Nor do you have to worry about tainted food if you follow the precautions given in a canning book.

Expensive? If it was, this frugal home canner sure wouldn't do it. On an average, it costs me 10¢ to can a jar of vegetables and meat (provided I grow the produce and hunt or home raise the meat) and even less if I can on our wood range, which I often do during the cool mornings of autumn.

And that jar can be anywhere from a half-pint to a half-gallon of food. Store-bought canned vegetables and meat cost a lot more than that. Just yesterday I priced eight ounces of canned chicken breast, on sale, at $2.19. That translates to $4.38 a pint vs. 10¢ for a pint of my home-canned chicken. And even if I bought the chicken from a butcher, then canned it, I could put up a pint for half the cost of that store-bought canned meat. And besides the reduced cost, there are no chemical additives in anything I can.

To successfully can, all you need are some basic equipment and instructions and you can enjoy clean, chemical-free, inexpensive, and nutritious vegetables and meat all year long.

Canning tools: good canning book, jar lifter, rings, lids, funnel, and jar. A pressure canner is also necessary.

Equipment

A good **canning book** is a must for all home canners. I have four, not because canning is difficult or that I am stupid, but because each provides a lot of different recipes and ideas. The processing and safety tips in each book are the same, but I'm always open to new ideas and you should be too. But until you become experienced you should not free-lance, that is, change the recipes, as incomplete processing times can result.

Jars are a must, of course. Some folks will swear that you cannot process meat and vegetables in other than brand-name canning jars and that if you use pickle, mayonnaise, salad dressing, or other jars, which a canning lid and ring will fit well, they will break in the pressure canner. Not so. I've used these "orphan" jars for over 35 years, along with Mason and Kerr jars. I can see absolutely no difference in the instance of breakage. So a note on a bulletin board or in a free shopper, or just plain telling everyone you know, will usually result in a lot of free jars.

Examine each jar as you wash it at home for any minute chips or cracks, especially in the rim of the glass. Chips will usually result in the jar not sealing or a larger crack developing. And cracks, of course, weaken the jar and cause it to break as it processes.

A **pressure canner** is necessary to can all meat, fish, poultry, and meat products such as soups, stews, spaghetti sauces, etc. This is a fairly large expense for many frugal folks, costing about $125 for the larger, more work-worthy size. But, when you figure it will last for over 20 years, without maintenance, it is one of the best buys of a lifetime. Remember, you can use it to put up nearly anything that you would see on a store shelf or that you may hunt or fish for yourself.

Vegetables and meat products must be processed in a pressure canner to raise the temperature of the product you are processing and hold it at that level for for a considerable time. This ensures that you will kill all the bacteria.

Water not under pressure, as is used in simple water-bath processing, boils at 212° F. This is fine when canning fruits and tomatoes which have high acid content that kills microbes that may survive the boiling. But it is not adequate for low-acid vegetables and meats. Still, it was the method used by our grandmothers, as they did not have pressure canners as young women. And the food they canned did seal and was usually okay to eat. Usually. But I won't gamble my family's lives on "usually." Food poisoning is nothing to fool with, so I, and all intelligent home canners, process all meat and vegetable products in a pressure canner.

Jar rings (sometimes called bands) and lids are a basic, as well. Jar rings are used to hold the lid in place during processing. They *do not* help keep the jar sealed during storage. A properly sealed jar will remain sealed, without its ring, even when handled. In fact, jars should *not* be stored with rings on them as dampness can collect under the rings and promote rusting, making the ring useless for further use, and the jar lid may rust too, which will ultimately cause the seal to fail and the food to spoil.

Jar lids need to be of high quality. Never use el-cheepo lids from Asia that you've never heard of before. The three most dependable brands are Mason, Kerr, and Bernardin. The lids are boxed a dozen to a box, and they consist of a disk of lightweight metal, rimmed with a rubberized compound which, under heat, effectively seals the jar. They are *not* reusable and should be discarded after one use. Boxes of lids will store for years, remaining good. Self-reliant people should stock up on jar lids.

Other handy equipment to have around are a **canning funnel, sharp knives, mixing bowls, a jar lifter, chopping board, and a lid lifter** which neatly picks individual jar lids out of a pan of boiling water.

Canning steps for vegetables and meat

1. Have all the equipment on hand and ready.
2. Inspect the jar rims again for nicks.
3. Fill the jars.
4. Wipe off the jar rim.

5. Put the lid into place.
6. Screw the ring on firmly, but not forcefully.
7. Place the jar into canner.
8. Put the canner lid on, securing it firmly, but leaving the exhaust vent open.
9. When a steady stream of forceful steam comes from the vent, close it off.
10. Wait for the pressure to build to correct readings, then begin counting the processing time.
11. When time is up, shut off the heat, then allow pressure to drop to zero.
12. Remove the canner's lid away from yourself, so steam does not scald you, and remove the jars.
13. Set jars on dry, folded towels away from drafts until they cool.
14. Examine for seal using one finger to press on center of the lid. If it gives, it is not sealed and you must reprocess it using a new lid.
15. Remove the rings, wash the jars, and store them in a cool, dark, dry place.

While many foods are most easily canned using the hot pack method (where partially or wholly cooked food is placed in hot jars, then pressure canned), most foods I can are placed in the jars cold for ease and speed of processing a batch. Read your canning book, then decide which method is best for you and the food you are processing.

When getting ready to can a batch of food, have all your equipment clean and ready to go. The jars do not need to be sterile but must be freshly washed and clean. It is good to remember that in canning, cold should not be mixed with hot. That is, don't put boiling food into cool jars, cold food into hot jars, or set hot jars on a cool surface. I learned a lesson after many years of canning: every once in a while, a jar bottom would break during processing. Finally, I discovered that if I warmed up the canner before setting warm jars of food into it to process, I drastically reduced this breakage. Just turning the burner on a few seconds before placing the first jars in did the trick. Match the canner's bottom temperature with the jar temperatures.

Place a small pan of water on to boil. Separate the jar lids and drop into the water. Boil the lids, then remove them from the heat, but keep them warm.

Place the jars to be filled on a folded towel, then carefully fill each jar. The folded towel not only moderates the temperature from the table or counter surface, but it also catches spills making cleanup a snap.

Using a canning funnel helps keep foods from dripping onto the jar rim. You want to prevent this, especially with meats and poultry, as grease on the jar rim (or even a tiny bit of green bean) will keep the jar lid from sealing onto the jar rim correctly. An unsealed jar equals spoiled food.

Tips for canning meat and vegetables (Low acid foods)

1. Always use a pressure canner for all meats, fish, poultry, wild game, vegetables, and products containing these products such as soups, stews, sauces, etc.

2. If unsure of processing time, process the jars for the ingredient which requires the longest time. For instance, spaghetti sauce needs to be processed for the time given for meat, not tomatoes.

3. Can only fresh food. Never use questionable food for canning.

4. Remember, hot + cold = broken jars.

5. Never take shortcuts in processing time.

6. Following canning book directions results in wholesome, long-keeping canned food.

7. Get into the habit of checking and rechecking for nicks and cracks in jars. You'll save frustration, food, and money.

8. Don't try to pressure-can with arty jars that use zinc lids, or glass tops with wire bails, etc. You can't tell if they are sealed or not. A dangerous practice.

9. Don't experiment with recipes for canning until you are experienced and understand canning fundamentals completely. There are hundreds of tried and true recipes out there for you to gain experience with. (Spices may be varied to one's taste without endangering processing.)

10. Don't can meat with bones or fat intact, excepting fish or poultry. The bones and fat impart an unpleasant flavor at times, especially in game meat or mutton, and the bones take up unnecessary room in the jars. Also remember that fat is the #1 enemy of jars sealing.

11. Before eating or tasting a newly opened jar of food, visually check it for normal appearance and odor first. If there is any frothing, cloudy juices, unusual odor, or if a jar gushes or is not sealed when opening, then discard the contents where animals cannot get at it. This food is a definite risk. When it passes inspection, boil it for 15 minutes, just to be sure. This will kill bacteria that might make you sick.

Cut-up or whole green beans, potatoes, corn, other vegetables or meat, poultry, and fish may be placed in the jar raw. This is the raw pack which I most often use. Canning books have gotten away from raw-packed meats. I believe it's because the writers felt that home canners would become sloppy and possibly cause incomplete processing, resulting in meat which might harbor harmful bacteria. It is possible, but personally I get tired of folks trying so hard to keep me safe from my own responsibilities. And when I have an elk to can—and an elk is a lot of meat—I need to get it processed fast. So I still raw pack pieces of boneless meat. I am not advising others to do what

A variety of foods canned in the pressure canner: left to right: beets, hominy, squash. chili, corn, carrots, elk meat, baked beans, asparagus, potatoes, and wild mushrooms.

I do; I am only explaining how I do it. You may well choose to hot pack partially cooked meat.

I place fat-free boneless steaks, roasts, stewing meat, and just plain chunks of meat into a clean jar. (I use everything from half pint jars to half gallon jars, but I always process jars of a like size together—I don't mix sizes.) A teaspoonful of salt may be added but is not necessary. Water is not usually added, so the jar rim is carefully washed with a warm damp cloth, the hot lid is put in place, and the ring screwed down securely but not overly tight. The jar is now ready to put into the canner.

Hot-packed meat, such as partially cooked roast, steak, stew meat, boiled chicken and meat products, such as stew, chili, soup, etc. are put into warm jars. Liquid is usually added, i.e., broth or soup, the rim carefully wiped, the hot lid placed on, and the ring tightened.

Hot packing is great and convenient for canning large batches of spaghetti sauce, chili, stew, baked beans, canned dry pinto beans, etc. Just cook and dump into jars, then process. Okay, I'm simplifying, but once you get the hang of it you'll see it becomes that easy.

All raw meat should be heated or "exhausted" in the jars, which are placed in a pan of water deep enough to heat the jars thoroughly, while the water boils, but not so deep that the water boils into the open jars. Bring this pan to a slow boil and check with a meat thermometer inserted into the center of a jar. You need to heat the meat to 170° F, then quickly remove the jars from the bath with a jar lifter, place them on a folded towel, wipe the rims clean, and put the lids and rings firmly into place. Then place the jars in the canner and exhaust the canner. This means you should ensure there is a steady stream of forceful steam escaping the vent, not just spurts now and then.

After the canner is hot, i.e., exhausted, close the vent and begin raising the pressure until it reaches the desired processing pressure. Remember that most canning books give an average processing pressure of say 10 pounds. But if you live at an elevation higher than 1000 feet, you must bring the pressure up higher. Check your canning book for your exact pressure needs. Begin to count the processing time.

Keep the pressure at the correct reading by adjusting the heat under the canner or moving the canner gently on a wood range's surface or adding wood to the fire, as needed. If you let the pressure fluctuate, it will suck the fluid out of the jars. The resulting food will still be edible, but may be dry-tasting, or food bits may get under the jar lid making a proper seal impossible.

After the food has processed long enough, turn off the heat or remove the canner from heat. Allow the pressure to return to zero, then carefully remove the canner's lid—away from you, so escaping steam does not scald your arms or face. (Don't get in a hurry, thinking to just leave the jars in the canner with the lids on to cool. The jars will not seal correctly.)

Carefully set the hot jars, still boiling and bubbling, on a dry (never damp or the jars may crack) folded towel in a draft-free area to cool. Soon the telltale musical "pings" will let you know they are sealing. Never fool around with the hot jars or you may disturb the seal.

When the jars are perfectly cool to the touch, remove the rings, and wash them for next time. Then wash the jars with warm soapy water, rinse and dry them, and then store them in a cool, dry, and dark place.

Canning green beans

Pick the beans, wash them in cool water, and prepare to can them immediately. The beans may be canned whole, Frenched, or however your family likes them. I usually can a variety, from whole to Frenched, with the bulk cut into convenient chunks an inch or so long. Cut the beans, removing any tough strings, as well as the stem and pointy end, if desired. Using a canning funnel, dump the raw, cut beans into clean jars placed on a folded towel.

Pour two inches of water into the canner and place the basket or inner kettle into place. The canner must never boil dry or it will warp.

Some reliable food processing books

The Ball Blue Book (the Guide to Home Canning and Freezing), Alltrista Corporation Direct Marketing Department PK31, P.O. Box 2005, Muncie, IN 47307-0005, $5.95, including shipping. IN residents add 5% tax

Putting Food By, by Hertzberg, Vaughan & Green, Stephen Green Press

Stocking Up, by Carot Hupping, Rodale Press

Other great books are available, of course. Check out your local book store (or their catalog) and the library. Your county extension office, usually located in the courthouse, can usually provide free (or very low cost) canning publications and leaflets.

In the meantime, have enough lids separated and boiled. Also, have boiling a large pan of water with which you will cover the beans.

Fill all jars to within one inch of the rim. This is called "head space" and is necessary for proper processing and storage. In canning, you do not want to cram as much food into a jar as it will hold. Some foods expand as they process, and all need a certain amount of head room to process and keep well. Always follow your canning book's directions exactly.

You may add a teaspoon full of salt to each jar if you want to enhance the flavor, but it is not necessary.

Pour boiling water into each jar, just covering the beans. Then carefully clean off the rim of each jar with a warm, damp cloth to remove any food bits which might prevent the jar from sealing, and check for nicks in the rim with a clean finger. Place the lids and rings into position. Do not over-tighten the rings. The ring only holds the lid securely into place for processing, and does not have anything to do with how well the jar seals.

Bring the canner up to the same approximate temperature as the jars, then carefully place the hot jars into the canner, taking care not to thunk them together. Leave space between jars to allow for steam to circulate during processing.

Tighten the canner lid, raise the heat to high, and allow the canner to exhaust. When a steady, forceful stream of steam blows from the vent, close it and let the pressure build up. When it reaches the correct pressure (10 pounds for altitudes less then 1,000 feet above sea level, but see your canning book for higher elevations), begin timing. Pints of green beans will be processed for 20 minutes, and quarts for 25 minutes.

At the end of this time, turn off the heat or remove the canner from the heat and allow the pressure to return to zero. When it does, unfasten the lid and carefully lift it away from you, allowing hot steam to escape away from your arms and face. Then remove the jars carefully with jar lifter, again not thunking them together, which could result in cracks. Place the hot jars on a dry folded towel in a draft-free area until they cool.

Canning ground meat

Any ground meat or ground meat products such as chili, spaghetti sauce, taco meat, etc., should be cooked before it is canned or it will not have a good texture. The meat will clump together in lumps. So, in a large frying pan fry the meat in as little grease as possible. (Grease is the #1 enemy of jars sealing). Add the spices you desire, then the tomato sauce, beans, chopped onions, or whatever.

Have clean canning jars on hand, kept hot in water. Also have a sufficient number of boiled lids on hand so that the process proceeds as quickly as possible.

Using a canning funnel, carefully fill each jar to within an inch of the rim (one inch head space), wipe the jar's rim with a warm, damp cloth and inspect the jar again for any minute nicks.

Then screw the band snugly on over the hot lids and place each hot jar into the warm canner. Again, be careful not to thunk the jars together as it could crack them.

Turn up the heat with the canner vent open, and wait until a steady stream of forceful steam exits the vent. When this happens, close the vent and wait until the pressure arrives at 10 pounds. (Again, if you are canning at altitudes over 1,000 feet above sea level, check your canning book, as the pressure must be increased with the increased altitude.) When the correct pressure is attained, begin to count the processing time. Be careful not to let the pressure fluctuate as it can blow liquid out of the jar.

Pints will be finished in one hour and fifteen minutes and quarts in an hour and a half. I process half pints, which are very handy for casseroles, etc., for one hour and fifteen minutes.

When the jars have processed for the correct amount of time, turn off the heat or carefully remove the canner from the heat, and allow the pressure to return to zero. (Do not try to hurry this by fooling with the exhaust valve or you may end up with broken jars or jars that do not seal.)

Carefully remove the cover away from you to avoid steam burns, then take the jars out carefully and place them on a folded, dry towel in a draft-free place to cool.

When completely cool—overnight is best—remove the rings. Then carefully wash each jar in warm soapy water, dry them, and store them in a cool, dark, dry place. This meat will last indefinitely, regardless of what you have been led to believe. Δ

Notes